PENGUIN TRUE CRIME

SUDDENLY AT THE PRIORY

Born in 1908, John Williams was educated at Bromsgrove School and London University. He served in the Royal Artillery during the Second World War and in 1947 was appointed Librarian at the newly founded Administrative Staff College in Henley-on-Thames. In 1956 he became a full-time writer. His books cover criminology and history and include *Heyday for Assassins*, a study of eight major assassinations, *Hume: Portrait of a Double Murderer*, *The Ides of May: The Defeat of France, May–June 1940*, *The Home Fronts, Britain, France, Germany, 1914–1918* and *The Guns of Dakar*. He contributed to the script-writing and research of the two BBC television series *The Great War* and *The Lost Peace*, and the *World at War* series for Thames Television. John Williams died in 1976.

JOHN WILLIAMS

SUDDENLY
AT THE PRIORY

FOREWORD BY
JOHN DICKSON CARR

PENGUIN BOOKS

PENGUIN BOOKS

Published by the Penguin Group
27 Wrights Lane, London w8 5TZ, England
Viking Penguin Inc., 40 West 23rd Street, New York, New York 10010, USA
Penguin Books Australia Ltd, Ringwood, Victoria, Australia
Penguin Books Canada Ltd, 2801 John Street, Markham, Ontario, Canada L3R 1B4
Penguin Books (NZ) Ltd, 182–190 Wairau Road, Auckland 10, New Zealand

Penguin Books Ltd, Registered Offices: Harmondsworth, Middlesex, England

First published by William Heinemann Ltd 1957
Published in Penguin Books 1989
1 3 5 7 9 10 8 6 4 2

Made and printed in Great Britain by
Richard Clay Ltd, Bungay, Suffolk

CONTENTS

CONTENTS

PART TWO: *Trial by Inquest*

PART THREE: *Guilt and Nemesis*

ILLUSTRATIONS

FOREWORD

WHEN MURDER-FANCIERS draw up their chairs to the fire, each settling himself to a night-long discussion of his favourite homicide, there always enters a ghostly procession of what the late William Roughhead called "the lost ladies".

In fact, you can seldom have a good case without a fascinating woman. They distract us as much in debate as they do in real life. Shadowy, smiling, they glide in and lean across our chairs.

Was she guilty? Was she not guilty? Did she think about murder—but refrain? Or was she only a dimpled innocent lurking amid the curtains? She may have died on a scaffold a hundred years ago, or drawn her last breath yesterday under a (figurative) heap of lilies. It doesn't matter. We still pound the table and yell.

And my own favourite among all the charmers of yesterday, I confess, is Florence Bravo.

She was pretty, she was alluring, she was both emotional and enigmatic. After reading all those columns in the *Daily Telegraph*, I see her as the most delightful of persecuted heroines, moving to a rustle of silks and a turn of blue eyes. Besides, the Bravo Case itself has few rivals in the history of crime.

First, it is a notable detective-story. There are as many suspects, all with motives, as crowd the stage in a play by Miss Agatha Christie. Poison is the weapon; and poison, *pace* De Quincey, is still the best method because it is subtle, secret, the heart of mystery.

Second, all these events take place against the starchiest background of Victorian respectability. Behind lace curtains lurks demoniac possession, and a twilight conservatory is a-buzz with lies and murder. Now everybody, for whatever reason, heartily enjoys this. Perhaps we still suffer from the delusion that men who wore whiskers could never have had emotions. Or perhaps, atavistically, it is only the pleasure felt by all right-minded people when they see some pious, unctuous hypocrite (I mention no names from this narrative) slip on the stairs and land with his face in his own top hat.

In fact, if I were writing of this affair as fiction, I should make the murderer turn out to be——

But the case is not fiction, and to theorise is none of my business. I wish only to speak a word of commendation for Mr. John Williams's book, *Suddenly at The Priory*, which is the best reconstruction of the Bravo Case I have ever read.

Mr. Williams, like a good journalist, gives us facts. He has a sharp eye for character, and a penetrating way of presenting it. He does not moralise; he understands. Always keeping a tight grip on the story, he unfolds its sweep from the background to the tragic and (to me, at least) completely unexpected solution.

Anyone who writes a foreword for such a book is in the horned and difficult position of a critic who reviews it. If he says too much, he betrays the secret. If he says too little, he confuses his reader without provoking curiosity.

You may agree with the solution presented here, or you may disagree with it. But it is impossible not to consider it a strong case, with evidence which may make necessary a whole re-arrangement of values and motives. Either the mystery is solved—or else it grows blacker and murkier. It is based on no mere deduction, though we must never underrate deduction; here is documentary proof. We may say anything concerning Mr. Williams's ending except disregard it.

Charles Bravo, to my mind as nasty a bit of work as ever lived, swallowed a fatal dose of antimony. Despite ingenious theories, the first of which appeared long ago in Taylor's *Medical Jurisprudence* and the last of which was suggested a year or so ago, accident or suicide must be ruled out.

He was deliberately murdered, by someone either living in his house or with easy access to it. Here are problem, question, answer. The verdict is yours to decide.

JOHN DICKSON CARR

AUTHOR'S NOTE

FOR EIGHTY YEARS the Bravo Case has remained one of the greatest unsolved mysteries in Victorian crime annals. But as tantalising as the question "*Who* murdered Charles Bravo?" has been the enigma "*Why* was he murdered?" All the more obvious motives—pinned to one or other of the several suspects —have been probed again and again, but none has seemed wholly convincing. Yet someone killed Mr. Bravo and somewhere in the tangled story the motive was there, overlooked perhaps because more subtle and unexpected than could be guessed. I approached the case from that angle, and now I believe I have found something that provides a compelling motive, in the hands of the person concerned, for Charles Bravo's murder. Moreover, in following a hitherto unexplored line of inquiry, I have discovered indications of further villainy by the same person. This throws a new light on the whole affair and shows it as more sensational and far-reaching than had been thought. Except in that part of Chapter Seventeen which offers the solution, the facts of the case are strictly adhered to; and the entire dialogue is (with a few trifling exceptions which do not affect the accuracy of the story) reproduced from published accounts of the various official inquiries.

My main source for *Suddenly at The Priory* has been *The Balham Mystery; or, the "Bravo" Poisoning Case*, issued in seven weekly parts (price 1d. each) in 1876. This popular illustrated account (the "broadsheet" several times quoted from in the text) remains the most indispensable record of the case. Use has also been made of reports in *The Times*, the *Daily Telegraph* and various other contemporary journals.

Books I have consulted include: *The Bravo Mystery and other Cases*, by Sir John Hall (John Lane, The Bodley Head); *Six Criminal Women*, by Elizabeth Jenkins (Sampson Low); *How Charles Bravo Died*, by Yseult Bridges (Jarrolds); *Without Prejudice*, by Sir Chartres Biron (Faber & Faber); *Echoes of Causes Célèbres*, by Arthur Lambton (Hurst & Blackett); *Recollections of Forty Years*, by L. Forbes Winslow (John Ouseley); *Verdict in Doubt—the Bravo Case*, by F. J. P. Veale (Merrymeade).

I would like to acknowledge in particular the help and advice I have had, directly or indirectly, from the following people: Mr. Frank Ricardo, J.P., who lent and allowed me to reproduce family photographs; Mr. H. Sargeant, F.L.A., Librarian and Curator, Portsmouth Libraries & Museums, who provided long transcriptions from local papers; Mr. Edmund V. Corbett, F.L.A., Librarian, Wandsworth Public Libraries; Mr. J. W. Lucas, F.L.A., Librarian, Malvern Public Library; Mr. Austin Stone of Malvern; Mr. Karl Jung and Mr. Walter Wirdeier of Cologne; Mr. J. R. Archer-Burton, O.B.E., Chief Constable of Hastings; my brother Mr. Christopher Williams, Chief Constable of Hunts and Ely; Mr. L. C. Nickolls, M.SC., F.R.I.C., Director of the Metropolitan Police Laboratory; Dr. F. G. Tryhorn, D.SC., F.R.I.C., Director of the North-Eastern Forensic Science Laboratory; Professor Cyril Polson, Department of Forensic Medicine, University of Leeds; Mr. F. Herron, late of New Scotland Yard Library; officials of the Home Office, Public Record Office, and Office of the Treasury Solicitor; the Coroner's Office, County of London (Western District); the Diocesan Registrars, Bishop of London's Registry, Westminster; officials of Brompton Cemetery.

FOR SONIA

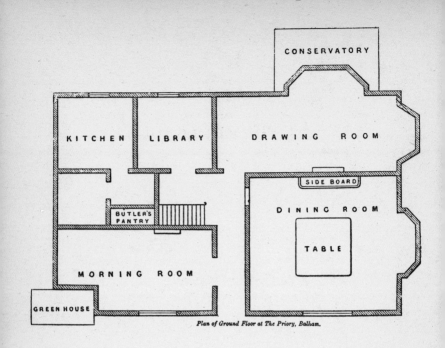

CONSERVATORY

KITCHEN LIBRARY DRAWING ROOM

BUTLER'S
PANTRY

SIDE BOARD

DINING ROOM

TABLE

MORNING ROOM

GREEN HOUSE

Plan of Ground Floor at The Priory, Balham.

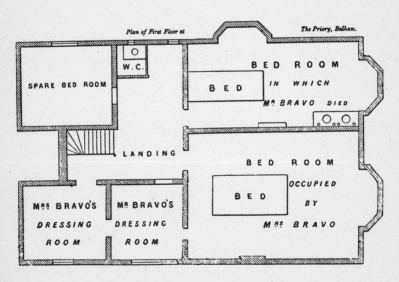

Plan of First Floor at *The Priory, Balham.*

SPARE BED ROOM

W.C.

BED ROOM

IN WHICH

BED

MR BRAVO DIED

LANDING

BED ROOM

OCCUPIED

BED

BY

MRS BRAVO'S

MR BRAVO'S

MRS BRAVO

DRESSING

DRESSING

ROOM

ROOM

Plans of The Priory as it was in 1876

PART ONE

DRINK, LOVE AND TRAGEDY

CHAPTER I

ROMANCE AND DELIRIUM TREMENS

ON THE 21st September, 1864, the bells of Buscot Church, near Faringdon, Berkshire, pealed out to mark a fashionable and romantic wedding. Florence Campbell was marrying Lieutenant Alexander Lewis Ricardo of the Grenadier Guards.

Both came from wealthy families. Florence, aged nineteen, was a daughter of Robert Campbell, a merchant from Sydney, of Buscot Park, a picturesque property near Faringdon, dominated by its elegant Adam-style mansion, Buscot House. Mr. Campbell, who moved in solid City circles and was a member of the Reform Club, was also something in the county, being a J.P. and having become High Sheriff of Berkshire in 1863. Florence's mother, whom her father had married in 1835, was Anne, daughter of James Orr, and Florence had two sisters and four brothers. Alexander (sometimes called Augustus) Ricardo, aged twenty-one, was the son of the late John Lewis Ricardo, of Lowndes Square, and Exbury House, Hants, and Lady Catherine, daughter of General the Honourable Sir Alexander Duff and sister of the 5th Earl of Fife. His father, who had died in 1862, was M.P. for Stoke-on-Trent and a prominent business figure, having been chairman of the International Telegraph Company (which he had founded) and several railway companies.

Florence and Alexander had met and fallen in love shortly before in Montreal. And standing there in the church that September day they were an attractive couple; the bride pretty, petite, blue-eyed and gloriously auburn-haired, and the groom tall, darkly handsome, upright and dashing in his Guardsman's uniform. Money, position, looks; they seemed to have everything: and impressionable Victorian mothers who saw them thus could be forgiven for shedding a sentimental tear at the thought of what an ideal match it was. The tear was opportune, but it should have been shed for quite another reason.

Just when Florence discovered that Alexander drank is uncertain. Perhaps in the blissful honeymoon days in the Rhineland he was intoxicated with her alone; or perhaps his frequent brandies-and-sodas—if indeed he took them then—seemed to her a fine manly habit. But as the months went by, the truth slowly dawned on her. And by 1867, when he left the Army as a captain, the early glamour had worn thin under his constant tippling. At twenty-four Captain Ricardo, Grenadier Guards retired, was a confirmed alcoholic—confirmed though not yet entirely hopeless: for at his young wife's tearful entreaties he could still renounce the bottle for a spell. That year he abstained for four months and, to Florence's delight, seemed a different man.

Alas, the abstinence was only temporary. And during their gay and varied social round—the season in London, country-house visits, travel abroad—Alexander was too often the worse for drink.

Their home at first was Hockham Hall, Norfolk, but in 1868 the lease fell in (or possibly Alexander got into money difficulties) and they moved to Shute House, Axminster. And that same year they toured the continent, sampling the beauties of the Rhine. Sometimes they went to stay with Alexander's mother, Lady Catherine, at Chester Square, and sometimes they visited Florence's parents at Buscot Park, or her brother William at Sudbury, near-by. They were here in December, 1869, when news of Lady Catherine's sudden illness and death

4

sent them hurrying to London. Alexander was very fond of his mother and her loss was a heavy blow; but at least the money that he now inherited from her improved his shaky financial position as a married half-pay captain with extravagant habits.

For a time they stayed on in Chester Square, and Florence grew increasingly worried as Alexander's alcoholic bouts became more frequent. At last she decided to get him away from the associations of the Chester Square house and the temptations of his West End clubs and drinking haunts. She thought that a change of scene, a quiet prolonged stay by the sea, might pull him together. So on Christmas Eve, 1869, they left Belgravia for Bournemouth. But the salty air and the scent of the pines were no antidote for the drunken Alexander's condition. He drank more than ever, and in his cups he was mostly morose and sullen—not, she thanked providence, violent again, as he had been on those two occasions at Bingen on the Rhine and Zurich, on their recent continental trip, when he had actually struck her. But in April, 1870, he began terrifying her afresh, showing all the distressing symptoms of delirium tremens. It was now too much for poor Florence to handle alone. She did what many an unhappy young wife does at times of grave domestic crisis: she wrote home to her mother.

Mrs. Campbell was brisk and helpful. She suggested their both going to Malvern: there were healing waters and good doctors there and she thought that Florence would benefit by the change and Alexander might be weaned from his habit by a strict medical régime. But here Alexander's uncle intervened. In his view Florence should start off alone, leaving her husband behind for a time. He hated being away from Florence and the separation might discipline him. So, at the end of April, while Alexander was installed in a room at the St. James's

Hotel, Piccadilly, with his manservant Field to look after him, Florence travelled to Malvern with her two maids.

She stayed at Malvern House, a quiet private hotel; and, thoroughly unnerved by her recent ordeal, the first thing she did was to consult a doctor. In fact she consulted two, Dr. Fernie and Dr. Gully, partners in a well-known Malvern practice. Things continued restfully for her for about three weeks; and then Alexander, bored by his own company and— to do him justice—miserable without Florence, suddenly turned up with Field and removed her from Malvern House to a furnished villa, Orwell Lodge.

He too, persuaded by Florence, consulted Dr. Gully (so it was said); and at first he behaved with refreshing sobriety. Seeing him so improved, Florence took new heart. Had he abandoned his horrid brandy? Was he going to mend his ways at last? She hardly dared believe it; and it was just as well that she did not build any extravagant hopes. For before two weeks were out Alexander was back at his old habits. Then one awful day in June, in a drunken outburst he stormed out of the house and took a train to London without leaving any address. Frantically Florence telegraphed her mother, and Mrs. Campbell arrived at once to console her. They agreed that Florence should remain at Malvern in case Alexander came back, while Mrs. Campbell returned to Lowndes Square. And a few days later to Lowndes Square came Field, inquiring about Florence and, on being questioned by Mrs. Campbell, telling a sorry tale about his master. The Captain, he said, was in rooms in Wigmore Street, seriously ill from the effects of drink. And there she found him in a pitiable state and seemingly in an advanced stage of alcoholism. The immediate thing to do was get him better care: and she had him removed to an address which she had ascertained was owned by an old servant of his, in Elizabeth Street, Westminster.

Next day Florence, summoned by her mother, arrived at Lowndes Square. Whether she visited her husband at Elizabeth Street is uncertain, but she saw him soon enough, and in most unedifying circumstances. At seven-thirty one morning, when the Lowndes Square *ménage* was hardly stirring, a hansom rattled up to the house and from it emerged Alexander, a staggering drunken wreck. He reeled up the steps, banged on the front door and was admitted by a terrified maid, incapable, incoherent and horribly intoxicated. To Florence and her mother, rushing downstairs half-dressed, it was a nasty shock. If they had not been so concerned with his deplorable state they might have reflected on the effect that this outrageous early morning irruption had on their neighbours in the prim stuccoed square. But what they did at once was send for a doctor, who took one look and diagnosed delirium tremens.

Under treatment Alexander recovered somewhat in a few days, and expressed a wish (to which Mrs. Campbell was no doubt very glad to accede) to be moved to his late mother's house in Chester Square. Florence went there to look after him, and succeeded by tears and warnings in inducing him to remain teetotal for much of that summer: so that in August he was fit to travel back to Malvern, in whose curative waters Florence and her mother still seemed to have faith.

Installed now at another furnished house, Stokefield, they took up the routine that had been so rudely broken by Alexander in June. They—and especially Florence—consulted Dr. Gully again, took the baths, strolled round the quiet walks of Malvern, while Florence built fresh hopes on her husband's reformation. But it was not to be: the demon drink was too strong for Alexander Ricardo and he resumed his bouts with growing frequency, until he was more often drunk than sober. While he stopped short of actual violence, in drink he was sullen, bullying, vindictive; he would shut himself in his room

7

and refuse Florence admittance. And in between times he would become maudlin and promise tearfully to reform. His health, it was clear, was rapidly deteriorating. And poor Florence, what could she do in those difficult autumn months but make allowances, get what help she could from her doctor, and treat her incorrigibly sick husband as patiently as she knew how? But at last in November she could stand it no more. With a married sister as chaperon, she fled to the welcoming shelter of the Priory House, Dr. Gully's residence, and wrote to her mother imploring her to come and take her away.

Mrs. Campbell arrived and escorted her weeping daughter to the haven of Buscot Park. For Florence this was the end: she could not go on living with Alexander: their married life was finished. Alexander stayed for a while at Malvern with his servant, Field, and then left for London, later returning briefly to Malvern to collect some belongings and finally departing for the continent. Florence's parents, to make sure that she had indeed seen the last of him, advised her to apply for a legal separation; and to this, despite letters from Alexander begging her to come back to him, she agreed. So, on 31st March, 1871, just before Alexander's departure abroad, the separation was drawn up, signed by Dr. Gully and Florence's solicitor, Mr. Brooks, as trustees. Under it Florence received an allowance of £1,200 a year.

Fate was soon to make that separation irrevocable. Three weeks later Florence received a laconic telegram announcing Alexander's sudden death on 19th April at Cologne. The cause was not disclosed.

At twenty-eight Captain Ricardo, who had everything to live for, had, it seemed, drunk himself into his grave, the victim of a sustained alcoholic orgy that his nearest and dearest had been powerless to prevent. It was strange that no one had sufficiently foreseen the tragedy. At Bournemouth, Buscot,

Malvern, Wigmore Street, Lowndes Square—everywhere the sinister symptoms, culminating in delirium tremens, had been apparent. And yet, seemingly, he had been allowed to go on from bad to worse, and die a miserable outcast, away from friends and family in a foreign city.

For Florence, young, innocent, refined, the romance so brightly heralded by the wedding-bells of seven years before had turned into a nightmare. Perhaps no one could blame her for refusing to pay Alexander's debts on the grounds that there had been another woman with him at Cologne when he died. Certainly no one could blame her if she lost her girlish illusions about marriage. And if she lost these she gained handsomely in another way. The settlement that Alexander had made on her at their marriage had never been rescinded, and on his death she came into a fortune of £40,000.

CHAPTER 2

INTERLUDE WITH THE DOCTOR

So, at twenty-six, pretty Florence Ricardo put on widow's weeds for the husband whose death she could not mourn overmuch, and consoled herself with an income of between £3,000 and £4,000 a year. Whither for her now? Was she, after a decent interval of widowed seclusion, to enter the marriage lists again, sadder and wiser? Or was she to forswear men altogether and remain a rich, fancy-free and unattainable widow—once bitten twice shy? In fact she did neither. For while Florence was not ready for marriage again, she certainly had not done with men. So she took that other course—the wayward path of illicit love. And yet it was not a matter of looking around for some new and handsome young admirer with the romantic appeal that had first endeared Alexander Ricardo to her: the admirer, as she well knew, was there already, waiting for her. True, he was old enough to be her father and he was not as dashing as a Guards officer or a young Mayfair man-about-town would have been; but there were hosts of women to vouch for the mellow cultivated charm, the fascinating bedside manner, of that well-known Malvern physician, Dr. Gully.

James Manby Gully, M.D., was in his early sixties when Florence met him in 1870. Clean-shaven, ruddy-cheeked, bald but for the neat silvery hair brushed back from his temples, he had a keen, handsome face and an intensely lively expression. He was distinguished as a pioneer of the Water Cure in Britain.

But he was more than just a noted doctor with an enormous practice bringing in thousands a year; he was a personality, a character of the mid-Victorian era, and was or had been friend as well as physician to Dickens, Bulwer Lytton, Disraeli, Carlyle, Tennyson and many others who swore by his hydropathic treatment. Charles Reade had even put him into his novel *It is Never too Late to Mend* as "Dr. Gullson". With a colleague, Dr. Wilson, he had virtually made Malvern as the Mecca of the Water Cure, which they had introduced there in 1842 after visiting Graefenberg in the Bavarian Alps and seeing some of the remarkable cures of Vincenz Priessnitz. This Austrian had, as a peasant, suffered grave internal injuries in an accident and had been given up as hopeless by the doctors. But by a seeming miracle he had entirely healed himself by the application of cold spring water—a technique learned from an old mountain goatherd. He had then set up as a healer of others.

Gully and Wilson had returned wholeheartedly converted to the cure by water and determined to establish it in England. Having toured the country to find a suitable place they finally came to Malvern, which seemed to them to have just the properties needed. Starting a hydropathic centre there at the old Crown Inn, they met with rapid and spectacular success. And their singular and uncomfortable treatment—in which the patient lay for hours wrapped in soaking sheets, underwent douches, lateral and horizontal showers, cold baths, sitz-baths, foot-baths, plunge-baths, compresses, friction with dripping towels, and drank gallons of water daily from the local hill springs—was undoubtedly beneficial to the gouty, dyspeptic and alcoholic sufferers who flocked to Malvern in search of health through the new Cure. Undeterred by opposition from conservative medical quarters, Gully—more notably than Wilson—stoutly defended the treatment; and when the partnership split up after a few years Gully carried on alone at the old quarters, now renamed Graefenberg House, taking an assured place as the country's leading hydropathic doctor.

But Dr. James Gully, whose book, *The Water Cure in Chronic Disease*, became a standard work, had other interests too: he was devoted to phrenology; and in 1839 his drama, *The Lady of Belleisle; or a Night in the Bastille*, adapted from a play of Dumas, was produced at Drury Lane. But above all it was his personality that made him famous. A contemporary record says: "What made him the man of influence he soon became was his very agreeable presence, his polished manners, and the charm of his companionship and converse enriched with the stores of a large and varied experience. Added to all this, he possesses a strong will and great force of character, and being also an easy-going man of the world, his society has always been much in request by all who knew him."

When Florence had faced Dr. Gully across his consulting-room desk at the Priory House, Malvern, a year before in 1870, she was not seeing him for the first time. For years he had been a friend of her parents and she had first met him when she was staying at Malvern with her parents as a twelve-year-old. But that had been long ago and probably, she thought, he had forgotten all about her. She remembered him, though, as having been very kind to her and her sisters, having them to tea and making much of them. Doctors, like parsons, have unrivalled opportunities of exercising personal attraction over people peculiarly placed to respond to it, and Dr. Gully had this quality to the full. No wonder then that Florence, as she had falteringly told him her troubles and sought his medical advice the year before, had come under his spell. There was the link, newly recalled, of family friendship; but more potent, there was his soothing understanding manner, his magnetic personality. He listened so well and spoke so wisely, so reassuringly.

He seemed to Florence to invite confidences, to be interested in her problems alone. He was like some favourite uncle—and at the same time she found a boyishness about him, a humorous twinkle behind the eye-glasses, that hinted that he could be excellent company beyond the confines of the consulting-room. It was a relief and a release for Florence, borne down by the tragedy of Alexander, to be able to talk to someone like him. She left him after her first consultation with the feeling that she had found a friend as well as a very competent medical adviser. And Dr. Gully, what could he think of this attractive patient, the little Florence that he had known years before, now grown up and coming to him with stories of a dipso-maniac husband? How could he help, as her visits went on and Alexander's malady developed, throwing in with his medical attention a good deal of interest that was not strictly pro-fessional?

In those anxious months at Malvern the friendship had pro-gressed until the doctor and his pretty married patient began to be talked about. Whispers of their indiscreet association had even reached Mrs. Campbell, Florence's mother, when she had visited Malvern—but she was inclined to pooh-pooh them as groundless gossip. Ricardo himself, reputedly a jealous man, expressed no objection to the social meetings of the two (as Florence herself asserted) and even encouraged them to go out together. After all, the doctor was sixty-two, and his pro-fessional prudence should be a guarantee against the least impropriety.

In late March or early April, 1871 (it seems uncertain whether she had spent the whole time since the previous November at Buscot, or gone abroad for two or three months), after a few days in the genteel suburban comfort of the Crystal Palace Hotel Florence had gone to Tooting as the guest of Mr. and Mrs. Brooks so that she could look for a suitable small house in the neighbourhood. It was at their house, Brooklands, that she heard the news of Alexander's death. Technically she was now a free woman; free to choose her friends, lead her own life, forget as soon as possible her wretched years with Alexander. As a young widow, suddenly bereaved after an unfortunate marriage, she was entitled to every sympathy. She was desperately lonely and needed companionship. All the same it might have been wiser for Florence, in her new-found freedom, to go a little slow and eschew for a while the company of the fascinating doctor. Ordinarily there would have been no harm in her meeting him during her mourning period: what more natural, for instance, than for her medical adviser and friend to call briefly and offer his condolences? But it did not happen like that. It was no formal, isolated call that Dr. Gully paid. With Alexander hardly dead a month he came and took lodgings near the Brookses' house and straightway visited Florence, thenceforward making frequent trips from Malvern on the same errand. It was certainly no way to kill the Malvern gossip of the previous autumn. His visits, in fact, soon drew pointed comment from Mrs. Brooks, and this led to a sharp quarrel with Florence in which the doctor heatedly intervened, threatening to bring a slander action against Mrs. Brooks. Remonstrances came too from Florence's mother, uneasy and suspicious now at the rumours that she could no longer ignore. Unquestionably, by her indiscreet conduct Florence was alienating herself from her family: and there now cropped up a further cause of estrangement. In May, under the advice of 'others' (whose identity may only be guessed), Florence took legal action against her father in respect of his administration of the trust under her family marriage settlement. It was infinitely regrettable that she was setting her family against her just when she needed them most.

But now Florence made another friend, one who was to

exercise as powerful an influence on her as anyone in her life: the lady who was daily governess to the youngest daughter of Mrs. Brooks. Jane Cannon Cox, a widow of uncertain age but perhaps in her forties, was a typical phenomenon of the Victorian era: an impoverished relict forced to eke out her slender means by teaching other people's children. Daughter of an East India merchant named Edouard, on whose death she had become a governess in the families of two clergymen, in 1858 she had married an engineer and gone with him to Jamaica. Widowed and left with three boys in 1867, she had returned to England two years later to set up as a schoolmarm in Suffolk. After a few months of this, however, she had come to London and introduced herself to a Mr. Joseph Bravo, wealthy partner of a merchant, Mr. Soloman, whom she had known in Jamaica; and he and his wife had received her very kindly. On Mr. Bravo's advice Mrs. Cox had invested most of her small capital in a house in Lancaster Road, Notting Hill, which she had let out in rooms; and with his help she had placed two of her sons at St. Anne's Asylum School at Streatham, an institution for the children of distressed gentlefolk. Then in May, 1871, lodging in Streatham with a Miss Child, she had advertised for a post as governess and been engaged by Mrs. Brooks.

In so many ways Jane Cox seemed just the person that Florence, in her lonely unsettled state, was looking for. Everything about her suggested the trusted sympathetic confidante. There was discretion in the quiet, almost mouselike manner, submission in the downcast bespectacled eyes. (Less obvious, because masked by the modest, self-effacing air, were the calculating shrewdness and inflexible strength of character of this hard-working, penurious widow with the jet-black scraped-back hair, sallow skin, and almost oriental look.) And so Florence took an immediate liking to Jane Cox, a sentiment that seemed to be fully returned. After all, though so different in background and circumstances, both had their widowhood and loneliness in common; and perhaps they were drawn together by the fellow-feeling that life had treated them unkindly. It may be too that Mrs. Cox, thus early, saw prospects of a post with Florence, who she knew was intending to set up house on her own.

Florence had been ill in April (being attended, for some reason, by a doctor from Worcester) and when she was better a change of air was indicated. So it was arranged that she should go away in June, taking her hostess's two daughters. And they went, of all places, to Malvern.

Was it so strange that Florence should return, a mere two months after Alexander's death, to the Worcestershire spa where they had recently spent the last few months of their unhappy life together? It would indeed have been if the place had recalled to Florence only the sordid picture of the sick captain's disintegration: in that case doubtless she would never have trod its streets again. But Malvern meant something else to her: it meant Gully. For her the doctor's warm, engaging—and yes, she now confessed it to herself, thrilling—personality had quite blotted out the painful Malvern memory of Alexander. Stokefield was forgotten in favour of the Priory House. And the elderly physician who in the crisis of last summer had proved such a friend in need had since then become infinitely more. How long had Florence thought of Gully in terms of love? Perhaps, subconsciously, ever since the day when she had first set foot in his consulting-room: Heaven knew, her heart had then long been empty of love for Alexander. But could one, at twenty-six, love a man of sixty-three, and a married man (even though his wife, much older than himself, was a chronic invalid)? Could anything worthwhile come of such love? Was it worth risking her good name and the affections of her family by continuing the association? It was a perplexing situation for Florence, lonely, bereaved and in need of guidance as she was. Emotionally she was staking a lot on Dr. Gully—who, for a rich attractive young widow, did not seem a very eligible choice. To seek him out by going to Malvern was doubtless her considered answer to the problem, a gauntlet thrown down to the gossips, a challenge to family and friends, who were genuinely concerned at her conduct. Her visit proved the prelude to an intimacy which—born and nurtured, as it was, round the affliction of Alexander—seemed ill-starred from the first.

How much Florence actually saw of the doctor while at Malvern and what plans they made for the future is not recorded; but soon after returning to Brooklands in September she started looking in earnest for a house of her own. Much as she enjoyed being with Mr. and Mrs. Brooks, she felt that she was beginning to trespass on their hospitality; and anyway she dearly wanted independence, privacy, a place where she could entertain her particular friend with no questions asked. She soon found just what she wanted, a solid, detached villa in Leigham Court Road, Streatham. Fond of comfort and well able to afford it, she took steps to engage a very adequate staff —a butler, a cook, two maids and a gardener. It was rather perverse of her to call it Stokefield, for her memories of that Malvern residence where she had last stayed with Alexander cannot have been of the happiest. Christmas passed and in January, 1872, it was time to leave. So, with a grateful good-bye to her kind hosts and an *au revoir* to her friend Mrs. Cox, Florence quitted Brooklands—but she did not immediately take up residence at Stokefield. To enjoy a kinder winter climate than England's and a companionship more unfettered than was feasible at home she went on a six-week trip to Italy with Gully, accompanied by Gully's man, Pritchard, and her own maid Fanny. And when they came back it was not to go their separate ways, she to Streatham and he to Malvern. The doctor now took up his abode in Leigham Court Road, in a house (to which his attention had been drawn by Florence) almost opposite hers. Having terminated his partnership with Dr. Fernie, he had left Malvern for good at Christmas. All pretences were now down. Here indeed was devotion, publicly proclaimed. For, whatever Dr. Gully's ultimate intentions towards Florence, it was a compelling attraction that made this clever and respected physician throw up his prosperous practice now (even though his retiring age was not far off), sever his long and honoured association with Malvern—and indeed hazard his whole professional reputation—to be near a woman (and a patient at that) thirty-seven years his junior.

From then on Gully was constantly in and out of Stokefield. Inevitably his frequent calls at the house across the road were noted from behind the lace curtains of the near-by villas— noted and commented on. Florence was to state later, when the whole story was dragged before a gloating public, that their relationship was then an "innocent" one. It may well have been then—but did either of them bother sufficiently about the "appearance of evil"? Perhaps they did not care. On the other hand, perhaps Florence did worry a little about the equivocal position; for in May she asked Mrs. Cox, with whom she had been keeping in touch (almost alone among the outside world except her aunt, brother and sister-in-law), to become her companion. Flattered and delighted to be offered such a domestic plum (£80 a year to start with, all found and not a great deal of work to do) Jane Cox wasted little time in accepting. She could not come at once: there was Mrs. Brooks to consider; and she had planned, on Florence's recommendation, to take her boys to Malvern for the summer holidays. But early in August she arrived at Stokefield with her boxes, fresh from her Malvern vacation and ready to take up her duties.

So began the queer four-year partnership of Florence and Mrs. Cox, for, despite the official mistress-employee relationship, partnership it was. From the first it was "Florence" and "Jane"; and at once the unobtrusive black-clad ex-governess took an assured place in the *ménage* as housekeeper, chaperon and confidante, lending an air of respectability to a situation that was beginning to need it, there when she was wanted, discreetly absent when she was not. There were few secrets that Florence did not share with her, and what Mrs. Cox was not told she had sharp eyes to see or the wits to guess. In her way she was fond of Florence, as Florence was of her; and in any case £80 a year and a cushioned live-in position like this were not to be sneezed at. Without doubt it was a situation that suited everybody.

The rest of the year passed quietly, with the doctor now almost a member of the household. He was there to lunch on most days, and often to dinner too, enjoying a *tête-à-tête* with Florence in the drawing-room afterwards. In return she frequently visited his house, generally with Mrs. Cox but sometimes without her. Jane Cox could not but notice the great intimacy between them, but tolerantly ascribed to Dr. Gully no more than "gentlemanly familiarity". Her later description of the doctor as a "fascinating man, one who would be likely to interest women very much", was as good as a confession that she had a soft spot for him herself; and thus when she spied them kissing, as she sometimes did, it was with an indulgent eye—especially as Gully was not above exercising a little of his charm on her; likewise she turned a deaf ear to the scandals about the goings-on at Stokefield and the house across the way that began to run around the neighbourhood.

Mrs. Cox was no fool. It must have crossed her mind before long that Florence and Dr. Gully were lovers—for lovers they certainly became, if not in 1872, at least some time in the first half of 1873. But whatever she suspected, perhaps she absolved the pair from guilt in view of the fact that they could not marry (even if they wanted to) because Gully had a wife, much older than him and a chronic invalid, living in a home at Brighton. Indeed, it seems that they themselves talked of marriage some time about now; and a vague understanding was even arrived at that they might make a match of it on the death of Mrs. Gully.

If Mrs. Cox's presence as duenna toned down the flagrancy of the couple's association it also meant that as lovers they could never be entirely alone together. They did have one undisturbed interlude at Christmas, 1872, when Jane took her boys away to Brighton; but otherwise there was no respite from her capable but ever-watchful attentions. Not, that is, until August. That month, accompanied by Florence's maid Humphreys, but without Mrs. Cox, they went to Germany. And there at last, in the romantic atmosphere of Kissingen, the pretty little Bavarian spa where they spent most of their time, they enjoyed each others' company unknown and among strangers, away from prying and censorious eyes. Not that they gave cause for undue comment, even here. Their rooms at Madame Manteuffel's *pension* were separate and they signed their own names in the register. It was an idyllic phase for both, the elderly doctor who should have long put aside such romantic flights, and the rich lonely young widow neurotically hungry for a love compounded of passion and fatherly affection that she could not have found in a younger man. Strolling along the chestnut-shaded Kur-Garten bordered on one side by the ancient Kurhaus, or looking down on Kissingen's wooded valley from the tower of the historic castle of Bodenlaube, they found a deeper intimacy, a more intense relationship, than they had had the chance to know before. But, for Florence at least, it was not all undiluted pleasure; for on Gully's recommendation she was taking the cure. She had what she described as the "horrid" baths—a glutinous mixture of iron-impregnated peat-soil mixed with mineral water. After half an hour in this steaming and repellent brew, "just like liquid manure", she had to take a hot bath to get clean. And on top of that she was forced to swallow three glasses of mineral water first thing in the morning and another in the evening. It was, as she told Mrs. Cox in a letter dated 23rd August, definitely "not agreeable".

But the letter is worth noting for other reasons than its description of the cure.

My dearest Mrs. Cox [it ran]— . . . Will you tell Rance [the gardener] that I have no intention of building a greenhouse, and will have nothing ordered from Mould or elsewhere without my order . . . I told M'Grath that he was not to sleep in the house, and *my order is to be obeyed*. Please tell him this. Will you write to Mrs—— for me and demand my recipe book back; . . . and tell her that unless she returns it I will write to her mistress . . . Will you find out if she comes to Stokefield, as I gave strict orders she was not to come at all, and you can tell Barton that it is as much as his place is worth if she comes to my house. I never gave Anna permission to have her sisters, and am writing to her about it. If all's well I shall be home on the 24th or 25th September. Will you kindly get me eight laying hens of the Brahma breed by that time from the *Exchange and Mart*—that will lay through the autumn and winter . . . Will you in the course of next week compare Watt Pegg's prices for coals with Pigott's, as I should like the cellar filled before I return. I am anxious to hear of the safe arrival of the cheque I sent you; please acknowledge it at once, and if it fails to reach you write at once to the London and County Bank, Great Malvern, to stop its payment at the Worcester Bank. As I have endorsed it anyone could cash it; but I hope you will get it all safe. . . .

With kindest love,—Yours very affectionately,

FLORENCE RICARDO

It was a revealing letter. Here, by the look of it, was no pathetic clinging Victorian vine, no poor little rich girl incapable of making up her mind or running her own affairs. Five hundred miles from home, she found time amid the pleasures and distractions of Gully's company and Kissingen's scenery to rule Stokefield with a rod of iron. Her injunctions and threats breathed determination to stand no nonsense, have her orders obeyed, watch every penny of her money. The whole letter signified indeed that Florence Ricardo was—in domestic affairs at least—a woman who knew what she wanted and was prepared to get it.

They returned at September's end, after over a month away, with Florence refreshed by her mineral cure and Gully in the best of spirits. And then, early in November, Florence became ill. She thought at first that the baths at Kissingen were responsible. But when the trouble was beyond mistaking it turned out lucky for all that Gully's presence dispensed with the need for calling a strange doctor: for Florence was suffering from a miscarriage. Dr. Gully, who had the closest personal interest in her case, was naturally worried to distraction; and for a few nights while Florence, weak and in pain, tossed feverishly on her bed, he slept at Stokefield. Incredibly, Mrs. Cox professed ignorance as to what the malady was. She asked Florence, who replied that it was "an unusual natural illness"; and even Dr. Gully kept up the deception by telling her that it was "a kind of tumour" which he had successfully removed.

It was a strange show of reticence or false modesty by Florence —and even the doctor—to one so obviously co-operative, devoted and discreet. But more inexplicable was the pretended ignorance of Mrs. Cox, a woman in her forties and mother of four (a daughter had died in Jamaica). Misplaced tact could hardly have been carried further.

With Florence satisfactorily convalescent, things at Leigham Court Road settled down largely to the old routine. But her illness wrought a change in her relations with Dr. Gully: they ceased to be lovers. This was at Florence's wish. She was still as devoted as ever to the doctor and delighted in his company and conversation; he was lively, entertaining, with a fund of information and anecdote about almost everything, courteous, solicitous—in fact the ideal escort and companion. And her affection for him was tinged with deep gratitude; she remembered what a welcoming refuge his society had been—and still was—in her estrangement from most of her family and friends. But the sequel to the Kissingen holiday had shocked her; she felt now that in giving way to passion her relations with James Gully had taken a wrong turn. After all, he was nearly forty years older than herself, and sex should play no part where there was such disparity of age. Henceforth, therefore, though they need see each other no less than before, she determined their association should be platonic.

Another change was at hand too. Florence was thinking of moving to a larger house. She felt a little cramped in Stokefield. She had the money; why not use it on something grander, more imposing? Not too far out, of course, for shopping in London; perhaps in that nice rural part on the edge of Tooting Bec Common. The Priory, Bedford Hill Road, Balham, was the complete answer to what she was looking for. She realised that as soon as she saw it. Losing no time in signing the lease, in March, 1874, she moved in with Mrs. Cox.

23

That lady was delighted: here, with every conceivable comfort, was a domain really worth running.

There was no doubt about it; Stokefield, though adequate, had been a modest place compared with this. The Priory was a castellated fifteen-room mansion in pseudo-Gothic style, with two lodges and ten acres of grounds. Florence had it magnificently refurnished throughout and engaged a domestic staff of eight to look after it. There were also three gardeners, and a coachman and groom. The whole thing was on a lavish scale: it was as if, after three years of widowhood and semi-seclusion, Florence had suddenly resolved to enjoy to the full the fortune that Alexander had left her.

Alas, she was in no position to make new friends; and perhaps that made her cleave all the more closely to the only old one she had. Dr. Gully had gone abroad shortly before her move, and now on his return about a month later he too left Leigham Court Road, his lease being up, to remove to a house a stone's throw from The Priory, which he newly furnished from top to bottom. With sentimental hark-back he called it Orwell Lodge—the name of the villa where Florence and the ailing Alexander had spent their first weeks at Malvern. So Balham too had its Priory (though in this case Florence had taken the name over with the house) and its Orwell Lodge. Malvern memories died hard.

Soon after settling into her new home Florence went away with Gully for a fortnight to Southsea. Mrs. Cox went with them, but no servants, and they stayed in lodgings. And then, summer at The Priory. As in Leigham Court Road, the doctor was a constant visitor. Florence gave him his own key to one of the garden gates and he lunched and dined there regularly as he had at Stokefield. Two or three times a week they took the air together in Florence's smart new landau. She would pick him up near his house and they would drive up to town for an afternoon's shopping or into the country that lay then just beyond the spreading villadom of Clapham. No doubt the new neighbours in Bedford Hill Road and the big houses near-by drew the worst conclusions from all this, but whatever the appearance may have been, Gully, as Florence had ordained after Kissingen, was no longer her lover. He had protested but she had been firm; and he was content to continue their friendship on her terms rather than not at all. But what sort of life was it for Florence? Sociable by inclination, she perforce made no contacts in the neighbourhood, had lost touch with old friends and would have been totally cut off from her family but for the occasional visits of her aunt, Mrs. Thomas Campbell, and her brother William and his young wife, Augusta, who gave her welcome news of her parents. Did she ever, yawning over an evening's crotchet with Mrs. Cox in the plush comfort of The Priory's drawing-room, or driving with the doctor in the quiet Surrey lanes, regret the choice she had made? Her carelessness of "virtue" was indeed proving its own reward. But if she sometimes wished things were otherwise, there were always Gully's unfailing attentions and solicitude to fall back on. When she was ill in May, of the same ailment that had affected her in April, 1871, at the Brookses' house, there he was to treat her with efficacious pills compounded of oil of savin. And when she felt in need of a change in September, there he was to escort her on a health-giving trip to Matlock and Buxton, with Mrs. Cox of course in attendance. The bond between them, even if now, on her side at least, devoid of passion, seemed as strong as ever.

But, soon after this, Florence did make some new acquaintances, in the shape of those kind friends of Mrs. Cox's, Mr. and Mrs. Joseph Bravo. The Bravos had been consistently good to Mrs. Cox and she often used to go and see them at their house at Palace Green, Kensington. At Christmas she would take her boys there and Mr. Bravo could always be relied on to tip them half a sovereign. More than once he had advanced her money when her tenants at Lancaster Road were behind with their rents; and it was through him that her third boy had been admitted to St. Anne's, Streatham, in January, 1873. So that one day in December, 1874, when Florence was driving up to London for shopping, Mrs. Cox took the opportunity of accompanying her, to pay a call at Palace Green. Florence dropped her there, and on returning to pick her up was asked in by Mrs. Bravo. She was shown into the drawing-room and introduced to Mr. Bravo. There too was a personable young man in his late twenties to whom she was also presented. He was Mr. Charles Bravo, the barrister son of Mrs. Bravo and stepson of her husband. A handshake with him, a brief, polite exchange of platitudes over the tea-cups, and it was time to go. Florence was glad to meet these people whose kindness Mrs. Cox was so often talking about, but beyond thinking that they seemed pleasant and lived in a remarkably fine house, she made no special note of them. There was no reason then why she should.

Florence was proud of The Priory. She had given her colourful taste full rein in embellishing the interior, and now she had plans for improving the grounds and gardens. Nevertheless, because of her restricted and secluded life there the place sometimes palled on her and she was glad to get away from it. Dr. Gully, of course, eagerly fell in with this mood of hers: a little gentle travel with Florence as companion—even though Mrs. Cox came too—suited him perfectly. So gaily he joined the two of them on a three-week jaunt to the West Country early in 1875: Exeter, Edgcombe, Ilfracombe, but always, whether in hotel or lodging, with the proprieties observed. The trip whetted Florence's appetite for more distant travel. She had never seen Italy: could they not go there? It was arranged; and in March the three of them set off without servants for Rome, via the Dover-Calais packet, Paris, Mâcon and Turin. Staying at Rome's smart Hotel Bristol (a double room for Florence and Mrs. Cox and a single for the doctor), they saw the sights of the Eternal City in the early Italian spring; and under these foreign skies they recaptured something of the romance of that holiday at Kissingen. Mrs. Cox could not help noticing a more demonstrative affection between them than had been apparent at, say, Exeter, but she was prepared to swear that they were never alone together. From Rome they went to Naples and Venice; and at the beginning of May Florence and Mrs. Cox returned home, leaving the doctor to travel back later.

That pleasant excursion turned out to be the last that Florence enjoyed with Dr. Gully, either at home or abroad. When she and Mrs. Cox took a late summer holiday at Eastbourne in September it so happened that he was away on the continent with his son; and then, some three weeks later, when the two ladies had moved on to Brighton, something occurred to precipitate the break with Dr. Gully that Florence had now been privately contemplating for some little time.

She was driving along the Parade with Mrs. Cox, going to a ports meeting in which one of Mrs. Cox's sons was taking part, when a tall young man passed them and smilingly raised his hat. The ladies bowed in return, and Florence turned to Mrs. Cox and said: "Why, Jane, surely that's Mr. Charles Bravo?"

CHAPTER 3

ENTER CHARLES BRAVO

MR. CHARLES BRAVO it was—the young barrister whom Florence had met briefly at Palace Green ten months before and had not seen since. She recalled him at once, noticing him now indeed with a decided interest. He made a smart figure strolling along Brighton front that autumn afternoon, a figure that might catch the eye of any young woman. For Charles Bravo was an attractive, upstanding young man; his handsome clean-cut features were well set off by neat mutton-chop whiskers and his dress was fashionably dapper. It was odd, Florence reflected as she gazed at him, that he had made so little impression on her before! Much the same thoughts were in Mr. Bravo's mind as he looked at her. She stopped the carriage to greet him, and they exchanged the remarks suitable to the casual encounter of slight acquaintances. He was staying, he said, with his parents in the New Steyne. She and Mrs. Cox were on a short holiday, she rejoined, and were in rooms in the King's Road. He hoped they would see something of one another, said Bravo; in fact he would be delighted to be allowed to call on her. By all means, said Florence. And then she drove off with Mrs. Cox to the sports ground and he resumed his walk.

So, by a chance meeting on Brighton promenade, came the new man into Florence Ricardo's life. If she did not already sense when they parted that she had made an impression on Charles Bravo she was soon well aware of it. As good as his word, he called on her without delay, and from then on saw her every day; and by the end of a week it was obvious that Charles Bravo was head over heels in love. Of course, his entrée to her company was aided by the fact that Mrs. Cox had known him for years as the stepson of her benefactor and a pleasant young man who was always kind to her boys when they called at Palace Green: and Florence, who was flattered at the conquest she had made, found this acquaintanceship useful too. She could learn from Jane all about this high-spirited, attractive new friend. And what she discovered pleased her. Charles Bravo's background, connections and prospects seemed as satisfactory as his personality was agreeable.

Charles Delauney Turner Bravo was just short of thirty years (a few weeks younger than Florence), having been born in November, 1845, at 39 Upper Charlotte Street, off the Tottenham Court Road. His father, Charles Turner of Jersey, whose only son he was, had died when he was a boy and his mother had then married Mr. Joseph Bravo. This wealthy merchant had carefully brought up and educated Charles, who at twenty-one had assumed the surname of Bravo. From King's College, London, he had gone to Trinity, Oxford, where he graduated in 1866 and took his M.A. two years later. He read for the Bar, and was admitted a barrister of the Middle Temple in April, 1870 (just when Florence was having those distressing experiences with her drink-addicted husband at Bournemouth). With chambers in Essex Court, Temple, he became attached to the Home Circuit, and lived with his parents at No. 2 Palace Green, the princely red-brick mansion behind Kensington Palace where Florence had first met him. He was clever and ambitious, and besides being determined to succeed in his legal career had some thoughts of getting into Parliament.

So much Florence learned from Mrs. Cox in those early days

of Charles's courtship at Brighton. Of his engaging impulsive nature she did not need Mrs. Cox to tell her. As they went out and about together on that October holiday, generally with Mrs. Cox in attendance—but, whenever they could throw her off, alone—this was obvious. Something else was obvious too: by the way things were going, the persuasive, ardent Mr. Bravo would soon be throwing himself at her feet and asking an all-important question. This was all very gratifying and exciting for Florence, but when the proposal of marriage came, what on earth was she to answer? Was she in love with him? Even if she could not fully return his affection, was he not a catch that she, in her position, would be mad to turn down? One thing was very clear to her: before she could even contemplate marrying Charles Bravo she would have to resolve the increasingly difficult problem of her relationship with Dr. Gully.

Her relationship with Dr. Gully . . . for months now this question had been on her mind, perplexing and worrying her; and the more she thought about it, the more she felt that it could have no future. She had considered her own equivocal situation. Was she to go on for ever platonically bound to this elderly admirer, warm as was her regard for him? Could the queer purdah-like association, with the sterile tedium of life at The Priory varied only by occasional trips to watering-places, compensate her for eternal estrangement from her family and friends? She had heard that summer from her aunt, Mrs. Thomas Campbell, of her mother's serious illness, and this had strengthened her growing wish to be reconciled to her parents, to get back into the family fold and be done with her dubious way of life.

And now Charles Bravo had come along, to give her, as it were, the chance of being an "honest" woman, to offer her substance in place of shadow.

There was only one thing for it: pondering the problem

during restless nights in her King's Road lodgings Florence came to the final decision to break with the doctor.

A chance to tell Dr. Gully came unexpectedly soon, but Florence found her decision easier to make than to carry out. The doctor, newly returned from abroad, suddenly arrived in Brighton to see her. To him, of course, everything was as it always had been and he had no suspicion of his impending fate: he was looking forward to meeting Florence again and telling her about his continental trip. He stayed the night not at her lodgings but at a quiet boarding-house, Markwell's Hotel, near-by; and in the morning, after a chat in her sitting-room at King's Road, they took a ride together (accompanied by the inevitable Mrs. Cox) along the front. Florence, unable to bring herself to tell him, was feeling awkward and unhappy; and her embarrassment was not lessened by their passing Charles Bravo in the street. As Florence acknowledged his gay salute the doctor asked who he was. She explained as casually as she could that he was the stepson of Mrs. Cox's good friend at Palace Green. Luckily the doctor showed no interest and the matter dropped, to the relief of Florence, who had very good reasons for not going into *that* particular subject just then.

Dr. Gully returned to Balham that night as unaware of Florence's decision as when he had arrived. Florence could hardly be blamed for not telling him. Her distaste for sending an old and valued friend packing so unceremoniously—especially when that friend might be expected to protest rather strongly—was understandable. But, ashamed of her weakness, she sat down almost at once and told him his fate in a letter. She was breaking off their association, she wrote, because, after five years, she could bear separation from her family no longer; her mother was ill and she must see her; but her parents would never take her back until she put him out of her life. There it was, done at last; and as she signed and sealed this sentence of dismissal she felt happier than she had done for months.

And now, of course, she could give her mind more un-reservedly to Charles Bravo.

For Dr. Gully had left Brighton ignorant of something else too. Shortly before his visit Charles Bravo had proposed; and, while Florence had not said yes, they had arrived at a very satis-factory understanding. Things could hardly have turned out better for Florence; for she had just brought herself to the pitch—and this was something she had been dreading—of con-fessing, on Mrs. Cox's advice, her association with the doctor when Charles had forestalled her by producing a skeleton out of his own cupboard. There was something he must tell her, he said. He had, he acknowledged with shame, kept an 'estab-lishment' at Maidenhead for the last four years. He knew he was unworthy of her love but if only she could forgive him he would be the happiest man alive; and he would of course sever all connection with the Maidenhead woman. To Florence, though she accepted this startling avowal with becoming gravity, it was wonderful news: now the way was clear for her to confess her own fall from grace. With a "past" of his own, Charles was hardly in a position to be high-handed about hers.

It was obviously the psychological moment to disclose her own secret. Even so, for some reason best known to herself (perhaps she did not feel quite sure of Charles yet), Florence let the moment pass, contenting herself with a gentle intro-duction to the full story which she knew she must tell sooner or later. And all she said now was that she had had a long attachment to a friend called Dr. Gully, and been constantly in his society ever since she had first lived in Leigham Court Road. Bravo was interested because he had often wondered whether such an attractive woman as Florence could have escaped male attentions during her widowhood. He laughed and asked how old Dr. Gully was. Evading a precise answer she replied that the doctor was an old family friend whom she had known from the age of twelve.

And that, for the time, was that. Charles seemed quite unperturbed; his reception of her half-confession was, Florence felt, a good augury for the way he would receive the rest of it —perhaps after they were formally engaged. Thus they reached their understanding; he the pursuer, professing ardent love, she the pursued, frankly more hesitant and cautious. Perhaps she did not want to appear to be too indelicately rushing things. And she was not quite happy about his mother, of whose devotion to her only son she had learnt a good deal from Charles. In this vein, and in admiration of his frank disclosure to her, she wrote to Charles in London just after writing to Gully.

113, *King's Road, Brighton, Oct.* 21, 1875

My dear Charlie,—After serious and deep consideration I have come to the conclusion that if you *still hope* and wish to gain my love we must see more of each other, and be quite sure that the solemn act of marriage will be for the happiness of both. This is what I think you ought to *tell* your mother. I would never enter any family where I was not welcome. I have no fear of not gaining her affection; but of course she must know me and judge for herself. All I can *say* is that you have behaved in the noblest manner, and that I have no doubt of being happy with you; but of course, before giving up my present freedom, I must be quite convinced it would be for our mutual happiness. Need I tell you that I have written to the *Dr.* to say I *must* never see his face again; it is *the* right thing to do in every respect, whatever happens, whether we marry or whether we do not. I shall ever have

a great regard for you, and take a deep interest in your welfare, for I think you are a very good man. Write and tell me what you think of this letter, and with every kind wish, ever your sincere friend, FLORENCE RICARDO
P.S. Of course this is sacred. I remain here till Monday.

To this Charles replied:

> 1, *Essex Court, Temple, Oct. 22, 1875*
> My dear Florence,—You are quite right. I approve thoroughly of what you say and do; and I may tell you that I am in danger of losing my chief jewel, my modesty, when I consider that you, whose opinion I most value, give me such high praise. It was but the other day that I was wishing that I knew where a commodity of good names was to be bought—and now I have them free—given . . .
> Ever your sincere friend, CHARLES BRAVO
> P.S. I will be in Brighton to-morrow.

Well might Charles feel smug at Florence's eulogies. For his own confession had been a gamble that might have ruined his chances. Instead, here he was, being told he had behaved in the noblest manner for confessing. Reading the letter in his Essex Court chambers, to which legal business had temporarily called him, he felt highly satisfied at the way things were going. For just as it had not escaped Florence that marriage with Charles Bravo was a passport to respectability embellished with the wealth of Palace Green, so Charles was aware that marriage with Florence would bring him fortune as well as a beautiful and desirable wife. And if she was prepared to overlook his peccadillo he was certainly ready to dismiss her friendship—especially with an elderly admirer like Gully.

Meanwhile that elderly admirer, back in his Balham villa,

had had Florence's letter. Receiving the tidings right out of the blue, the poor man was flabbergasted. A dear friendship such as theirs, cut short like this by a stroke of the pen! It was unthinkable! Why, he had seen Florence only a couple of days before, and not a hint had she dropped. He appreciated her desire to be reconciled with her family, but was there no way of effecting this without their parting? He would write to her, go down and see her again and beg her to reconsider her decision. These were the doctor's immediate thoughts as he read and re-read the letter: shock, incomprehension, hope, chased themselves through his mind. Finally he slept on it (the letter had come on Saturday evening); slept on it, in fact, for two nights; and on Monday, in calmer mood, wrote a reasonable and kindly reply, proposing that he run down to Brighton and talk things over with her. Florence telegraphed back, suggesting that he travel down with Mrs. Cox, who had been in town and was returning next morning. The faithful diplomatic Jane, she thought with appreciation, could temper the wind to the shorn lamb on the journey. So when Mrs. Cox's Brighton-bound train stopped at Croydon the doctor was on the platform looking out for her. And with the train speeding towards the Sussex coast the two of them spent the next hour or so in close and earnest conversation.

Florence was there to meet them at the station. After rather stilted greetings Dr. Gully suggested they had a private talk: was there a suitable place near-by? A small hotel outside the station seemed convenient, and there Florence and the doctor went, leaving Mrs. Cox to wait in the ladies' room at the station. No wonder poor Florence was nervous and upset as the door of the private sitting-room closed on them. For now not only had she to tell the doctor, face to face, that she had done with him, but she had to deal him an entirely new blow in the matter of Charles Bravo. Tearfully she stressed again to

35

the grave and silent doctor what she had said in her letter about her wish to be reunited with her family, her mother's illness and the impossibility of reconciliation unless she gave him up. And then in trepidation she broached the other subject. Mr. Charles Bravo, she said, the young man whom doubtless he would recall meeting in the street last time he was down, had been paying her marked attentions; and she herself liked him well enough. He asked whether they were engaged, and she said no. But she begged him, as a dear friend, to see her position and future as she saw it. It was, as she had known it would be, a painful interview, but in the end Dr. Gully seemed to take it all very philosophically and said that whatever was for Florence's happiness he wished her to do. With that they left the hotel, rescued the patient Mrs. Cox from the cold comfort of the station waiting-room and drove back to King's Road for a rather subdued lunch. In the afternoon Dr. Gully left for London, a man who had much to be dejected about, but who must also have foreseen that sooner or later this was bound to happen to him.

Charles was back in Brighton now and Florence hastened to tell him all about the interview. His conclusion on the matter was that, with Gully disposed of, there was nothing to stop Florence accepting his proposal. Florence evidently thought the same; for at the end of October, on the eve of her return with Mrs. Cox to Balham, they became engaged.

Florence was a happy and satisfied young woman. Rapturous love may not have come to her, but she had gained a very presentable fiancé with admirable prospects; she had extricated herself from a difficult relationship; and having lost no time in telling her parents of her dismissal of Gully, she was back in the family circle. Her father wrote her an understanding and forgiving letter, and on 30th October she replied thus from The Priory:

My dearest Father,—Your kind and affectionate letter gave me great pleasure last night, and I look forward with sincere and heartfelt joy to meeting you all again. My past has been a very sad one, but it will be for ever blotted out and forgotten, and believe me when I say how much I regret ever having caused you or any of your family pain with regard to the last few sad years of separation. With much love to yourself, and all at Buscot, ever your affectionate child,

FLORENCE RICARDO

Though Florence did not mention her engagement her parents heard of it very soon afterwards. Mr. Campbell made inquiries about Charles Bravo's position and prospects and professed himself satisfied. Both he and Mrs. Campbell felt that Florence could show no better evidence of regained respectability than by getting herself married to a good husband.

Now was the time, Florence judged, for her full confession. Charles, more passionately in love with her than ever, would surely not draw back now. After all, she had paved the way by mentioning her strong attachment, and there was his own affair with that Maidenhead woman. Hot-blooded, impetuous Charles was, she felt more and more certain, no prude in these matters; and he might even desire her the more because she had been desirable to another man. So, on a visit of his to The Priory, she nerved herself to tell him. And falteringly the story came out—the visits to each other's houses, the trips at home and abroad (albeit with Mrs. Cox generally in attendance), the guilty episode at Kissingen; and yet it was not quite the whole story; for, feeling that there was no point in overlabouring her guilt, she omitted the intimacies that had occurred before Kissingen. Having thus unburdened herself, Florence tactfully left the room to let Charles take it in and consider whether he wanted to rescind his proposal. Returning after twenty minutes she told him with commendable unselfishness that she had no wish to hold him bound by his offer. But one look at his face was enough to show her that she had no need to worry. There was understanding in his eyes and a tender smile hovered about his mouth. With immense relief she heard him say that she had acted nobly and generously in confessing to him.

"I am quite satisfied to make you my wife," he said, "but of course you must never see Dr. Gully again."

And he made her swear before God that she would never divulge the secret to anyone else. She promised eagerly and they sealed the compact with a kiss. Now there were no secrets, no shadows, between them.

The pleasure at Buscot Park over the announcement of Florence's engagement was not echoed at Orwell Lodge. Dr. Gully had left Brighton believing, from what Florence had said, that there was no engagement in the offing; and when, about 10th November, he received a little note from Mrs. Cox telling him of it, he expressed his resentment in letters to both Mrs. Cox and Florence. To do him justice, he wrote again soon afterwards apologising for his strong words; they were, he said, due to his being so upset at the news. And was it so very strange that this friend—and more than friend—of five years' standing should feel that insult was added to injury when he found himself first summarily discarded and then supplanted?

Behind all the developments, the comings and goings, of those eventful days at Brighton had lurked, like an unobtrusive shadow, Mrs. Cox. Quietly watching every move and knowing Florence's mentality pretty well, she had seen early how matters were going. And as Dr. Gully stepped out of the picture and Charles Bravo stepped in, one thing was clear to her: that, on the analogy of the old adage that two's company and three's none, if Charles married Florence she herself might be out of a very comfortable job and lose the valued companionship of a mistress who in these last years had become almost a crony. She had nothing against Charles but it was only human for her to look at it in this way, for £100 a year all found in a place like The Priory was something worth holding on to—a thousand times better than scraping along as a daily governess. But what could she do about it? Very little: Florence had a mind of her own and would not be advised by *her* against marrying Charles, whatever pretext could be cooked up. But Charles might feel less eager to marry Florence if he knew of her affair with Gully. So when Florence, herself undecided, asked Mrs. Cox's advice as to whether she ought to tell Charles "all", Jane strongly urged her to do it. But alas for the housekeeper's hopes, Charles's own confession—made first —completely nullified the effect of Florence's. (Incidentally, Mrs. Cox strenuously maintained later that at the time she encouraged Florence to confess she was unaware that Florence's relations with Dr. Gully had ever been "guilty", and that Florence had only told her of this just before they left Brighton. Was this part of the same blinkered modesty that had prevented her acknowledging that Florence's post-Kissingen illness of 1873 was a miscarriage?)

The secrets of Florence's past were still not allowed to be forgotten when she returned with Mrs. Cox in the last days of October to The Priory. Now, in the opinion of Florence's mother, and her aunt, Mrs. Thomas Campbell, it was Charles's mother who ought to know them. And, naturally, Mrs. Cox heartily concurred. The matter was put to Charles at Mrs. Thomas Campbell's Surbiton home early in November. Florence and Mrs. Cox had driven over from The Priory and Mrs. Campbell was there too. Florence told her mother that she had disclosed her association to Charles, and Mrs. Campbell then took Charles into a corner of the drawing-room and tackled him.

"I have learned from my daughter," she said, "that she has told you all the circumstances of her life that have been the cause of her estrangement from her family."

"Florence has told me everything," answered Charles shortly, "and I'm satisfied."

Mrs. Campbell then urged on him the necessity of telling his parents, and especially his mother.

Charles flared up at this. "Sooner than do that I'd leave the country."

Mrs. Campbell was not daunted. She begged that if he would not tell his mother himself he should let Mrs. Cox do so. Her sister-in-law added her entreaties.

Annoyed at this persistence Charles said heatedly: "We're both old enough to judge for ourselves, and the name of Dr. Gully will never be mentioned by me again!"

But still Mrs. Campbell would not give up. Once more she appealed to him, and Charles, now pale with resentment, refused point-blank to mention a word of the affair to his mother.

Mrs. Campbell saw that enough had been said and the subject was dropped. But she had not finished. After the party she wrote to Mrs. Cox—who doubtless had not missed much of the discussion—imploring her to try her utmost to get Charles to do the right thing. Mrs. Cox said she would do what she could: was not this an extension of her own tactics at Brighton? Even now the possessive Mrs. Joseph Bravo was showing an antipathy to Florence, and if she heard of Florence's past she would certainly veto the marriage.

One evening soon afterwards when Charles was dining and staying the night at The Priory—his mother objected to his going home late as he caught cold easily—she tactfully brought the matter up.

"Charles, I do hope you'll tell your mother all about Florence," she said. "I think she'd be very grieved if she heard anything of it afterwards."

But Charles would not consider the idea. His mother would come round, he said, after the marriage.

"Well, will you let me tell your mother?" asked Mrs. Cox.

Charles turned on her. "You know what the consequences would be. The marriage would be broken off."

Petulantly he added, like a punished small boy threatening to get his own back: "And then I should leave the country and no one would see me again!"

The silly threat reflected the impotence that Charles felt against his dominating strong-willed mother. And Mrs. Cox knew as well as Charles that if Mrs. Joseph Bravo said no to the marriage, then it would not take place. She saw now that there was no shifting him, though she did have one more try, equally vain, at Palace Green, where she and Florence spent ten days at the end of November. It was obvious now that nothing would induce Charles to bring certain ruin on his hopes of marriage—and it was equally clear that, as a man of the world, he viewed Florence's past lapse very lightly. He had forgiven her and the affair was dead and buried. All he wanted to do was forget it.

Yet he did once, at this time, express one tiny doubt to Mrs. Cox. He asked her if she thought there was any probability of Florence going wrong again.

"I think a woman who has once gone wrong is likely to be all the more particular afterwards, don't you?" he said.

Reassuringly Mrs. Cox agreed. She did not think Florence would transgress again.

How then stood Mrs. Cox's future, with Florence's past

secure and the marriage plans as strong as ever? Shortly before the wedding she was relieved of all her worries. One Sunday when Charles was down at The Priory he spoke to her about her position after the marriage and said quite simply: "I don't wish you to leave." That same afternoon she ran into Charles and Florence as they were strolling in the garden. Evidently they had been discussing the matter further, for Florence told her they had both made up their minds for her to stay. It was welcome news, a handsome recognition—on Florence's part at least—of the ever-discreet and unobtrusive service given during the years with Gully. And as for Charles, he may have been influenced by his mother, who had already told Mrs. Cox that she did not wish her to go: Charles was not strong, she said, and it would be very nice for Florence to have a lady friend in the house; she could be so useful in so many ways. It seemed, then, that in Mrs. Cox's case the old adage fortunately had no meaning.

Florence passed the ten days at Palace Green with mixed feelings. The visit was her formal introduction to her future parents-in-law, and as such slightly formidable. Mr. Joseph she found friendly and charming: he seemed thoroughly happy about the marriage. But his wife, while playing the hostess politely enough, Florence felt to be lacking in warmth and cordiality. And no wonder, for Florence was the very last woman whom this possessive and adoring mother would have wished her son to marry. Charles was there, of course, to support his fiancée; and Mrs. Cox, quite at home in the house, could be relied on to smooth over any awkward moments. But altogether Florence was not sorry when they returned to Balham. Perhaps the most satisfying impression she brought away with her was of the richness and smooth luxury of the palatial Bravo mansion.

By way of return, Florence introduced Charles to her father, and her brother William and his wife Augusta. With his easy manner and social graces she had no fear of his not being a success. And meeting this frank and charming young barrister the Campbell family agreed that it was likely to be a very good match.

Meanwhile preparations were going ahead for the wedding. It was to be at All Saints Church, Ennismore Gardens, and the reception was to be at 31 Lowndes Square.* The date first fixed was 14th December, but for some reason—possibly Circuit business—this did not suit Charles and at his request it was changed to the 7th. Florence was busy shopping, visiting dressmakers, calling at Lowndes Square to see how arrangements were proceeding. And every time she drove down Bedford Hill Road she passed, at the bottom on the right, the house whose name proclaimed the past that she was trying to discard—Orwell Lodge. Florence had not seen its occupant since the uncomfortable Brighton meeting. The last time her carriage had stopped there she had not been in it: Griffith, her coachman, had on her orders been returning to Dr. Gully all the presents that he had given her and bringing back to The Priory all her gifts to him. As far as she was concerned the break was absolute: even the little portrait of the doctor that she had carried in a locket around her neck went the way of all the other mementoes. And Gully for his part felt the same. His last link with Florence was, as far as anyone knew, severed when he gave Pritchard, his butler, the key to the garden gate of The Priory and asked him to return it to its owner.

Then, ten days before the wedding, something happened which caused her to seek the doctor's company once more.

It was to do with the marriage settlement. Mr. Brooks, her solicitor, was drawing this up to include her various moneys

* The Ricardos' old town house. Mr. Campbell had acquired it in 1867 from Lady Catherine on her moving to 46 Chester Square.

43

(her husband's bequest and £20,000 settled on her by her father) and the lease of The Priory, when he received her tele-graphed instructions to bring in all her personal effects too. As the law then stood, everything possessed by a woman passed, on her marriage, to her husband unless previously secured to her by a settlement. When Charles heard of this move he protested violently, and one evening at The Priory told Florence in an angry outburst that unless these personal effects were left out of the settlement he would not marry her. He had not the slightest objection to her settling the money on herself, he said, but he was not going to come into the house and sit on a chair that was not his! Florence was deeply upset: she had never seen Charles so worked up. She wondered what on earth to do. It seemed vital that she immediately sought advice—and whom should she turn to but that elderly friend who had so often counselled and comforted her before.

Early next morning she sent Fanny Griffith, once her maid and now the coachman's wife, with a message to Dr. Gully, asking him to come at once to the coachman's lodge to see her on an urgent matter. Fanny hurried off while Florence waited at the lodge; and in ten minutes the doctor arrived. As they exchanged brief greetings at The Priory's familiar entrance gates there might in other circumstances have been room for sentiment. But not now. Gully was more mystified than any-thing at being so suddenly summoned from banishment. And Florence was too worried and unhappy over her dispute with Charles to indulge tender memories.

They went into the lodge parlour and Florence told him her trouble. Gully's answer was short and to the point.

"Don't squabble about the furniture," he said. "You shouldn't wish your husband to come into a house of which he's not master."

Meekly Florence accepted the advice. And that was virtually

all that passed between them—save one little concession to the past.

In parting, Florence said in a small voice: "I've told my future husband all that has occurred between us."

"I hope it will turn out well and that you'll be very happy, my dear," Gully replied gruffly. With that he kissed her hand and said good-bye. And that really was the end. As far as was known, they never met again.

If sentiment was lacking in that last rendezvous, at least it was spiced with irony. Dr. Gully had after all behaved very decently: he had given Florence his parting blessing; and it is not often that a discarded lover, on taking leave of his ex-mistress, advises her on a matter to the advantage of her future husband.

Florence acted at once on his suggestion and got Mr. Brooks to alter the settlement. What were a few sticks of furniture, a handful of jewellery, the cobs and the rest of her personal possessions, she reflected, compared with a husband like Charles? And it was not as if the money were all on her side: Charles's stepfather had contributed handsomely to the match by settling £20,000, to take effect on the death of the survivor of the parents, first on Charles, and then—if anything should happen to him—on herself. So now, with the ghosts of the past laid, there seemed no possibility of dispute between them, and every prospect of a long and happy marriage.

CHAPTER 4

A WEDDING AND A PROPHECY

On 7th December, 1875, driving from the family house in Lowndes Square to All Saints, Ennismore Gardens, Florence Ricardo entered on her marriage to Charles Bravo. It was a happy occasion: the bride looked radiant, the groom proud and handsome. Did Florence's thoughts, as she stood at the altar beside Charles, go back to that other wedding of eleven years before at Buscot Church? Did she reflect on the queer unorthodox course her life had taken since then? She was very different from the young girl of nineteen who had pledged herself to Alexander Ricardo, no longer sheltered, romantic or innocent, but, with her bright complexion, her wide-set blue eyes and striking auburn hair, still as beautiful and appealing as ever. Her small figure was a shade rounder, more mature, but the years had treated her kindly, leaving little mark of the experiences that had in that decade or so made her a woman of the world. She knew something about men now, knew too what she wanted from life; and this knowledge, reinforcing the egotism, the independence, the latent hardness of her character, had well equipped her to order her own destiny. Watching her now as she was united with her second husband, her parents felt content with what seemed to lie in store for her. Wayward and self-indulgent she might be, but the poor girl had learned her lesson, and marriage to a fine, steady fellow like Charles Bravo was the very thing to ensure her a serene, untroubled future.

The only person there who might claim to know Florence better was Mrs. Cox, and what that reticent lady, with her impassive expression and blank spectacle-shuttered eyes, might think, guess or foresee was her secret and hers alone.

The reception over, the couple left Lowndes Square, amid the congratulations and good wishes of family and friends, for Victoria and thence to Brighton, where they were spending their honeymoon. Everything had gone wonderfully; but both Charles and Florence were conscious of one small damper on the celebrations: Mrs. Joseph Bravo had absented herself from the wedding. This over-possessive mother had in the end felt unable to bring herself to witness her adored son taken off by another woman. All she would say was that she hoped that in time she might be disposed to look more kindly on Florence.

There was another absentee from the ceremony, probably noticed by neither Florence nor Charles. George Griffith, long in service as Florence's coachman, was not there. It was regrettable, for Griffith was an old retainer and the only one among Florence's staff who had been with her at Malvern. And before being in her service there he had been for some years with Dr. Gully. He had known Florence's first husband and, while in Gully's employ, recalled seeing him, in company with Florence, dining at the doctor's house. He had accompanied Florence to Streatham, left her for a time on marrying her maid, Fanny Plascott, and returned to her service when she moved to The Priory. He it was who used to drive Florence and the doctor in her landau on their excursions to London and elsewhere. And then misfortune had befallen Griffith. The previous December, while driving Florence and Mrs. Cox in London on the day of the Lord Mayor's Show, he had collided with a wine cart in New Bond Street. The roads were crowded that day and the traffic was difficult; but, though Griffith himself strongly denied it, the accident was said to be his fault. And when Charles heard of it he urged Florence to get rid of him: the man was obviously not careful enough to drive in London. So Griffith got a month's notice and was due to leave at the beginning of January. It was the end of a long association in which he had seen the mistress with the captain, the doctor and now the new gentleman, Mr. Bravo. And Griffith, however he viewed the first two, regarded Charles Bravo, the author of his dismissal, with little favour. No doubt he was disappointed with Florence too. At all events George Griffith was not at the wedding.

Instead, he was in the tap-room of the Bedford Hotel, Balham, the public-house that stood at the bottom of Bedford Hill Road just beyond the railway bridge. As he sat moodily alone with his mug of porter in front of him, Mr. Stringer, the manager, spoke to him.

"Hallo, George, haven't you gone to the wedding?"

"No," answered Griffith, "I'm going to Wandsworth, to the County Court, to pay a summons for some vegetables supplied by Mrs. Hale up at New Park Road, Brixton Hill. The fact is, I'm in a bit of a hurry."

Taking a pull at his drink he added: "Missis will be sure and have a lot of brandy before she goes to the wedding."

Then he spoke of Charles Bravo.

"Poor fellow," he said, "I shouldn't like to be in his shoes. He won't be alive four months!"

And, wiping his mouth with the back of his hand, George Griffith got up and left the bar.

CHAPTER 5

PRELUDE TO POISON

1 Undertones at The Priory

IT WAS a startling pronouncement, and Mr. Stringer scratched his head, completely taken aback. It was as well that no one else heard Griffith utter it. If Mr. Stringer later repeated it in the bar parlour of the Bedford Hotel, at any rate it never reached the ears of the folk in the big house at the top of Bedford Hill Road. Had it done so, no doubt it would have been put down to nothing more than George Griffith's rancour at being dismissed. George was known to be a queer fellow, good with horses (if one charitably overlooked his recent trouble in New Bond Street) but a bit simple otherwise.

By the time Charles and Florence set foot in The Priory as a married couple Griffith had left, to take up another post with Lady Prescott at Herne Bay. They had not as a matter of fact gone straight there from their ten-day honeymoon at Brighton. They had first visited their respective parents, staying at Palace Green for Christmas and spending a few days at Buscot at the beginning of January. The visits were a pleasant overture to the serious business of settling down to married life. But while they were at Palace Green something very peculiar happened which greatly upset Charles. He received an anonymous letter. It had been addressed to him at the Temple, and it accused him in coarse language of marrying Florence, ex-mistress of Gully, for her money. His first thought was that the doctor himself had sent it, and in Florence's presence he showed it to Mrs. Cox, asking her to look at it and see if she could recognise Gully's handwriting. She, however, was able to say (though it was doubtful how she knew) that it was not in the doctor's hand; and then, on her suggestion, Charles threw the thing in the fire. Thus, before it could be seen by anyone else and its author identified, this abusive little note went up in smoke and its secret was lost for ever. But it left behind a disquieting reminder that someone disliked Charles; and he could not get it out of his head that Gully was responsible.

The affair rankled with him, and a few days later, at Buscot, he mentioned it to Mrs. Campbell, calling it "a vile letter".

"All anonymous letters are vile," said Mrs. Campbell, trying to make as little of it as possible. "If I were you I'd disregard it entirely."

Charles apparently took her advice, for he at once resumed his cheerful mood and spoke of it no more.

And so, on 6th January, 1876, they came to The Priory, Bedford Hill Road, Balham; that charming mansion in a sham Gothic style popularised by Horace Walpole's Strawberry Hill which Florence had leased some two years before from the Hon. Mr. Byng and to which she now brought Charles Bravo as its first lord and master.

The Priory exists still, but its semi-rural glory has long departed. The name has gone and now it is merely No. 197, Bedford Hill. And what was a spacious residence of some fifteen rooms (eleven bed, four reception and a conservatory) is now divided up into six self-contained flats. The two lodges which, housing the coachman and the head gardener, commanded the front and back entrances, have long since disappeared; and the ten acres of grounds in which the house stood have been entirely built over. But it was a fine property when Mr. and Mrs. Charles Bravo crossed its threshold in

January, 1876, a creeper-clad, three-storey pile, turreted, cream-stuccoed and the height of Regency elegance.

The Priory's previous occupant had been a wealthy partner in a firm of City bankers, and while he had done much to improve the grounds and gardens Florence had lavishly renovated the interior. Indeed the whole place was a repository of high-class mid-Victorian taste. The dining-room, on the right of the entrance-hall, was massively dignified. Its vast eight-foot sideboard with mirrors, table with seven extra leaves, twelve chairs upholstered in crimson morocco, and dinner-wagon were all in magnificent Spanish mahogany; and for ornament it had a ponderous marble-cased clock and several fine bronzes. Behind this lay the drawing-room, gorgeous with its suite in rich blue satin and hangings to match, its chimney glasses, amboyna and ebonised cabinet inlaid with ivory, whatnots and Sèvres and Dresden china ornaments, its pair of candelabra, two marble busts on pedestals and seven-octave semi-grand pianoforte in walnut by Collard and Collard. Giving on to the drawing-room was the conservatory or fernery, abounding in rare plants, some worth twenty guineas apiece. Opposite the drawing-room, at the back of the hall on the left, was the library, in choice oak throughout and thickly carpeted, with several hundred volumes "for the delectation of the studious occupants of The Priory". Then, opposite the dining-room and on the left of the front hall was the morning-room or boudoir, Florence's sanctum, *recherché* in crimson silk with matching draperies, a cabinet, centre table, and a wealth of *étagères*, whatnots, *jardinières*, and pouffes and tasselled cushions tastefully toning in with the colour scheme, a glittering collection of Venetian glasses, a seven-octave cottage piano by Broadwood and a steel and ormolu fender and fire implements. A mass of wool rugs covered the carpeted floor. Abutting on this room was a greenhouse.

A well-fitted kitchen and a small butler's pantry completed the ground-floor rooms. Upstairs on the first floor were the three principal bedrooms and two dressing-rooms. Above them were the servants' quarters and Mrs. Cox's room. And again in the main bedrooms Florence had given her taste full scope. There were suites in finely marked Spanish mahogany with ebonised mouldings and carvings, and in light satinwood and mahogany; there were pedestal duchesse tables and brass and iron French and Arabian bedsteads. The servants' rooms above were suitably furnished in pine and japanned woods. A choice and ample cellar—this may have reflected a certain liking for drink in which Florence had been increasingly indulging and which her mother had noted and reproved her for, or may have been laid down because Charles was something of a connoisseur and enjoyed a good glass of wine—included champagne, still and sparkling hock and moselle, old pale brandy, still and sparkling burgundy, St. Julien claret, Amontillado and old gold sherry, old crusted and light tawny port. And profusely decorating the main rooms, the hall and staircase were religious prints and pictures. It was said that "Messrs. Gladstone, Newman and Spurgeon, were they visitors at The Priory, would each and all of them have found some effort of more or less inspired pictorial art to flatter their religious proclivities".

From the windows of The Priory one looked out, through the 'venetians', over well-tended gardens. Indeed, seen from the upper windows the gardens seemed to merge into the rural background of Tooting Bec Common, from which they were separated only by an unobtrusive laurel hedge. On this secluded side, with its quiet walks used mainly by nursemaids and cyclists, was the rose-covered lower lodge occupied by the gardener. In the centre of the side lawn stood a noble great oak, a hundred and fifty years old. (It stands there still, a stark and sorry shell of its former self.) Around the lawn were wide flower-beds full of choice summer bedding-plants and varieties of dwarf standard roses. In addition there were a pinery, a vinery, melon pits, a well-stocked kitchen garden, strawberry beds and fruit trees. Behind the house was a five-acre paddock bordering on Tooting Bec Common and Streatham Hill. Its protective barrier of fine elms not only maintained the property's park-like features but also, it was emphasised, helped "to mask from view that dreaded innovation by occupiers of eligible suburban residences, the passage of railway trains". (But despite this jealously guarded seclusion, The Priory was briefly visible to railway travellers between Balham and Streatham Hill Stations, and also to passengers on the Crystal Palace High-Level line and Brighton-bound passengers from Victoria and Clapham.) Finally the stables, so recently vacated by the unfortunate Griffith: to the care of the four stalls, loose-box, harness-room and carriage-house Florence had devoted as much attention as to any other part of her property; for she was a keen horsewoman and drove a dashing phaeton, for which she kept two spirited cobs, Cremorne and Victor. (The horses for the landau were jobbed from a local stable.) And to run the house she had, under the competent Mrs. Cox, an inside staff of Rowe, the butler, a footman, five maids and a cook; while outside she employed a coachman, a groom and three gardeners.

This was the impressive *ménage* to which Charles Bravo came in the New Year of 1876. He knew it of course already, but the longest he had spent here was a night: now it was his home. And accustomed as he was to the opulence of Palace Green, the country-house splendour of The Priory was something different, even a little overwhelming at first. Surveying the plushy comfort of the drawing-room, the fussiness of the boudoir, the sprouting exotics in the fernery, he sighed

privately for the dull masculine heaviness of his favourite Pall
Mall haunt, the Junior Carlton Club. Inside and out the place
was run on such lavish lines. The expenses, he reflected as he
looked around, must be huge. For Charles was careful where
money was concerned. He believed in knowing where the
money went and in getting good value for it. Not that he was
involved to any great extent in the household expenditure; for
it had been arranged before the marriage that Florence should
continue to finance the entire upkeep of The Priory except for
the stables, which would be Charles's charge. And as his
income was about £1,000 a year—£800 from his stepfather as
the yield on his settlement capital, and £200 as his earnings at
the Bar—he should not be unduly pushed, especially as his
stepfather never refused a request for cash. But in this money-
conscious side of his character he was like Florence, who loved
spending, loved the power that her wealth had given her, but
in her open-handed disbursements on the things she wanted
never lost sight of the pennies that could be saved. The Priory
was her pride, her property, and she was prepared to spend on
it up to the hilt—though not beyond. And it was not long
before Charles was enjoying this satisfying sense of possession
too: soon he was taking an active interest in the running of the
grounds and gardens, expansively talking of his new home as
"the estate". But just as his devotion to the place never quite
equalled Florence's, so he never quite lost the feeling that the
scale of living at The Priory was too high.

But such mundane thoughts of finance were soon dismissed
in the early days of married bliss. Charles was entirely happy
in his new-found state, and so was Florence. To add to their
contentment they were without the company of Mrs. Cox,
who was away on a short holiday. Then, suddenly, misfortune
struck them: at the end of January Florence had a miscarriage.
Mr. Harrison, a surgeon from Streatham Hill who had

attended Florence before, was called in; and Mrs. Cox, now returned, was at hand to nurse her as devotedly as she had after Kissingen. Charles hovered about the sick-bed helpless and concerned, and with relief saw her restored to reasonable health. But she needed a change; and in mid-February had a week or so at St. Leonards, though business kept Charles from accompanying her.

For the rest, those first months went on placidly and uneventfully enough. Charles, his high-spirited, ebullient self, went regularly to his Essex Court chambers, though he often bewailed that he got so few briefs. And once he was away on Sessions. They entertained fairly frequently. Barrister friends of Charles's like Frederick MacCalmont, who shared his chambers, and Edward Hope came to be proudly introduced to Florence, and Florence's relatives and Mr. Bravo dined there, and all who came noted how happy and devoted the pair seemed. They remarked too how admirably Mrs. Cox appeared to fit into the scheme of things, so friendly with Charles and Florence and running the house (though always under Florence's close supervision) so capably. Not that Charles and Florence never had a tiff. Once they got very near quarrelling about household expenses. Charles, prompted by his mother (who had never quite relinquished her beloved son to this "other woman" and greedily gleaned every detail from him, on his frequent visits to Palace Green, of life at The Priory), urged Florence to economise by giving up the personal maid whom she had had up to the time of her marriage. Florence resented this and was for refusing: but finally agreed —chiefly, she said, so that Charles should not be further bothered by Mrs. Joseph about it. More half-heartedly Charles, again at his mother's instigation, suggested that she get rid of her beloved ponies. This time he had touched a really tender spot. Florence indignantly refused, declaring that she had always lived within her income and that what she did with her money was her own concern. Charles, far from happy at being his mother's mouthpiece in these matters affecting Florence's expenditure, did not press the point. Yet, much as he regretted his mother's hostility towards Florence and her interference in Florence's affairs, he remained uneasy at his wife's extravagant spending. That early concern of his was specially liable to crop up again whenever he was subjected to one of his mother's lectures on economy; and coming home and reckoning up the total of what it must be costing to run The Priory, he more than once found himself working out how the outlay could be pruned, by reducing gardening expenses, perhaps, or cutting down the staff.

But judging from the tone of the letters that they wrote each other when Florence was at St. Leonards, and Buscot, where she went for a short stay in mid-March, and those that they wrote their parents, such differences were nothing more than passing clouds in the general serenity of their marriage. Loving, light-hearted, bantering, full of family affairs and domestic chit-chat, they were the letters that any normal newly-married young couple might write.

Yet one letter of Charles's did suggest something different. Written to Florence at St. Leonards from Palace Green (where he sometimes stayed in her absence) on 15th February, it said:

My darling Wife,— . . . Looking back on the ten weeks of our marriage, I feel that many of my words to you, although kindly meant, were unnecessarily harsh. In future my rebukes, if it be necessary to say anything, which God forbid! shall be given with the utmost gentleness . . . I hold you to be the best of wives. We have had bitter trouble, but I trust every day to come the sweet peace of our lives will not so much as be disturbed by memories like those . . . I wish I could sleep away my life till you return . . . Come back as well as you can to your devoted husband, CHARLES

What were his "words" to her, his "rebukes"? Florence's liking for drink—engendered perhaps by the stress of her life with the dipsomaniac Alexander—which her mother and Mrs. Cox had already noted, had become evident to Charles, and he had reproved her for it. In urging her to control it he had suggested good red burgundy (his own usual drink) as preferable to the sherry to which she was addicted.

As for the "bitter trouble", this may have referred to the miscarriage which had blighted their hopes so early in the marriage. Or did it signify an altogether darker business—a devouring jealousy which even now may have been voicing itself in the privacy of Florence's silk-draped boudoir and behind the closed doors of the best bedroom, a secret to all except Florence, Charles and Mrs. Cox? The world was to hear about it later, but now no hint of it emerged to make family, friends or servants suspect the slightest thing was wrong. All who had known of Florence's past were convinced that it was dead and buried; and there was no reason for anyone else to know that it had ever existed.

Revealed in another letter of Charles's, written to Florence at Buscot on 11th March, was that queer streak of closeness that was part of his make-up. (Rowe, the butler, who was devoted to him, had noticed that the nearest he ever got to quarrelling with Florence was when she asked him to write cheques for items which he thought extravagant.) He wrote:

My own darling Wife,—I miss you dreadfully, and I would willingly give £100—if times were not so hard—to have you here now. . . .

It appeared again—rather more significantly—in a letter written to her four days later from Palace Green. Having mentioned an offer by his stepfather to give them "the barouche" if they put down the pair of cobs (so Mr. Joseph was in the "economy" conspiracy too!), he went on to say, "by giving up the cobs and Mrs. Cox we can save £400 a year". Poor Mrs. Cox! If by any chance she had got wind of this she would have been jolted into renewed concern about her future —would assuredly have speculated how she could secure it this time.

It was early in March—whether Florence was away at Buscot at the time is uncertain—that a rather disturbing thing happened to Charles. After breakfast one morning he felt very sick; and having to get off to work shortly he asked Rowe to fetch him some brandy. He took it and set out for his train. But on the way to Balham station the nausea came on again and he vomited violently. He managed to catch his train, though still feeling desperately ill; and at Victoria took a cab straight to Palace Green. Mr. and Mrs. Bravo, shocked at his washed-out appearance, pressed a pick-me-up on him, and he took a glass of curaçao and lay down. Soon, though weak, he felt well enough to go on to the courts at Westminster Hall. By the time he returned home that night he had recovered, and could even smile at the notion that his fellow-travellers that morning must have thought he had dined too well the night before. But it was a strange attack: as far as he knew he had had nothing to upset him and it was the first time in his life he had ever been seized like this.

Charles may have had an excellent constitution (even though Florence sometimes cosseted him, and had once got Mary Ann, the maid, to make him a red flannel garment which he declared was "a cross between a kilt, a sporran and a pair of bathing drawers"), but Florence, despite her bright complexion and general look of radiant health, was not robust. Early in April that trouble which had afflicted her twice before struck her down once more: she had another miscarriage. Their hopes of children seemed doomed to disappointment. This time Charles, in great distress, called in his cousin and intimate friend Royes Bell, a Harley Street surgeon, while again Mrs. Cox ministered as nurse. Pain and weakness, with some sleeplessness, kept Florence over a week in bed on a régime of sitz-baths and spinal washes, and Royes Bell advised a convalescence by the sea after Easter. The bracing air would, he was sure, tone her up and bring back the colour to her cheeks. Meanwhile Easter was spent quietly at The Priory. On Good Friday Royes Bell came down for the afternoon. And on the Saturday Florence went out for the first time since her illness. With Mrs. Cox she drove over in the carriage, Charles riding beside them on Victor, to St. Anne's School, Streatham, to ask leave for Mrs. Cox's boys to spend a day at The Priory; and it was arranged that they should come on Easter Monday. In the afternoon Charles was busy putting up, with Rowe's help, a newly-acquired tennis-net, after which he had vigorous games with Rowe, and Osman, the gardener, and another with the little daughter of a friend who came over from Norwood. Mrs. Thomas Campbell was there too. It was a pleasant day, marred only by the weather, which was consistently dull and disagreeable. Easter Sunday was passed in becoming peace and quiet, Charles having abandoned the idea of a tennis party on Mrs. Cox objecting that it was not quite the thing. He read *The Newcomes* in the garden instead. But on Monday, with Mrs. Cox's boys over from Streatham, tennis was on the programme; and The Priory's lawn that morning, as Charles and the young Coxes strenuously contested it across the net and Florence and Mrs. Cox looked indulgently on from their garden chairs, presented a happy scene of family enjoyment.

In the afternoon Florence's uncle, James Orr, and his daughter Peggy came over. Everyone was pleased that Florence was so much better: she was still retiring early, and that evening, as for the last ten days or so, Mrs. Cox and Charles dined alone together and he, after a short time in the morning-room, went up to see her and say good night.

After being in fine form all day, Charles was now feeling a little sorry for himself. That nagging toothache or neuralgia that he had had once or twice before had come on again. Slumped in a chair in front of the fire in Florence's room he nursed his aching jaw and said to the maid, who was tidying up:

"Mary Ann, I feel very cross!"

"Do you, sir? What's the matter?"

"I have the toothache, like you have sometimes."

He had in fact complained of it to Florence and Mrs. Cox previously, and Florence had asked Mary Ann the night before if she knew a "good thing" for it, mentioning that Charles had taken chloroform and some laudanum to rub on his gums, and also a glass of hot brandy and water before going to bed. Mary Ann could suggest nothing but the "tincture" that Florence had previously prescribed for her, but Florence said that he had found this ineffective. So in the end on this Monday night he took along some brandy and water to his room, trusting that this, together with Florence's laudanum, which he still had, would relieve him. And under this comforting combination the pain soon passed.

2 *The Fatal Tuesday*

Next morning, Tuesday, 18th April, Mrs. Cox was early astir. She was going to Worthing for the day to look for suitable accommodation for Florence's convalescence. The idea was to rent a small furnished house and take the servants and the carriage; and the party was to include Florence's sister-in-law, Augusta, who had not been well. Before nine, then, Mrs. Cox (carrying in her reticule a fortifying flask of sherry) left the house for Balham station. Florence rose more leisurely, to come downstairs dressed ready to go out, for she too was taking a trip. Charles, who was lunching in town with her Uncle James, had persuaded her to come up with him and do a little shopping. So at about half-past ten, in coldish weather with snow threatening, they started out in the landau with Parton, the new coachman, at the reins and young Smith the footman in attendance. After calls at Charles's bank in Stratford Place and Bensons, the Bond Street jewellers, they went on to Jermyn Street, where Charles got down at the Turkish Baths to go to his lunch appointment at St. James's Hall, Piccadilly, leaving Florence to drive on to the Haymarket Stores. At this well-known restaurant he lunched excellently off a steak washed down with half a bottle of burgundy and conversed amiably with his host; and walking down Piccadilly afterwards with Mr. Orr he ran into his barrister friend Mac-Calmont, who accompanied them both as far as the bottom of St. James's Street and then strolled on with Charles to Victoria, where he was catching the 4.05 train. Before leaving, he expansively invited MacCalmont to dinner that night, and when this proved impossible arranged for him to come down next day and play tennis. MacCalmont simply must try his hand on the new court that he had just laid out, he said.

Half an hour later Charles was back at The Priory, to find Florence already at home. She had returned about two, had a late lunch with a glass or two of champagne, and then, feeling tired after her outing, had lain down on the sofa in the morning-room. Here Charles kissed her affectionately and reported on his "jolly lunch" with her uncle.

Florence told him what she had done and then said teasingly: "Go up and see what I've got for you in your bedroom!"

Expectantly Charles ran upstairs, and found on his dressing-table a tin of choice tobacco. She had often complained of the rank mixture that he smoked, and this gift, selected with wifely care, was evidently her remedy. Tobacco, like a tie, is not always the most appreciated of a woman's presents to a man; but however he regarded this little offering as fit for serious smoking, he hurried down to thank her. Then he left her again, and shortly reappeared changed, to her surprise, into riding kit. He was in no mood at that moment to smoke a pipe, however fragrant; what he wanted was a good gallop to work off that substantial lunch. So, without stopping, he went out to the stables.

Here he spoke to George Younger, the groom.

"Have you exercised the cobs to-day, George?"

"I don't think they want exercising to-day, sir," George answered, touching his cap. "They went out in the carriage to Streatham yesterday, and then they went on to Clapham Junction. I wouldn't ride 'em if I were you."

But Charles insisted, and a few minutes later trotted out of the yard on Cremorne, saying as he went that he would take Victor out before dinner.

But it was an hour and a half before he got back, a sorry figure, pale, breathless, obviously shaken, his hat covered with mud. Parton and Younger looked at him open-mouthed.

"The animal bolted with me—took me nearly five miles, right over to Mitcham Common! He galloped so hard my hat blew off," he told the startled coachman.

They got him off the sweat-lathered Cremorne and he hobbled into the house. Florence was still in the morning-room and he joined her and fell into a chair. She stared at him.

"Why, Charles, what on earth's the matter? What happened?"

He told her that he had "come to grief" on Cremorne and then hunched forward in the chair, grimacing with pain. Rowe, who came in then to attend to the fire, was quite taken aback when he saw him. Florence suggested a hot bath, and helped by Rowe he limped slowly upstairs, his hand to his bruised side.

"I hope Cremorne didn't throw you, sir," said Rowe, concerned.

"Oh no, it didn't throw me." Charles laughed ruefully.

After his bath he felt better, though still stiff and shaken. But he noticed that Florence was looking tired and urged her to go to bed early.

"Oh, Charlie, do let me stay up and give you your dinner."

"Well, I will if you promise to go to bed immediately after."

"Then I will, Charlie." This with a sweet smile.

They went to dress for seven-thirty, but Mrs. Cox, who had caught the five o'clock express from Brighton, made the meal a little late that night. She came in almost on the half-hour and hurried up to Florence's dressing-room to see if she could help her, hastened to her own room for a quick toilet and descended to the morning-room, apologising for keeping them. Then Rowe announced dinner.

"The dining-room of The Priory is small," says a contemporary note. "The traditional party of eight would find ample accommodation, but a dozen or score of guests might experience some inconvenience." Small by spacious Victorian standards it may have been, but in fact this square, bay-windowed front room overlooking on two sides The Priory's pleasant lawns was one of the biggest in the house. Certainly its monumental sideboard and multi-leaved table could cater for more than modest entertainment. And on evenings when the trio were dining alone, as now, with Charles at the head of the table and Florence and Mrs. Cox facing each other on his left and right, leaving a wide expanse of empty tablecloth below them, the room seemed over-large, its darkly opulent furnishings a shade oppressive, its imposing gilt-framed oils on the rich-papered walls a little heavy, its chandeliers too brilliant. It was not a room for a small family group—especially when, as on this particular Tuesday evening, the usual domestic gossip seemed inhibited by an unwonted air of restraint.

For despite the fact that it was Florence's first evening down since her illness and that Mrs. Cox was full of her Worthing trip and the houses she had seen, it was not a scintillating meal. Charles, owing no doubt to his jolting on Cremorne, was dispirited and glum, and when the master of the house is out of sorts the family generally knows it. So, with the deferential Rowe handing the dishes and Smith the footman assisting, they went through one of those excellent but unexciting dinners that Ellen Stone the cook could be relied on to produce— whiting, roast lamb, anchovy eggs on toast. Charles declined the fish and busied himself with a letter, just delivered, that Mrs. Cox had brought in.

It was from Joseph Bravo at St. Leonards, enclosing a "sold" note from Charles's stockbrokers relating to Caledonian Railway stock. Mr. Bravo senior had seen from this that Charles had just sold stock—at a loss of £20—which he had told his stepfather a few days earlier he had bought for investment. Mr. Bravo strongly disapproved of such Stock Exchange transactions and bluntly said so in his letter.

This did not add to Charles's good-humour. His face darkened with annoyance as he crumpled the letter up.

"I'll write the governor a shirty letter," he growled, "I won't be interfered with in this way!"

Over the lamb, of which he partook, the conversation turned

on Mrs. Cox's trip. She brought out a photograph of the house. Charles glanced at it.

"You've taken the house, then?" he asked curtly.

Mrs. Cox said yes and went on to mention that it belonged to someone from whom his parents had had a house and that they knew the name of Bravo. But Charles seemed uninterested, off-hand even, and Mrs. Cox looked at him over her glasses as if reproaching his brusqueness. Florence was silent. As the savoury was served Charles spoke of his runaway gallop, telling Mrs. Cox that he was so exhausted that he could hardly put his hand in his pocket to find a shilling for the man who had picked up his hat. All this time he had been helping himself pretty freely from the burgundy decanter, and by the end of the meal had drunk about four glasses. But if he showed a respectable thirst the ladies outdid him, for they accounted for nearly two bottles of sherry between them.

Dinner over, Charles and the ladies moved to the morning-room across the hall. Conversation was equally desultory here. Charles, still stiff and sore, was brooding over his step-father's "interference" and the loss of that £20; Florence, who had spoken little during the meal, was tired and preoccupied; only Mrs. Cox, as she sat there quietly sewing, seemed her impassive and indefatigable self. After twenty minutes Charles looked at his watch and saw it was about nine o'clock. He turned to Florence.

"Well, my dear, you know what you promised."

"Yes, Charlie, I will."

She rose and kissed Charles, and as she made for the door Mrs. Cox stood up too.

"Let me come and help you undress, Florence, it's early and Mary Ann will still be at supper for a while yet."

So, saying good night to Charles, she went out with Florence, leaving him alone.

At the foot of the stairs Florence paused.

"Jane, I'm so thirsty. Be a dear and get me a little Marsala in water and bring it up with you."

She went on up while Mrs. Cox went to the dining-room to do her bidding. Her dressing-room was along the first-floor landing on the right of the stairs, beyond her bedroom with its green baize outer door; and she was here, starting to undress, when Mrs. Cox arrived with the tray. The door closed and for the next twenty-five minutes the two were alone and un-disturbed in their preparations for the night. Then Mary Ann, her supper finished, came quietly up with a can of hot water and tapped on the door. Florence opened it in her dressing-gown. She spoke to the maid.

"Oh, Mary Ann, fetch me a tumbler of Marsala and water from the dining-room, please."

So down Mary Ann tripped to satisfy this still unquenched thirst of Florence's for the sweet, rich wine (albeit diluted), got it out of the cellaret, and was just leaving the dining-room with it when Charles emerged from the morning-room opposite, on his way to bed. He passed her in silence—and she thought this rather unusual as he always had a cheerful word for her—merely turning round twice to look at her on his way upstairs. How pale he was, she thought, and how angry he looked. Charles may well have looked angry at that moment, for he guessed whom the wine was for. That weakness of Florence's again! Hadn't he taken her to task for it often enough before? So now he strode straight into her dressing-room and, in front of Mrs. Cox, said in French (for the matter was not for Mary Ann's ears):

"Florence, you've sent downstairs for more wine. You've drunk nearly a bottle to-day!"

Having delivered this reproof he turned about without wait-ing for Florence to reply and made for the room at the other end of the landing where he had been sleeping apart from Florence during her illness. It was one door beyond the main bedroom, which Mrs. Cox was now temporarily sharing with Florence in his place. Meanwhile Mary Ann, who had tactfully hidden herself in the main bedroom until she heard Charles pass and his door close, came out and met Florence and Mrs. Cox coming in, told Florence that her wine was waiting for her and went along to tidy the dressing-room. Then she returned and saw Florence in bed, with Mrs. Cox sitting beside her. Quietly she spoke to Mrs. Cox.

"Will Mrs. Bravo be wanting anything more to-night?"

"Have you brought the little tray? Then there'll be nothing more, thank you, Mary Ann. But be sure and think of Skye." (Skye was one of Florence's pet dogs). "Good night."

Then the outer baize-covered door of Florence's room closed and all was silent on the gas-lit landing; and Mary Ann, on her way downstairs, was calling softly for Skye when Charles's door suddenly burst open and he appeared in the doorway in his night-shirt.

His face was white, his eyes staring, and he seemed in acute pain. Gasping, he called out loudly and urgently: "Florence! Hot water!" Again he shouted, louder and with a touch of panic in his voice: "Florence! Hot water!"

CHAPTER 6

ACCIDENT? SUICIDE? MURDER?

1 *Tuesday*

FOR A MOMENT Mary Ann stood looking at Charles in horrified surprise. Then, as no one else seemed to have heard, she dashed back upstairs and into Florence's room and said urgently:

"Mr. Bravo's ill!"

Her words were addressed to Florence, but Florence's eyes were shut and she did not stir: she appeared dead to the world. It was Mrs. Cox, still fully dressed beside the bed, who responded. She hurried immediately into Charles's room with Mary Ann close behind her.

They found Charles standing by the open window to the left of his bed. He was vomiting out of it on to the leads below, and as Mrs. Cox went to him he gasped between spasms of retching:

"Hot water! Hot water!"

Jane Cox turned to Mary Ann in the doorway and sent her to the kitchen for hot water. Looking round she saw a chloroform bottle on the mantelpiece—empty. Charles was now slumped down on the floor, half-sitting, half-lying. She realised that the immediate need was for an emetic; but meanwhile she must get a doctor.

She ran down to the butler's pantry and pushed open the door, calling to Rowe:

"Tell Parton to go for Mr. Harrison. Mr. Bravo's ill!"

Rowe doubled off to the coachman's lodge and Mrs. Cox, upstairs again, found Mary Ann with the mustard. Hurriedly she ordered:

"Mix and make haste!"

Mary Ann was flustered. She asked Mrs. Cox how much mustard to put in and Mrs. Cox cried impatiently:

"Here, give it to me. I'll do it myself."

And she forced some of the mixture through the clenched teeth of the now semi-conscious Charles. He was immediately sick into a basin, which Mrs. Cox passed to Mary Ann, telling her to empty it and bring it back.

It says much for Jane Cox that in this sudden dire emergency she did not lose her head. She seemed to know exactly what to do. Calmly and quickly she rapped out orders to Mary Ann—to put Charles's feet into a bath of mustard and water and rub them as hard as she could, fetch spirits of camphor, go down and make strong coffee to keep him awake.

And while Mary Ann was briskly massaging his feet she was shaking him and saying:

"Wake, Charlie, do wake!"

Looking for the camphor, Mary Ann went into Florence's room and found her still asleep. If she had drunk so heavily at dinner and taken her double night-cap afterwards to ensure sleep she had seemingly succeeded. Otherwise she could hardly have slumbered on through the alarms of the last ten minutes, let alone Charles's first loud cry. But Mary Ann now thought it her duty to rouse her.

She touched her. "Oh, madam, do come quickly. Mr. Bravo's very ill."

Florence opened her eyes. She seemed almost drugged. She stared at the maid and mumbled:

"What's the matter?"

As Mary Ann helped her into her dressing-gown she repeated the question and appeared hardly able to take in what she was saying. Together they went next door into Charles's room. The sight of him lying on the floor looking so deathly, with Mrs. Cox bending over him rubbing his chest, instantly cleared the wine-fumes from her fuddled brain and jolted her fully awake. She stood at the door, her eyes round with horror and gave a strangled cry.

"What is it, Jane? What's happened? Have you sent for a doctor?"

Mrs. Cox looked up. "Yes, Florence, Mr. Harrison."

Florence was astounded. "Mr. Harrison! He lives right over at Streatham! Why didn't you send for Dr. Moore—he lives much nearer!"

Then, in her dressing-gown, she ran distracted downstairs to find Rowe. She met him coming in on his return from sending Parton for Mr. Harrison and shouted to him hysterically:

"Go and bring someone! Do something, Rowe! Fetch Dr. Moore."

Off Rowe hurried to Dr. Moore's house, a bare quarter of a mile away. Giving him Florence's message he said that his master had had a fit, and the only thing he could tell the doctor was that Charles had been out riding that afternoon and had been run away with.

In ten minutes they were back at The Priory and Dr. Moore was shown straight upstairs, to find Charles in a chair, unconscious. Florence, now fully dressed, and Mrs. Cox were with him, and Mrs. Cox was rubbing his chest with liniment. They had changed his night-shirt and tried to give him coffee but he had brought it up almost at once.

Anxiously Florence spoke. "Oh, Dr. Moore, my husband has been taken ill and I don't know what is the matter with him. He had his dinner as usual."

Without a word Dr. Moore, a bald, middle-aged, rather handsome man, clean-shaven but for a pair of bushy mutton-chop whiskers, examined the patient. He looked up after a few minutes, his face serious. Charles's heart had almost stopped, his pulse was imperceptible, his skin cold and clammy, his pupils dilated; in fact to the doctor he looked to be *in extremis*. He suspected poison but had no idea what it might be. With Rowe's help he moved Charles to the bed, had mustard plasters applied to his chest and feet and tried to give him brandy but found him unable to swallow.

He asked Florence and Mrs. Cox if they could account for Charles's illness, and both mentioned his mishap on Cremorne, Florence adding that he had been suffering lately from neuralgia. He bent down over Charles again and when he straightened himself there was no mistaking the meaning of his grave expression.

Florence clenched her hands together. Her face was white. "Doctor, you don't mean that you apprehend anything serious?"

"Madam, I fear I do. In fact I doubt very much if your husband will recover."

Florence burst into tears. Mrs. Cox went over and quietly tried to comfort her. The companion-friend seemed entirely mistress of the situation, truly a tower of strength in this sudden crisis.

It was she who went down to receive Mr. Harrison when he arrived about eleven. Meeting him at the door she told him briefly what had happened and how she had treated Charles; and she finished her account by saying:

"I'm sure he has taken chloroform."

Mr. Harrison, a younger man than Dr. Moore, well-groomed and affecting a pair of neatly trained dundrearies, was of course no stranger to the Bravos or Mrs. Cox. He had last called at

71

The Priory to attend Florence for her miscarriage in January. And now he hastened upstairs behind Mrs. Cox to the spare bedroom where Charles was lying. Dr. Moore met him at the door and they consulted together for a few moments and then went in.

He bowed to Florence, who was standing beside the bed, and then examined Charles. He shook his head slowly. Like his colleague he regarded the symptoms most seriously. Charles was completely collapsed and insensible; and after briefly conferring again, the doctors took the view that a large vessel near the heart had given way. Mr. Harrison suggested ether but Dr. Moore said that the patient would never be able to take it. Then they tried giving brandy and water by the mouth, and when this was unsuccessful they injected some. This at least had the effect of stimulating the heart after a time.

But at that moment, as he looked down on the unconscious and hardly breathing Charles, Mr. Harrison agreed entirely with Dr. Moore: he saw no hope of recovery. He turned to Florence.

"I fear, Mrs. Bravo, your husband is very gravely ill. I hardly think he will live an hour."

Florence bowed her head, trying to control her grief; and again Mrs. Cox was at hand to console her.

Looking at Charles again and remembering what Mrs. Cox had said, Mr. Harrison thought of chloroform as a possible cause of the seizure—but the odd thing was that he could not smell it on Charles's breath. Still, he mentioned the possibility to Dr. Moore, and they searched the room for signs of that or any other drug. On the mantelpiece they found the empty chloroform bottle that Mrs. Cox had noticed, and they also discovered a bottle containing laudanum and another containing an ammonia and camphor compound. Yet there was no smell in the room to indicate that chloroform had been used, nor would these other drugs have brought on such total collapse as Charles was suffering. It was puzzling.

Charles stirred uneasily for a moment, and Florence, in tears, threw herself down on the bed beside him and cried:

"My dear Charlie, what is the matter? Do speak to me, Charlie dearest!"

She was in great distress, sobbing bitterly as she stroked his damp forehead. It was a moving scene for all of them there, but the doctors had to think of the patient and Mr. Harrison spoke:

"Mrs. Bravo, I fear I must ask you to get up. Lying near your husband like that, you'll interfere with his breathing."

So, with the doctors watching anxiously over the unconscious Charles for any sign of a change, and Florence and Mrs. Cox—the one weeping uncontrollably and the other so admirably self-possessed—standing at the foot of the bed, the minutes ticked by in the quiet sick-room. Outside on the landing Mary Ann and Rowe waited, and in the servants' quarters the rest of the staff, their bedtime long past, were speculating in shocked undertones on their master's sudden seizure.

Florence broke the silence.

"Do you really think Charlie is dying?"

Both doctors nodded gravely and one of them said in a low voice:

"Yes, Mrs. Bravo, I am afraid he has little chance."

Then she had an idea. Urgently she said:

"We'd better send for Royes Bell. I know that Mr. Joseph Bravo would like it. Ought we perhaps to send for him and Charles's mother too? I know that if anything happens they'll never forgive me."

Whatever breach of medical etiquette this might involve, both jumped at the suggestion of another doctor. Nonplussed

73

for a diagnosis—except that they suspected some kind of poison —and therefore unable to prescribe a treatment, they would have welcomed half a dozen colleagues around the bedside at that moment.

It was therefore decided to fetch Royes Bell; and at once Mr. Harrison wrote him a note asking him to come at once and to bring someone with him, as Mr. Bravo was "suffering from failure of the heart's action". Parton was roused and in a few minutes he was off in the carriage to 44 Harley Street. Florence, impatient for Royes to join them, realised with dismay soon after Parton had gone that he had taken the hired horses. The cobs, she bemoaned, would have been so much quicker. She was now so overwrought and on edge that Mrs. Cox persuaded her to go and rest on her bed for an hour. It was after midnight, and Royes could not be back for some time.

2 *Wednesday*

In the sick-room the vigil of the two doctors and the tireless Mrs. Cox went on in a silence only occasionally broken by Charles's unconscious moanings and the fall of a coal in the brightly burning fire. One-thirty, two o'clock, two-thirty . . . and then the rattle of wheels in the drive told them that Royes Bell had arrived. The doctors left the room to meet him and found that he was not alone. He had brought with him Dr. George Johnson, whom he had called for at his house in Savile Row. George Johnson, M.D., F.R.S., was Professor of Clinical Medicine at King's College Hospital and Senior Physician there. With his steady gaze, firm clean-shaven features and rather stern manner, he looked the picture of an eminent and experienced doctor; beside him Royes Bell, dark and handsome, appeared quite youthful despite his luxuriant beard. The four of them conferred outside the room and it was agreed that Dr. Johnson should take charge of the case.

They went in and the two newcomers examined Charles, who was still unconscious, with a feeble pulse, and breathing heavily. About twenty minutes later his condition took an alarming turn: his pulse rose and he began to pass and vomit blood. To Dr. Johnson this immediately told a story of irritant poison, confirming the suspicions of the first two doctors. And soon after this he opened his eyes and moved uneasily.

He looked up at Florence. Piteously he said: "Kiss me, my wife."

Florence bent down and kissed him.

"What have you taken, Charlie, to make you so ill?" Her voice was imploring.

Charles was obviously in great agony. His face was twisted and he was writhing; and his voice rose to a scream:

"Oh Christ have mercy upon me!"

He even in his extremity begged Florence to read the burial service over him.

Dr. Johnson put his hand on the sick man's brow and asked him in a low firm voice:

"Mr. Bravo, what have you taken?"

Royes Bell echoed the question: "Yes, Charlie, what did you take?"

Poor Charles was confused and so desperately distressed that he could hardly speak.

"I rubbed my gums with laudanum and may have taken some."

"Laudanum won't explain your symptoms, Mr. Bravo."

"Well, I've taken nothing more." This in almost a whisper.

Royes Bell was now beckoned outside by Mrs. Cox. He

followed her to the dressing-room at the far end of the landing. She quietly closed the door and then made an astounding statement:

"I feel you ought to know that Charlie said he had taken poison and told me not to tell Florence."

Royes was dumbfounded—and annoyed. He spoke sharply:

"You'd better tell Dr. Johnson that. It's no good sending for a doctor if you don't tell him what's the matter!"

He turned on his heel and went back to Dr. Johnson in the sick-room.

"Mrs. Cox has something very important to communicate."

Dr. Johnson went back with Royes to the dressing-room, curious to know what this important communication might be. Mrs. Cox quietly repeated her statement, but now with a slight variation.

"When Mr. Bravo was taken ill he said to me: 'I've taken some of that poison, but don't tell Florence.'"

Dr. Johnson frowned. "Didn't he tell you any more than that? Didn't you ask him what he had taken, or when he'd taken it, or why?"

Mrs. Cox was not very helpful. "No, Dr. Johnson, he told me nothing more than that."

Royes was standing by and heard her reply. Recalling the incident later, he had the impression that she had implied that Charles had taken chloroform, but could not be sure.

Dr. Johnson returned at once to Charles's bedside. He looked down at him sternly.

"Mr. Bravo, Mrs. Cox tells us that you've spoken to her of taking poison. What is the meaning of that?"

Charles opened his eyes and answered weakly. There was puzzlement in his voice.

"I don't remember having spoken of taking poison."

The doctor pressed the point. "Have you taken poison?"

"I rubbed some laudanum on my gums for neuralgia and may have swallowed some of it."

"That will not explain your symptoms."

"If it wasn't laudanum I don't know what it was."

But Dr. Johnson persisted. It was vital to discover the truth.

"Well, have you any poison in the house?"

"Yes, several. Chloroform, laudanum, Condy's Fluid and —yes—some rat poison in the stables." Another paroxysm of pain tore at him and he cried out in distress.

While Florence and Mrs. Cox tried to comfort him the two doctors looked round the room as their colleagues had done earlier. All they found was a blue fluted chloroform bottle, empty, a bottle containing a little laudanum, a bottle of camphor liniment about three-quarters full and a bottle of Condy's Fluid. None of these, they knew, would have caused such acute and serious symptoms. And they could find no cup or vessel that might have contained poison.

Meanwhile Mr. Harrison had been pondering over Mrs. Cox's statement to Royes Bell and Dr. Johnson that Charles had confessed to her that he had taken poison. He challenged Mrs. Cox about this and asked her why she had not told him on his arrival.

"I quite thought that I had, Mr. Harrison."

"You certainly did not. You told me you were sure he had taken chloroform!"

And there, for the time, the controversial little matter rested.

At five o'clock, with daylight breaking, Mr. Harrison, Dr. Moore and Dr. Johnson departed, leaving Royes Bell in charge. Charles was still conscious and suffering severely, but there was nothing more that they could do just then, and the two local doctors were tired out by their seven-hour watch. Dr. Johnson took with him some of the vomit to be tested for arsenic—the most likely poison that he could think of.

Royes, Florence and Mrs. Cox were around the bedside in the gradually lightening room. Charles was tossing restlessly, groaning occasionally. Suddenly he said:

"Royes, am I going to get better?"

"I hope so, Charlie, but you're very ill indeed."

After a pause Charles spoke again.

"Royes, I wish you'd read some prayers for me."

His cousin was so affected that he could not trust his voice. And when he said nothing Charles falteringly recited an extempore prayer himself, in which he prayed for the three around the bed, and followed it with the Lord's Prayer. He seemed to realise that he was dying.

Soon after breakfast Florence telegraphed for Charles's parents, who were staying at Warrior Square, St. Leonards-on-Sea: "Charlie is seriously ill. He wants to see you. Come at once." About ten o'clock Mary Ann came in to tidy the room. Florence and Mrs. Cox were there.

Charles turned to the maid with a ghost of a smile.

"How are you, Mary Ann?"

"Very well, sir, thank you. And how are you feeling now?"

"Not much better, Mary Ann." And then, ruefully: "We shan't have our trip to Worthing now."

Mary Ann said that she hoped indeed they would. But Charles shook his head.

"No. My next trip will be to Streatham churchyard."

Mary Ann could not restrain her tears, for she was fond of her master and it was terrible to see him struck down like this, and suffering such awful pain.

He looked up at his wife.

"When you bury me, Florence, make no fuss over me."

Sobbing, Florence replied:

"Oh, don't say so, Charlie. But I won't if it's your wish."

Charles seemed more than ever certain now that he would die. To Royes he said:

"Oh, Royes, I'm dying. Shall I linger long thus in such pain?"

For Royes, standing by almost helpless to ease his cousin, it was a terrible situation. If only they knew what he had taken!

About noon Charles asked Florence to give Royes his watch and be kind to Rowe, who had been constantly in and out of the room helping to move him and make him comfortable. Then he told Royes he wished to make a will.

Royes protested gently.

"Is it necessary, Charlie?"

But Charles was determined, and Royes sent Mrs. Cox to fetch writing materials. And then in a faltering voice he dictated to Royes his last will and testament:

"I give all that I possess to my wife Florence, whom I appoint my executrix."

The will was witnessed by Royes himself, and Rowe.

He then enjoined Royes to ask his mother to be kind to Florence, to whom he had shown the greatest affection ever since his seizure. He had said to her:

"You must marry again, but not a word of the past."

And on another occasion he had begged her to take care of Katie, the child (not his) of his ex-mistress.

After making his will he seemed a little happier. But several times that morning, as he had tossed and murmured uneasily, Royes had wanted to ask him a question. They were cousins and closest friends, and surely Charles would tell him if he had anything on his conscience—if, for instance, he had taken poison. At last when they were alone together for a moment he spoke:

"Charlie, have you anything on your mind?"

Charles's guileless answer seemed to dispose of that suspicion altogether.

"No—I've not led a religious life."

So the hours dragged by, with Charles plagued by a raging thirst, constantly sick and purging, and rarely free from agonising abdominal pain. Florence and Mrs. Cox were by his bedside, giving Royes what help they could, and Mary Ann and Rowe were never far away. The rest of the household went about their duties hushed and tense, waiting anxiously for any news from behind the closed door upstairs. This sudden illness of their master, so well liked by all of them, had been a shock.

About three o'clock there was renewed activity. Almost at the same time Dr. Johnson, Mr. Harrison and Dr. Moore returned; and a little later Mr. and Mrs. Joseph Bravo arrived with their old servant Amelia Bushell, who had known Charles from a small boy. They had caught the first available train from St. Leonards.

In the hall Florence and Mrs. Bravo greeted each other with less reserve than they might normally have shown. The barriers were down a little: common sorrow and anxiety had put a truce to the aversion that had built up so formidably between them. And Mrs. Bravo could not help noticing the pallor and the red-rimmed eyes that bespoke Florence's exhaustion and grief—and her affection for Charles.

As they were going up to Charles's room Florence turned to Amelia.

"What a dreadful thing, Amelia! The only thing by which I can account for it is that Mr. Charles took lunch at St. James's Hall with a friend and had something cooked in a coppery pan which has disagreed with him."

She had also expressed this thought to Mrs. Cox and Mary Ann, having apparently known someone at Epsom who had been poisoned in this way.

Charles Bravo, about the time of his marriage to Florence, 1875
(*Picture Post Library*)

Florence at the time of her marriage to Charles (*Picture Post Library*)

Mrs. Joseph Bravo now made a request of Florence that might have tried the patience of any wife. Remarking that she had looked after Charles all his life and would be the best nurse for him now, she asked that she might take Florence's place as chief attendant in the sick-room, and have Amelia to help her.

Biting down her resentment Florence reluctantly agreed. It was no wish of hers to make trouble, and distress poor Charles at such a time. She even made another concession to Mrs. Bravo by giving up her bedroom (next door to Charles's) to her and her husband and moving her own things to Mrs. Cox's room upstairs.

Charles, quite conscious though still sick and in great pain, knew his parents at once. As he turned his head and smiled at them, saying in a weak voice how glad he was to see them, they were shocked to note his ravaged waxy features and sunken eyes. The doctors, too, making their examination, found him weaker. But what poison it was that was killing him they had no idea. They questioned him again, but it was useless. At last, in irritation, he turned to Dr. Johnson and said:

"If I knew what I was suffering from, why the devil should I send for you?"

That was all they could get out of him, and they left him to the care of Royes, Dr. Johnson having arranged to return early next morning.

That day Florence had twice been in touch with her family about Charles's illness but she had not actually summoned them to The Priory. Before the Bravos' arrival she had telegraphed to her mother at Buscot: "Charles is dangerously ill—internal inflammation—have telegraphed for his mother. Florence."

After their arrival she wired again, to her brother William: "Charlie rather better. Still very ill. Will telegraph you again should I wish you to come up. Florence."

William replied: "Very grieved to hear about Charlie. Telegraph how he is and whether you would like mother, Augusta or myself to come to you. William."

To this wire Florence made no reply that day, and the night passed with the Campbells anxiously awaiting further news. For Charles the hours of darkness only brought greater pain and weakness, with his symptoms persisting and his condition steadily growing worse. And early on Thursday morning Mrs. Campbell received another more ominous telegram.

3 Thursday

"If you wish to see Charles alive," it said, "you must come at once. I fear the worst. Florence."

That was bad enough, but as Mrs. Campbell and William were hurriedly preparing to go to Balham (Mr. Campbell had been ill and was hardly fit to travel) a second wire arrived with still graver news: "No hope for my darling. He cannot live long. Florence."

Speeding to Paddington on the 11.55 train from Faringdon, Mrs. Campbell and her son feared that they might not see Charles alive. And at The Priory the worried Dr. Johnson was confessing himself baffled and impotent. The test for arsenic on which he had built his hopes had proved negative and he was therefore back at the starting-point. And so much valuable time had been lost already that he now doubted whether anything could save Charles. Gravely he told Mr. Bravo that he regarded the case as fatal. Mr. Bravo thought it his duty to inform his stepson, but in doing so he felt bound to say that while there was life there was hope. Charles accepted the news stoically: he seemed quite resigned to dying. There was a limit to the pain and distress a man in the throes of deadly irritant poison could endure.

Mr. Bravo told Florence too. But at this late stage, when there seemed no hope left, she refused to accept defeat. She declared that as the medical men had given Charles up for dead she wished to try some other remedies that she had been advised were efficacious. She did not, however, say who had told her of them. They were a mustard plaster on the spine, cold water applications to the stomach, and small and frequent doses of arsenicum. When she proposed these to Dr. Johnson he vetoed the first two, saying that they would only add to Charles's pain; but he allowed the arsenicum. (Hitherto the doctor had prescribed chiefly iced milk and morphia.)

Dr. Johnson left at mid-morning and was back about two with Mr. Henry Smith, F.R.C.S., of Wimpole Street, whose wife was a sister of Mrs. Joseph Bravo and who had known Charles since boyhood and therefore had a personal interest in his case. While they were consulting with Royes there was another ring at the door. Royes's sister, Ann Maria, arrived with Alice, Charles's deaf-mute sister. Ann Maria had been staying with the Bravos at St. Leonards and had followed them up from there. They now took her to the sick-room. Charles was conscious and looked up at her and said "Kiss me". He then asked that Alice should kiss him. But he was so ill and exhausted that they did not stay long; and Ann Maria joined Florence for a walk in the garden.

They sat for a time in the conservatory and talked of Charles. Florence was in tears.

"We've been very very happy," she said, "and Charles has said he's never been so happy in all his life. We've never had a word together."

Looking at Florence as she spoke, Ann Maria was impressed by her simple sincerity and deeply moved at this newly-married wife's complete bewilderment at the sudden blow that fate had struck her: a bewilderment that left her quite unable to suggest a cause for Charles's symptoms. There was no word now of the "coppery pan" that she had mentioned the previous day to Amelia, and earlier to Mrs. Cox and the maid; no reference to poison; and certainly no hint of the possibility of suicide—just this touching emphasis on the untroubled bliss of their short married life.

But desperate as she knew Charles's condition to be, still Florence would not give up hope. Racking her brain for anything else that could be done for Charles, she thought of another doctor—the famous Sir William Gull, of whom she knew as the "first opinion" in London. Why not call him in? She mentioned the idea to Joseph Bravo, who, though enthusiastic for any course of action that might help his stepson, was doubtful about the question of medical etiquette. And certainly it was unorthodox to bring in another doctor like this. But neither Dr. Johnson nor Royes objected. At their wits' end, they were as ready to accept another view as Messrs. Harrison and Moore had been two days earlier. And so before lunch Florence had herself written, and given to Mrs. Cox to deliver to Sir William at 74 Brook Street, the following note:

Dear Sir,—My husband is dangerously ill. Could you come as soon as possible to see him? My father, Mr. Campbell, will feel so grateful to you if you can come at once. I need not tell you how grateful I will be to you if you can come at once. Yours truly, FLORENCE BRAVO

Dr. G. Johnson is coming in the course of the afternoon. Mr. Royes Bell, of King's College Hospital, is with his cousin, and acquiesces in my wish for you to come.

Calling in the great Sir William, even at the eleventh hour, was an excellent idea, but it was a pity that Florence in her haste had forgotten to allude to Charles's symptoms or the strong possibility—of which she must have been aware from the doctors' repeated questionings of Charles—of poison. It would have helped Sir William to know in advance what trouble he was being asked to treat. Nor did Mrs. Cox say anything to him when she delivered the note. For all she knew, Florence had explained the situation fully herself. However, Sir William obligingly promised to come with Dr. Johnson on his evening visit, and Mrs. Cox returned at once to The Priory.

Soon she was out again, this time to meet Mrs. Campbell and William at the station, where they arrived about tea-time. Their chief worry was that they had come too late, for the journey from Buscot had taken them about five hours. They were therefore almost relieved to hear from Mrs. Cox that though Charles was sinking he was still alive. In ten minutes they were in the sick-room; and Charles's wan features brightened at the sight of his mother-in-law, of whom he had always been fond. In a whisper he asked her to kiss him and said:

"You've been very kind to me."

He looked at his mother, who was standing beside the bed.

"Mother, will you be kind to Florence? She's been the best of wives to me."

At that candid moment the thought did not enter poor Charles's head that he might be embarrassing Mrs. Campbell; nor did his own mother's slightly grudging reply seem to him anything less than generous and whole-hearted.

"I'm never unkind to anyone, Charlie, and I assure you I'll be kind to her."

For him, at least, this was a promise to end all the animosities that he had so deplored, a guarantee of reconciliation. He closed his eyes, content.

About six-thirty Dr. Johnson arrived with Sir William Gull.

Sir William had been briefed by his colleague on the way from London, and now went straight to the sick-room with him, where he was introduced to Royes Bell.

Florence was not wrong in her estimation of this consultant—the sixth and most distinguished doctor to be called to Charles's bedside since Tuesday night. Sir William Withey Gull, Bart., was one of the greatest medical men of his day. It is said that he would have reached the top in almost any profession. With a vast fund of clinical experience and a flair for diagnosis he combined a forceful, commanding personality and a striking appearance. He was tall and erect, and his expressive eyes, the dark hair falling over his brow, and his firm mouth and well-modelled chin gave him an almost Napoleonic look. Just short of sixty, he was now at the height of his reputation and enjoyed an enormous practice (on his death fifteen years later he left £344,000), having less than five years before been awarded his baronetcy for helping to save the life of the Prince of Wales, gravely ill with typhoid fever complicated by bronchitis. He had the faculty of dominating any group in which he was present; and now as he came into Charles's room he took complete control.

Asking all except Dr. Johnson and Royes Bell to leave, he looked briefly at Charles, felt his pulse, which was barely perceptible, and turned down the bedclothes and examined his abdomen. He put the clothes back. Sir William was a man who did not mince his words and believed in telling his patients the truth. He told Charles bluntly that he was very seriously ill and had not long to live. Charles heard him apathetically. Then Sir William added:

"This isn't disease. You're poisoned. Pray tell us how you came by it."

"I took it myself."

"What did you take?"

Wearily Charles answered (he had heard the question so often before):

"Laudanum."

"You've taken more than laudanum!" Sir William spoke pointedly, with the greatest emphasis.

Dr. Johnson leant forward over the foot of the bed and broke in:

"If you die without telling us more than we know at present, someone may be accused or suspected of having poisoned you."

"I am aware of that, but I can tell you nothing more."

Charles was fighting pain and nausea and sometimes crying out with the distress of it, but he remained clear-headed, though he was weak to exhaustion. And what impressed the doctors most in their ruthless questioning of this dying man was his obvious sincerity. Why should a patient at death's door lie?

But again Sir William pressed him, and said that it might help them to find an antidote. And he added, as a further inducement to make Charles speak:

"That wouldn't be quite fair, as I fear no antidote would do you good."

But this too failed to draw Charles. He closed his eyes and turned his head away.

Sir William looked at Royes.

"Where was he sick?"

Royes indicated the window to the left of the bed. Leaning out, they could see the vomited matter still lying on the leads two or three feet below. Then Sir William gave the footman the unpleasant task of collecting it into a jar with a clean silver spoon. The jar was handed to Dr. Johnson and he took it with him to seal as the three of them went along to Florence's dressing-room to discuss the case.

Sir William said that in his view the patient was suffering from arsenic poisoning, possibly combined with some laudanum; but of this idea Dr. Johnson felt bound to disabuse him. He had heard by now, and had told Royes, that there had been no arsenic in the matters taken away for analysis.

They were interrupted by a knock on the door. Royes's sister was there and said:

"Charles wants to speak to Sir William Gull."

With Amelia and others she had gone into Charles's room when the doctors had come out, and almost at once he had started asking for Sir William: "I want to see Dr. Gull! I want to see Dr. Gull!"

Sir William went back alone with Ann Maria. Charles stirred as he saw him.

"Sir William, I wish to tell you now that I've told you the truth and nothing but the truth."

The eminent doctor said in measured tones:

"Mr. Bravo, that doesn't account for the condition you're in. There must be something else. You must consider the gravity of your situation and of all you say and do."

And he repeated as impressively as he could that Charles's end was near.

"I know that. I know I'm going to appear before my Maker. I can't tell you anything more. I took nothing but laudanum to rub on my lower jaw for toothache—like this."

And the poor man feebly put his finger to his gums to show how he had done it.

"Charles, dearest, tell us where you got it." It was Florence now who spoke, entreatingly.

The answer came, low and weak. "Out of your bottle, Florence." And Charles added that if there was anything else in the bottle he was unaware of it.

"It is not for me to press a dying man," said Sir William now, "but if we could only know what you've taken we might be able to give you an antidote."

"I've taken laudanum," Charles's voice rose. "Before God I've taken only laudanum! If it wasn't laudanum, so help me God, I don't know what it was!"

Could anyone present doubt now that Charles was speaking the truth?

Charles begged Sir William to give him something to ease his pain. Was there really no hope, he asked?

Sir William was frank. "Looking at your condition, Mr. Bravo, it wouldn't be right to give you any hope."

He felt Charles's pulse and sounded his faintly beating heart. "There's very little life left in you—in fact you're half-dead now!"

It was unpardonably blunt, but still Sir William clung to the notion that this was the only way to get the secret out of Charles—if secret there was.

Ann Maria, holding Charles's pillow for him, was in tears; and Florence, weeping too, leaned over and embraced Charles. They and all the others in the room felt that it was the end. Mrs. Campbell asked him gently if he would not like to see a clergyman, and suggested the Rev. Mr. Nichol, the rector at Streatham, but Charles just shook his head. Then he said:

"Let us say the Lord's Prayer."

And as everyone present knelt he recited the prayer in a low and halting voice.

Even Sir William Gull, who had attended so many death-bed scenes, was moved. But there was nothing more that he could do now; and he prepared to take his leave. Solemnly he wished Charles good-bye, told Mrs. Bravo that he had left a prescription for the night though he thought her son would be dead before morning, and withdrew. Even his great skill had been powerless to help fight a killing poison that Charles either could not—or would not—name.

When Sir William had gone, accompanied by Dr. Johnson,

Charles said good-bye to those who were gathered around the bedside—his mother and stepfather, Mrs. Campbell, his sister Alice, Royes's sister Ann Maria and Mrs. Cox—and asked them once more to join him in a prayer. And then they all left the room except Mrs. Joseph Bravo, Ann Maria, Florence and Royes. That evening Charles's death was a matter of hours.

4 *Friday*

Through the night the vomiting and pain and other symptoms persisted. About two-thirty on Friday morning Charles's breathing became laboured and Mrs. Bravo sent Amelia for Florence, who, tired out with almost ceaseless watching at the bedside, had gone at her mother's entreaty to lie down for a while in Mrs. Cox's room. Amelia found her asleep there with Mrs. Cox lying on the bed beside her. She said gently:

"Will you come down as Mr. Bravo's worse."

It was Mrs. Cox who answered: "Is he really?"

She roused Florence and together they went down to Charles's room. Charles was now unconscious. He had already spoken his last, turning to his mother and saying: "Ah, Granny." Florence stayed for a time and soon after five went in tears to Mary Ann's room and asked her to get up and make tea for Mrs. Campbell, Mrs. Cox and herself. When the tea was ready Mrs. Cox came out of Florence's dressing-room and told the maid that Florence wanted to speak to her.

She went in and Florence said:

"Mary Ann, Mr. Bravo is dead."

"Oh, madam, when did he die?"

"A few minutes ago."

Charles had died at about five-thirty in the presence of Florence, Mrs. Cox, his mother, Amelia, Mrs. Campbell and Royes. It was a merciful release. And though everyone at

The Priory was stunned by grief, along with the shock of Charles's death there was a sense of relief that his prolonged and terrible sufferings were over. Later that morning a terse telegram went out from Florence to her father at Buscot: "Charles died this morning at five-thirty quite peacefully." The reply came soon: "We're much grieved by sad news which was unexpected after your telegram. Augusta joins us in warmest sympathy. Can I be of any use? If so I'll come. Telegraph immediately." Mrs. Campbell wired back. "Mr. Bravo senior is here and will do all that is necessary. Keep where you are and take care of yourself."

But now that the emergency was past, the comings and goings of the doctors over, the sick-room tidied and put to rights, its door quietly closed on the laid-out body of the late Charles Bravo, there was time for those at The Priory to think. The master of the house, who three mornings ago had appeared so well and cheerful, so very much alive, was suddenly and unaccountably dead—killed, according to the doctors, by some powerful irritant poison. But what poison? Charles had maintained almost to his last breath and with every mark of truth that he had taken only laudanum, and the doctors were unanimous that laudanum was not the drug that had killed him.

Was it accident? There were no signs in the room (though perhaps some other part of the house might reveal them) of any bottle or container from which Charles might have inadvertently taken some lethal draught. And surely he would have known it if he had.

Could it have been suicide? To most of those who asked themselves this question in the hours following Charles's death the idea seemed utterly unthinkable, even abhorrent. High-spirited, sanguine Charles was the last person to kill himself; he had no troubles that anyone knew of—and again there was his solemn death-bed denial that he had knowingly taken anything but laudanum. And yet, running counter to this denial, there was one very strong indication of suicide—that admission of Charles's to Mrs. Cox about taking poison, which she had repeated (so she said) to Mr. Harrison and again four hours later to Royes and Dr. Johnson. But it was queer that Mr. Harrison had categorically denied that she had told him this, and that Charles himself had later had no recollection of having made such an avowal to Mrs. Cox. The only explanation of this little inconsistency seemed to be that someone's memory was playing them false or that what Charles had said had been misunderstood by Mrs. Cox.

And the third alternative—murder. Did anyone of those who had been around Charles's bedside during those harrowing hours even contemplate this third and most sinister possibility? Certainly a suspicious-minded person could argue that Charles's strenuous denial of having taken anything but laudanum suggested that he had been secretly given a lethal poison by someone else. But perhaps, with Charles so newly dead, such drastic thoughts had barely had time to obtrude themselves into that house of grief. And surely cold-blooded murder was too horrible a thing to envisage in connection with such a pleasant, lovable fellow as Charles Bravo—at least until the other alternatives had been examined and dismissed.

The only recorded conclusion that was uttered while the household was still bowed under the immediate impact of Charles's death came from Florence herself: it was supremely unhelpful. On Friday morning she declared to Ann Maria Bell that it was "very mysterious" and would "always remain a mystery".

CHAPTER 7

PRIVATE INQUEST

IT WAS CLEAR that after this puzzling and suspicious illness, which had exercised the wits of six doctors on and off over for fifty hours, the granting of a death certificate was out of the question. A post-mortem would have to be held. (Indeed, Mr. Joseph Bravo, not at all easy about Charles's seizure and death, pressed for one.) So on Friday, 21st April, Royes Bell warned the Surrey Coroner and arranged this. And next day, at St. Thomas's Hospital, the post-mortem was conducted by Dr. Joseph Payne, of Savile Row, in the presence of Dr. Johnson, Dr. Moore, Mr. Harrison and Royes Bell himself.

As Dr. Payne performed his gruesome work on the remains of Charles Bravo the four doctors who had stood so helplessly around his sick-bed now pressed round the slab with keenest professional curiosity to learn the secret that had baffled them. The dissecting scalpel revealed no signs of natural disease, but in the large intestine there was ulceration and extensive inflammation which could mean only one thing: irritant poison. The doctors looked at one another: this amply confirmed their suspicions. But before they could know any more they would have to wait for an analysis. And so, following the grim medical routine, Dr. Payne removed certain organs, placed them in sealed jars and entrusted them to Royes Bell to deliver to that eminent analytical chemist Mr. Theophilus Redwood, Professor of Chemistry to the Pharmaceutical Society of Great Britain, in Bloomsbury Square. The professor had already received from Royes Bell a bottle containing the vomited matter collected from the leads below Charles's bedroom window.

Meanwhile the inquest was being arranged. Florence, prostrate from grief and shock, was dreading the thought of it. The requirements of the law must be met, she realised; but, after all, Charles's death was her private and personal tragedy, and her only wish was that this inquiry, with its heartless probings, statements and harrowing reminders of the whole ghastly business, should be as quietly and quickly dispatched as possible. Consequently, on the 23rd, she got Mrs. Cox to write Mr. Broadbridge, the Coroner's officer, a little note which said: "Mrs. Charles Bravo writes to say that she wishes the inquest to be held at The Priory, where she will have refreshments prepared for the jury." Mr. William Carter, the Coroner in charge of the case, considered the matter. Here was this young barrister, in comfortable circumstances and of good respectable background, very probably a suicide. Nothing criminal seemed involved; and he could sympathise with the widow's desire to avoid further distress. Mr. Carter was a kindly man and had no wish to cause her unnecessary pain by dragging the case before an inquisitive and insensitive public. He therefore agreed with Florence's request; and on Tuesday, 25th April, the inquest was opened in the dining-room of The Priory.

As the officials, jurymen and witnesses solemnly made their way through the front door of the darkened house on the morning of the 25th the scene presented a mournful contrast to that of the previous Tuesday. It was just a week since the day of Charles's seizure, the day when, cheerful and apparently in the best of health, he had driven off to London with Florence and lunched with her Uncle James, had returned to have his misadventure on Cremorne, had taken his last dinner, with

Florence and Mrs. Cox, in this very room where the Coroner and jury were now assembling to inquire into his sudden death. Even now his body was lying in an upstairs room.

Few outsiders were present beyond those officially concerned. There were one or two curious neighbours and a few barrister friends of Charles's; his stepfather was there, and Florence's parents. But there were no reporters, for Mr. Carter, in his desire to respect Florence's wish for privacy, had been remiss enough not to notify the Press. As for Florence herself, she was upstairs in her room, unable to face the ordeal of appearing, even in her own house, and excused by the considerate Mr. Carter from giving evidence.

The first witness called was Mr. Joseph Bravo, who since Charles's death had been staying in the house and, according to Mrs. Cox, had been kindness itself to his stricken daughter-in-law. He stated, among other things, that from the time that he had arrived on the Wednesday until his stepson's death, Charles had never suggested the cause of his illness.

Mrs. Cox, clad in deepest black, then testified. With eyes downcast and in a low and barely audible voice she described the events in the sick-room, relating how at about nine-thirty (the time was actually rather later) she had seen Charles in his bedroom standing at the window, looking very ill. He told her at once that he had taken poison and asked her not to tell Florence. She then noticed on the mantelpiece two bottles. One was blue, labelled 'Chloroform—Poison' and had a little whitish fluid in it; the other, white, was labelled 'Laudanum'. He had used them, she said, for his neuralgia, from which he had recently been suffering. She asked how he had come to take the poison and he did not reply. However, she insisted that she had told Mr. Harrison what Charles had said. Charles and Florence, she concluded, had always lived on affectionate terms, and she knew no reason why he should commit suicide.

Amelia Bushell followed Mrs. Cox and stated that she did not, while in almost continual attendance on Charles since her arrival with Mr. and Mrs. Joseph Bravo on the Wednesday, hear him account for his condition.

Mr. Harrison then gave evidence, relating what had happened in the sick-room. But he stated that he had not been informed by Mrs. Cox that Charles had admitted taking poison, and Charles had denied, despite repeated questioning, having taken anything but laudanum.

After these four witnesses had been heard the Coroner adjourned the proceedings until Friday, the 28th, in order to give Professor Redwood time to produce his findings on the analysis. (There is, however, reason to think that the professor had already established what the poison was.) The first witness at the resumed hearing was Florence's servant, Mary Ann Keeber. Quietly she deposed that at ten o'clock on the Tuesday night Mrs. Cox had asked her to fetch some hot water for Mr. Bravo; and went on to outline the events of that night as she had seen them. She declared that he had called to Florence for hot water "as loud as he could". After mentioning that Charles and Florence had lived together very happily she stated that Charles had not used the word "poison" in her hearing and that Mrs. Cox had not spoken it on the Tuesday night either.

After Mary Ann had finished, the Coroner unexpectedly recalled Mr. Harrison. The jury wanted confirmation on two points. The first concerned the identity of the doctor who had taken charge of the matter to be analysed. The second was rather more crucial: it dealt with Mrs. Cox's allegation that she had told him that Charles had taken poison. He now emphatically adhered to his previous denial of this, saying: "I was not told the deceased had said he had taken poison. Mrs. Cox said she was sure he had taken chloroform."

Then came Dr. Payne, who described the post-mortem he

had carried out on Charles and the state in which he had found the body. He said that the autopsy had been performed at the request of "the family" (by which he meant the Bravo family), as had the analysis.

Royes Bell followed, stating that he had arrived at the bedside early on the morning of the 19th and remained with Charles almost uninterruptedly until his death. He said that Charles made no admission that he had taken anything other than laudanum.

Now Professor Redwood was called. This was what everyone had been waiting for. The temporary court-room, incongruous with its dinner-wagon and vast mahogany sideboard, was hushed as the famous pathologist, bearded and mild-looking, stood up and sorted his papers. The jury straightened themselves in their well-padded chairs and looked more alert as he cleared his throat and began his evidence. Only Mrs. Cox, her hands folded primly on her lap, seemed completely unmoved. But they had to wait a little before the professor reached the interesting part. First he went through the formality of stating who he was, what matters he had received for analysis, how he had gone about analysing them. And then it came. In his unemotional voice he said:

"I detected antimony in the vomited food."

Antimony. Few beyond the doctors present could have heard the name before, and fewer still known the nature of this deadly poison. And yet to all there it had a dread, chilling sound, more sinister in its implications than arsenic or prussic acid. To leave no doubt in the jurors' minds about what this poison was and what its effects were, this expert witness went on: "Antimony is a poison not commonly used as a poison. In all the articles delivered to me I found evidence of antimony. I detected nothing else, except in the vomited food a little lead. That I accounted for by his having vomited on the leads of the window. There is one form in which alone antimony could have been administered, and that is emetic tartar. It is soluble in water and tasteless. I apprehend that it is almost the only form in which it could be taken. We have not many well-authenticated cases of poisoning by antimony in large doses, but symptoms are recorded similar. The symptoms might be like chloroform. The effect of antimony is to produce prostration and vomiting, generally from half an hour to an hour after the taking. I got as much antimony from the vomited food as would make ten grains of emetic tartar. Upon the analyses and evidence my opinion is that death arose upon the taking of antimony into the body, and in sufficient quantity to cause death."

The professor sat down, and for a minute the court was silent while the Coroner made his notes. Then Mr. Joseph Bravo rose with a question. Might not the antimony, he asked, have been in the food partaken at dinner? Mrs. Cox was then called on to inform the court that the dinner that Tuesday night had consisted of fish, roast leg of lamb, spinach (she was wrong here: no spinach had been served) and eggs, and anchovy toast, and that Florence and she had eaten these without ill effects. Mr. Bravo then declared himself satisfied.

The Coroner was about to sum up when the clerk leant over and whispered to him: he had omitted to hear evidence on the state of the deceased's mind on the day of his seizure. He then asked anyone who could testify to this to come forward, and up stepped Frederick MacCalmont, Charles's colleague. MacCalmont spoke of his meeting with Charles on the Tuesday afternoon and affirmed him to be in his usual health and spirits. He remarked too on the excellent terms on which he and Florence had been, and said that in his opinion Charles had been a most unlikely person to commit suicide.

Again the Coroner was preparing to sum up when Dr.

Johnson rose, gave his name and said that as he had seen Charles several times when he was ill his evidence might be relevant. The Coroner seemed rather put out at this and replied tartly:

"We don't require any further evidence; it is quite unnecessary to examine you!"

Dr. Johnson sat down, blushing a fiery red at the snub. His colleagues glanced at him sympathetically. George Johnson, they knew, could have given useful testimony—it was confoundedly irregular of the Coroner to refuse to let a responsible medical man testify like this! Dr. Moore, too, had come to give evidence; but in view of this rebuff he kept silent. It was clear that some of the jury were uneasy. In fact there was a feeling in the court now that the Coroner was in a hurry— many thought in too much of a hurry—to record a verdict and be done with the case. But again he was thwarted in his aim to sum up. Mrs. Cox stood up this time, desiring to rectify an omission in her evidence. In describing the bottles in Charles's room, she said, she had forgotten to mention a bottle of liniment prescribed by Royes Bell.

What Mr. Carter said in summing-up is not officially recorded, but from the recollection of one person present he told the jury that they would have to say whether the poison spoken of by the medical men was taken by Mr. Bravo himself, or administered to him, or taken by accident. If they believed Mrs. Cox, he had taken the poison himself. If that were so, it was a case of *felo de se*, unless he was insane, of which there was no evidence.

The jury returned after a short absence to give their verdict, and the foreman proclaimed in a firm voice their finding "that the deceased died from the effects of a poison—antimony—but we have not sufficient evidence under what circumstances it came into his body".

An open verdict. That was that. The court broke up, and as

those attending made their way out of The Priory's dining-room that afternoon there were few who would have called it a satisfactory inquest. In not calling Florence, whose evidence would have been at least as important as Mrs. Cox's, refusing to hear Dr. Johnson, dismissing some witnesses over-hastily, in short in not covering the ground anything like as thoroughly as he ought to have done, Mr. Carter seemed badly at fault. And then there was that entirely unorthodox action of his in having a private word with Mr. Joseph Bravo when the court was cleared and the jury were considering their verdict. He had summoned him and asked him whether he had any suspicions of foul play. Mr. Bravo's reply had not been very reassuring.

"No, but there are drugs in nearly every room in the house!"

Mr. Carter appeared to have convinced himself early in the proceedings—or even before—that Charles had committed suicide and to be determined to call the minimum of evidence necessary to obtain that verdict. So eager had he been to fall in with Florence's wishes that he had conducted what was virtually a private inquest. Not only was the Press unrepresented but his own transcript of evidence was bald and incomplete. If Mr. Reid, Charles's barrister friend, had not taken down his own notes, some of the vital points in the testimony would have gone unrecorded. It was he, not Mr. Carter, who had reported Mrs. Cox's statement that Charles had said "Don't tell Florence" after admitting having taken poison; Mr. Harrison's denial that he had been told that Charles had taken poison (when Mrs. Cox had asserted that she had told him); much of Professor Redwood's description of antimony and its effects; and various other details. That the Coroner should have been so summary may have suited the bereaved Florence in her wish to avoid publicity; and his hopes for a suicide verdict were also shared by Mr. Campbell.

This was shown by a couple of calls he made before the second day's inquest. The first was to Mr. Joseph Bravo at Palace Green on the Thursday. Mr. Campbell explained that he had come to discuss the cause of Charles's death; and Mr. Bravo, who had known unofficially about the discovery of antimony since Monday, now told Florence's father about it and said that antimony was a poison used by people wishing to take the lives of others and that no one, as far as he knew, had ever used it to take his own life. Thus Joseph Bravo showed, only too plainly, that he would have no truck with the suicide theory, however convenient it might be to others.

Mr. Campbell's next call was on the Friday morning, before the resumed inquest had started, on Dr. Johnson at Savile Row. He told the doctor that he had been advised by Sir William Gull to come to him. Then he said:

"The question is, what verdict shall we get? I can get a verdict of suicide in five minutes."

Dr. Johnson was interested. "How?" he asked.

"By repeating Sir William Gull's opinion."

"Then Sir William believes it to be suicide?"

"Yes."

"Well, it may be suicide, but so far as I can see there is no evidence to show it, and the only possible verdict is an open one, that he died by antimony."

Dr. Johnson added that he thought of going to the inquest. With rather surprising vehemence Mr. Campbell begged him not to, and said he would telegraph to him whether to come or not. But no telegram came and the doctor attended the inquest in any case, in the hope of being able to give evidence —vain, as it turned out.

In Mr. Campbell's two little reconnaissances, made while the verdict was still *sub judice*, were clearly foreshadowed a coming clash of family interests (or convictions)—Florence's father canvassing for a suicide finding, Charles's stepfather (despite what he said later to the Coroner) suspecting murder. The open verdict arrived at can have satisfied neither entirely. Nor did it satisfy Mrs. Cox. For it was on her testimony and hers alone that the whole suicide theory was based. And in discarding suicide the jury had shown what they thought of that lady's evidence—and perhaps her integrity. But if not suicide—if Mrs. Cox was lying—what then?

CHAPTER 8

SUSPICIONS GROW

CHARLES BRAVO's funeral took place the next day, Saturday, 29th April. In an open hearse fringed with violet trappings the flower-covered coffin was borne from The Priory to Norwood Cemetery, where Charles was buried on the hill at the top of the right-hand road near a clump of trees, in a vault that was crowned by a single stone slab "prior to the erection of a tasteful mausoleum". Parents and friends attended, but Florence, still shattered by her grief, could not face this last distressing ordeal. She placed a wreath of flowers upon the coffin and then, white-faced and sobbing, from an upper window she watched the cortège move slowly down the drive of The Priory and then abandoned herself to her grief—a widow for a second time, bereaved after a mere four months of marriage. (Did George Griffith, in his stables at Lady Prescott's, hear of his ex-master's death and recall his own sullen prophecy of the previous December?)

Florence's health had been delicate enough before Charles's death and the sudden devastating shock of her loss had caused a relapse. Her father, who himself had been too ill to come to Charles's bedside but had arrived to stay at The Priory after the post-mortem, was seriously concerned at her condition and thought it imperative that she went away for a time. The Worthing trip was clearly off; there was no question now of the hoped-for convalescence with Augusta in a rented house with servants and the carriage. What Florence needed was absolute quiet and rest. So he and Mrs. Campbell talked with

Mrs. Cox, and on the day after the opening of the inquest she went down to Brighton to look for rooms for a few weeks' stay for herself and Florence alone. She found suitable lodgings at No. 38 Brunswick Terrace; and here she brought Florence accompanied by her maid, Mary Ann, a week later to forget— if she could—the tragic events of the last fortnight and regain her broken health. But the sudden mysterious death of Charles was not a thing to be put aside by a change of surroundings— and certainly Brighton, the scene of their brief courtship and honeymoon of but a few months back, was not the best place in which to seek such oblivion. Weak and ailing, Florence brooded on her loss. But amid her grief for the dead Charles she allowed some curiously calculating thoughts to obtrude themselves.

On 5th May, two days after arriving at Brunswick Terrace, she wrote to Mr. Joseph Bravo:

Dear Father Joseph,—I am astonished to hear from my solicitor, Mr. Brooks, that you had dear Charlie's drawers sealed, as, legally, nobody but myself has the power to touch one single thing belonging to him, he having left all he possessed to me, and I must ask you to see that nothing he possessed is touched by anyone. With regard to what he died possessed of, I must leave to you; he told me he had £200 a year of his own coming from investments, and of course his books, pictures and private property at Palace Green are now mine. His watch was left at your house, and by his own wish I give it to Mr. Royes Bell; please see that it is delivered to him. My father will take care that I have all my dear husband left to me. Poor fellow! How he would have grieved at all the unkind feeling shown to me. Hoping you and Mrs. Bravo are better, believe me, yours sincerely,

FLORENCE BRAVO

And then she added a strictly business-like postscript:

P.S. Poor Charles also told me that you promised to allow him £800 a year.

Next morning she heard from Royes Bell. What he wrote her is unrecorded, but evidently he said something—despite his statement at the inquest that Charles had not admitted taking anything besides laudanum—in favour of the suicide theory. This was reassuring, for sad though it was to contemplate Charles dying by his own hand, this was at least preferable to the sinister alternative that Florence knew was already in Mr. Bravo's and other people's minds after the unfortunate open verdict at the inquest. So at once she wrote to Mr. Bravo again:

Dear Father Joseph,—A letter received this morning from Royes Bell fully confirms my suspicions as to poor Charlie's suicide: hence his motive for reducing our expenditure, as he could not tell me how hard he had been pressed by that dreadful woman. I wish he had, poor fellow, for I should not have been hard upon him; but it is a most sad reflection upon his memory for me, and I intend to sift the matter. We have Sir William Gull's evidence, and I shall not allow the living to be under any imputation such as is cast upon them by such a wicked verdict. I leave it all in my father's hands, and shall abide by his decision. Yours sincerely,

FLORENCE BRAVO

"That dreadful woman" was Charles's ex-mistress at Maidenhead; and Florence must have known that she was jumping to conclusions in suggesting that this lady was pressing him for money. She had no evidence of this. Her eagerness to establish Charles's suicide, motive and all, was certainly leading her in her overwrought state to wishful thinking. But such a possible suicide pretext might, she felt, induce Joseph Bravo to rid his mind of the horrible notion that Charles had been murdered. And if she could banish his suspicions, win him over to her way of thinking, Charles might be allowed to rest in peace and his nearest and dearest left to their sorrow, undisturbed by these terrible doubts about his death that Mr. Bravo was busy fomenting.

Thinking thus, she had misgivings about her letter of 5th May. It must have sounded unforgivably brusque, hasty and high-handed, she reflected; hardly the sort of letter to enlist Mr. Joseph's sympathies. So on the 8th she wrote another in a much more conciliatory tone (and seemingly better-informed):

My dear Father Joseph,—The letter I wrote you on Friday was written under the impression that you had forced dear Charlie's drawers at the Temple, and I regret having been so impressed, as ever since I knew you I have only experienced kindness and consideration. Please try and think of me as your loving daughter, and do not address me as "Mrs. Florence Bravo", it pains me more than I can tell you, and it is only in legal documents that I must be so addressed. I hope you are all recovering from the dreadful and sad last fortnight. My life is a complete blank and I am very ill. With love to you and yours, ever your affectionate daughter, FLORENCE BRAVO

P.S. Have dear Charlie's photos been sent by mistake to you?

Florence discussed the suicide theory with her family, who, it seems, were at Brighton with her during the early part of her stay; and she even suggested that Charles might have helped himself to antimony from his stepfather's stables at Palace

Green—she had an idea that Joseph Bravo had told her father that he kept some there. But all her efforts, in those unhappy May days at Brighton, to paint Charles as a suicide were unavailing. Suspicion had already taken too firm a hold. She knew that before the Friday of the resumed inquest Joseph Bravo had learned of the presence of antimony and had on the advice of his brother-in-law, Mr. Henry Smith, been to Scotland Yard and that as a result Inspector Clarke had been detailed to make investigations; but she was unaware that on the Monday after the funeral Charles's barrister friend Edward Willoughby, profoundly dissatisfied at the implication of suicide, had also called at the Yard. And, as the first week of May passed, the doubts and speculations that had been buzzing among Charles's many friends in the Temple and the Junior Carlton Club—not one of whom could see this cheerful, optimistic and essentially extrovert young man, so suddenly struck down by antimony, as a suicide (let alone as having accidentally taken it)—quickly spread to a wider circle. Gossip reached Fleet Street, and on 10th May the matter first became public. That day, in the *World*, an article appeared entitled "A Tragedy?" Reporting the main facts of the case it quoted no names but referred to Charles as "a young barrister rapidly gaining a position at Westminster Hall, who had recently married". Next day, more fully and prominently, the *Daily Telegraph* came out with it. At breakfast-tables all over the country readers learnt for the first time the details of the mysterious affair at Balham and the names of those involved, including some of the doctors. In an accompanying leader they also read strong criticisms of the inquest. So the story of that last dinner at The Priory, the agonising hours in the sick-room, the ominous discovery of antimony, the suspicions, the sinister possibilities, leaked at last beyond the confines of Mr. Carter's private court-room and were public property. Here in this tale of poison in a plush domestic setting, with the hint of a sequel yet untold, were the makings of a first-class sensation such as the scandal-hungry public loved. Reading that day's *Telegraph* in her sitting-room in Brunswick Terrace, with Mrs. Cox beside her, Florence realised with horrified dismay that the worst had happened, that the parading of her private bereavement and grief, which she had dreaded from the first, had come to pass; and that murder, not suicide, was the surmise on everybody's lips.

And that was only the beginning. From then on, to a mounting public interest, the *Telegraph* featured the case almost daily, campaigning either for a new inquest or some other form of investigation. In its columns Dr. Moore and Mr. Harrison gave their accounts of what had happened; while reports from Drs. Johnson and Payne, and Professor Redwood, appeared in the *Lancet*, that of Dr. Johnson being reprinted in other papers. The professor's report threw light on the quantity of antimony that Charles must have absorbed. "I have calculated," he wrote, "that the antimony found in the vomited food submitted to me would be equivalent to ten grains of emetic tartar; but this would probably have been only a small portion of what was taken. . . . It may therefore be assumed that a very large dose of the antimonial salt was taken which would probably account for all the symptoms observed in the case."

The next issue of the *Lancet* had something to say on the vehicle in which the poison might have been taken. Referring to the burgundy, which had been suggested as a likely container, it decided that the tannin in this wine would precipitate the antimony to cause noticeable turbidity, and might also precipitate some of the wine's colouring matter. As for the table salt, another possible vehicle, the paper dismissed this on account of the large amount that must have been eaten to carry the quantity which Charles Bravo was reckoned to have absorbed. It also pointed out that poisoned table salt would have caused vomiting before the end of the meal.

To these expert speculations (which implied that Charles had not taken the poison dose at dinner) were added those of the laymen whose letters now appeared numerously in the *Telegraph* and other papers. Some offered one theory, some another, often conflicting, but all these, like the newspaper comments, were necessarily cautious in their statements. But what of the other letters that are never lacking when hasty and hostile public judgment singles out a victim—the anonymous letters that Florence now began to receive by the dozen at Brunswick Terrace? These did not mince their words but held her responsible for Charles's death, dragging in Mrs. Cox's name too. The writers had never stopped to ask themselves why—if murder it was—Florence should have done it, or Mrs. Cox for that matter. Cruel and monstrously unjustified the charges might be, but at least they showed where a section of public opinion was tending. Florence, terrified and heartbroken at the awful allegations, turned to her parents for help and asked them in desperation what she should do. Her father took a wise step. He advised her—the idea was said to come from their medical man, Dr. Walters of Faringdon—to come out into the open and advertise in the papers, offering a reward for information as to the source of the poison. With Mr. Brooks's help an appropriate notice was drafted which appeared as follows in the national press on 16th May:

FIVE HUNDRED POUNDS REWARD.—Whereas up to the present time it is not known where or by whom the antimony or tartar emetic which caused the death of the late Mr. Charles Delauney Turner Bravo, of The Priory, Balham, Surrey, was procured on or before the 18th April last, the above reward will be paid on behalf of his widow by the undersigned to anyone who will prove the sale of the said antimony or tartar emetic in such a manner as will throw satisfactory light on the mode by which Mr. Bravo came by his death on the 21st April last.—Any information to be given to Superintendent Williamson, Scotland Yard, London.— Brooks, Jenkins and Co., Solicitors for Mrs. C. Bravo, 7 Godliman Street, Doctors' Commons, London.

Five hundred pounds was a lot of money; enough, it might be thought, to induce anyone concerned to come forward except the murderer (if murder it was). Yet not a soul responded. It was disappointing, even a little surprising, but at least Florence had demonstrated to the public that the victim of these cruel slanders and innuendos was herself as anxious as anybody to clear the matter up.

Meanwhile, as the rumours circulated and the speculations seethed, Mr. Carter's jurymen were becoming increasingly dissatisfied at his handling of the inquest. Discussing the matter in their twos and threes they felt that what had been elicited from the witnesses had been entirely inadequate and that, while they themselves had given the only possible verdict in the circumstances, they had not heard nearly the whole story. They could not help taking the Press criticisms to heart as reflecting on themselves, and finally they decided that they ought to get together unofficially and go over the whole matter again. So they persuaded the foreman to call a special meeting. And on the day after Florence's notice had appeared these shrewd, conscientious business-men and shopkeepers of Balham assembled in a private room at the Bedford Hotel, that same tavern where George Griffith had drunk and moodily prophesied on the Bravos' wedding-day.

The foreman in his opening words rather significantly remarked that if there had been a jury less determined to do their duty, and less acquainted with the attendant circumstances, a verdict of suicide or death by misadventure would have been returned. He then invited his colleagues' views. Most of them had something to say and the criticisms chiefly centred on the incompleteness of the Coroner's depositions and the inadequacy of his questioning. But there was also some adverse comment on the evasiveness of Mrs. Cox. Indeed, as the jurymen went through the proceedings and listed the shortcomings of Mr. Carter, Mrs. Cox's name cropped up more than that of anyone else. There was no record, it was noted, that she had been called before the jury three times, that she had said that Charles Bravo had drunk burgundy specially decanted for him, that she had been very reticent about saying what had been done with the remains of the anchovy or bloater paste served for dinner that night. Especially did these jurors attack the Coroner's sketchy questioning in regard to Mrs. Cox's statement (unrecorded) that though Charles Bravo had told her at ten o'clock that he had taken poison, she never mentioned anything about it to the doctors in the house until two-thirty the next morning. One juror considered that it was vital to know all that had been said on that occasion, and thought it inexplicable that Mrs. Cox had not at once told a servant to run off to the nearest doctor and ask him to return with a stomach-pump as Mr. Bravo had taken poison. The Coroner was censured too for not calling Dr. Moore, the first doctor on the scene. And he was further criticised for omitting from his record an important statement of Mary Ann Keeber's about the emetic administered to Charles. Finally, one juror said that it would have been useful to know whether Mrs. Cox was ever confronted with Charles Bravo and whether he was ever told that she had stated that he had confessed to having taken poison. Another juror said that he could have had no suspicion (of

Florence) as they had it in evidence that his last words were "Take care of my poor dear wife".

Mr. Carter's jurymen left the Bedford Hotel more disquieted than they had been before. The inquest on Charles Bravo had been thoroughly unsatisfactory—but they knew this already. Now the whole story of the events leading to his death seemed more than ever bedevilled by loose ends and contradictions and riddled with question-marks: and more than one of them felt that if all the queries were fully answered a rather ugly picture might be revealed.

As appeared next day, 18th May, this thought was shared in higher quarters. In the House of Commons the Liberal member for Dewsbury, Mr. Serjeant Simon (later Sir John Simon, Serjeant-at-Law), rose at question-time to ask the Home Secretary, Mr. Cross, "whether your attention has been called to the unsatisfactory character of the Coroner's inquest on the late Mr. Bravo." In reply the Home Secretary admitted that irregularities had been committed and he declared himself to be "entirely dissatisfied with the way the inquiry had been con-ducted". While not yet able to announce what action would be taken, he said that all the papers in the case were being studied by the Law Officers of the Crown.

The Law Officers of the Crown. . . . So the dissatisfactions of a few doctors and jurymen, the private doubts of a handful of Charles's friends in their Temple chambers and Pall Mall smoking-rooms, sensationally echoed and magnified by the Press, had in a few weeks brought this suburban poisoning tragedy to the notice of Parliament and before the cold scrutiny of the legal gentlemen in Whitehall. Florence, learning this news at Brighton as she vainly waited for a reply to her advertisement, wondered desperately where the thing would end now. How much of her private life was going to be dragged out and trailed before inquisitive, unsympathetic

Dr. James Manby Gully, about 1876 (*Picture Post Library*)

Florence's companion, Mrs. Cox, "hard-working, penurious widow with jet-black hair, sallow skin and almost oriental look"

officials and a sensation-hungry public before the affair of poor Charles's death was allowed to be decently buried and forgotten? And it was not only her life with Charles at The Priory that she saw so ruthlessly exhibited: there was her "past", the intimate years with James Gully. She could lay her hand on her heart and say that everything was over between them, had been since they had parted here in Brighton seven months ago. After that last meeting of theirs at the lodge in December— and that was for a strictly business reason—she was prepared to swear that she had seen him only at a distance from the windows of The Priory, walking once or twice across the common. And Gully himself had been as determined to sever the connection as Florence was. He had ordered Pritchard, his butler, not to admit her or Mrs. Cox to Orwell Lodge, and in December had shut up the house and gone away for three months. When he heard of Charles's death his only comment was: "Ah, that's a bad business." He had, however, written to Mrs. Cox at Brighton saying how sorry he was to hear of Florence's loss and asking Mrs. Cox to convey his sympathies to her. Mrs. Cox, with her usual discretion, had thought it best not to carry out his request, and had merely shown the letter to Florence's brother, who was then at Brighton, and destroyed it. Perhaps she was wise in the circumstances not to reopen the communication between them, even on this innocent matter.

Like Florence, Mrs. Cox was wondering too where things were tending now. She knew that she had not made too good a showing at the inquest and was particularly aware that her story that she had told Mr. Harrison on his arrival that Charles had confessed to having taken poison had failed to carry conviction. Thinking over what she could do to strengthen her her position on 19th May, the day the report of Mr. Serjeant Simon's question appeared, she decided then and there to write to Mr. Harrison with the idea of refreshing his memory of the events of that Tuesday evening.

My dear Mr. Harrison [she wrote],—The reports and comments in the papers make me most unhappy. I do wish that you would try to remember what I said to you about the poison. It is so dreadful for it to be said that I never mentioned anything about the poison until Mr. Bell came.

I told you I felt sure he had taken chloroform, for I smelt it when he was sick; but when afterwards you said "It could not be chloroform", or "It was not", I said, "I feel sure he took chloroform, and the bottle is empty, and he said he had taken either 'some poison' or 'poison', I forget which;" and I also told you that I had given him mustard and water to make him sick, and that I had put his feet and hands in hot mustard and water, and mustard plasters on his feet. All this I did to keep him awake, as I thought, and you know you told me afterwards I could not have done better. Do try to remember, and say all you can for me. It is so dreadful to have such things said as they are now doing. I know you will, with your usual kindness, forgive my troubling you; and will you kindly reply to me per return post? With kind regards, believe me, yours truly, JANE C. COX

I did not tell Dr. Moore, because I was expecting you every moment, and I quite thought also he [Charles] would recover from the effects of the chloroform, and he would be so angry at my having told he had said he had taken poison.

The affair must have been weighing heavily on her mind, for there was anxiety in her appeal for an immediate and reassuring reply. Impatiently she watched for the post two days later, and sure enough it brought the awaited letter. The doctor had at least responded promptly. From his home at Streatham Hill he wrote:

Dear Mrs. Cox,—I am willing to do my best to relieve your mind. You did not use the word "poison" to me, nor did you say that he had told you he had taken it, but you did tell me that he had taken chloroform, and you told me so in such a manner as to imply that he was poisoned by it; but Dr. Moore and I hunted for poison all over the room before Bell arrived. As you may remember, we examined the liniment bottle, &c.: and directly the vomiting of blood commenced we became certain that it was an irritant poison, so that no difference could have been made in the treatment.

Believe me, yours very truly, GEORGE HARRISON

Mr. Harrison's answer was cold comfort for the worried Mrs. Cox. She folded the letter away, bitterly disappointed. All she could do now was to stick to her own story, as it was clear that Mr. Harrison was going to adhere to his. Pondering over the situation she saw the difficulty she might easily be in if the inquiry went further. If the doctor's word was accepted —as it was almost certain to be—she herself would be under the suspicion of distorting the truth for some sinister motive of her own. If only, she thought, the jury had taken the course that the sensible Mr. Carter had so obviously believed was the right one and declared poor Charlie's death to be suicide, all this bother would never have arisen!

Under these stresses and uncertainties Mrs. Cox stood up better than Florence. In her small lean frame she harboured a determined, resilient, utterly self-reliant spirit. She had faced and overcome obstacles before, and she could do so again if necessary. Florence too had known trouble, but she had had James Gully to share it with her: now in this new adversity there was no one—except of course Mrs. Cox. With her delicate, high-strung constitution undermined by her recent illness, the shock of her bereavement and now these present worries, she was near to breakdown. The anonymous letters, the Press reports, the horrifying publicity of the whole affair, preyed on her mind to make her morbid, hysterical, sleepless. In this state her mother, summoned by Mrs. Cox, found her; and early in June she did what she had done six years before when Florence had sent out a cry of distress from Malvern; took her back with her to Buscot Park.

But, before she went to Buscot, Florence, together with Mrs. Cox, made a highly important contribution to the official investigation into Charles's death that was now being held by those Law Officers of the Crown to whom the Home Secretary had referred in his Parliamentary answer of 18th May. She and Mrs. Cox went to London and made statements to the Solicitor to the Treasury.

Mr. Stephenson, the Treasury Solicitor, had already been directed to hold his investigation before the Home Secretary had made his announcement. He had thereupon arranged to examine as many people as possible who could throw light on the events surrounding Charles's poisoning; and he had done something else. He had, after asking and obtaining Florence's permission, instructed Professor Redwood and Inspector Clarke to search The Priory for poisons. It was a foregone conclusion that they would find nothing, for the five weeks since Charles's death was ample time for all traces of lethal drugs to have been removed. However, search they did, taking two days over it, and all they discovered were the contents of the homœopathic medicine chests in both Florence's and Mrs. Cox's rooms, and dozens of loose bottles which proved on analysis to contain harmless domestic medicines. Meanwhile an examination of the witnesses was going on, and on 27th May the *Daily*

Telegraph reported that, with thirty people questioned, the investigation was complete. The final paragraph of the report had a slight sting in it. "For various reasons," it said, "neither Mrs. Bravo nor Mrs. Cox, although questioned by the police [this referred to a brief interrogation at Brighton by Inspector Clarke], has been asked to give evidence."

This pointed announcement amounted to a challenge. It was only too clear what the public—and the authorities— would think if Florence and Mrs. Cox, the two key people in the whole affair, stood back now. Mr. Campbell realised the danger and strongly urged them both to go at once to Mr. Stephenson at the Treasury and make statements. It was imperative that they told their side of the story, he said, and removed once and for all the impression that they had anything to hide. The very worst construction would be put on their continued silence now that the matter had gone so far. With a shudder Florence agreed, and steeled herself for this further trial. Mrs. Cox too had to admit the sense of Mr. Campbell's argument; so, having thought out together what they were going to say, on 2nd June they travelled to London to see the Treasury Solicitor. It was an occasion when Florence blessed the calm competence and strength of Jane Cox: without her she could never have carried the thing through. Their first call was to Mr. Brooks's office in Godliman Street, where the solicitor wrote down their dictated statements. Then, with Florence's brother William to escort them, they drove to the Treasury chambers to be introduced by him to Mr. Stephenson. He received them with polite formality, looked at them across his desk, and said to Florence, who was to give her deposition first: "You understand you come here voluntarily, and that I shall ask no questions, but write down whatever you like to tell me." Florence inclined her head, and, pale and tremulous, faltered through her reading, while Mr. Stephenson took her words down; and at the end she seemed so affected that Mr. Stephenson, concerned that she might collapse, omitted to get her to sign the statement. Mrs. Cox followed, in that low, quiet voice of hers, thoroughly composed. When she had finished, the Solicitor passed the close-written sheets over to her and she added her neat signature "Jane Cannon Cox". Then she got Florence home to Brighton and put her straight to bed. Re-living the harrowing details of Charles's seizure and death—and delving, as she had to do, into the past that she had hoped never to disinter again—had been a nightmare ordeal for her; and next day she was prostrated with fever and delirium, too ill to be left alone. Dr. Dill, her Brighton physician, was called and he took a grave enough view of her condition to sleep for a night or so in the house.

Soon she was recovered enough to leave with her mother for Buscot, and when she went Mrs. Cox packed her bags and went too, to stay with friends near Birmingham. For Florence Brighton had proved a poor refuge from trouble. Instead of being allowed quietly to forget the past she had been constantly beset by new cares and anxieties. No wonder her health and peace of mind were gone. And it had been no tranquil holiday for Mrs. Cox either. But at least they had both done their duty in going to Mr. Stephenson. No one could say now that they were not co-operating in the task of sifting the mystery of Charles's death. But what they told the Treasury Solicitor did not help solve it, though certain sinister possibilities were clearly indicated by their sensational disclosures.

CHAPTER 9

"CHARLIE WAS MEAN AND JEALOUS"

1 *Florence's Statement*

FLORENCE began her statement to the Treasury Solicitor by describing her life from the time of her first marriage, and almost at once brought in the name of Dr. Gully:

"When I was nineteen years old I married Captain Alexander Louis Ricardo, of the Grenadier Guards, who died at Cologne on the 19th April, 1871. In the spring of that year [she meant 1870], at the instance of my mother, I went to Malvern with my husband, to be under the care of Dr. Gully, who had attended us all previously."

She then referred briefly to her stay at Malvern and her separation from Alexander:

"At this [Malvern] house I left my husband, and I never saw him again. I went home then with my mother to Buscot, and then remained abroad three months."

She mentioned her sojourn with Mrs. Brooks. "I there remained nine months, and then took a house of my own at Leigham Court Road, Streatham, taking with me from Mrs. Brooks's a Mrs. Cox, who was then daily governess to Mrs. Brooks's children. I remained about two years, and then took a lease of my present residence, The Priory, Balham.

"From the time of my being placed by my parents under Dr. Gully he took a great and increasing interest in me and my welfare, and I became attached to him and grateful for his care of me. He resided near me at the above houses, he having given up his practice at Malvern in or about the year 1871.

"In the autumn of 1875 I casually met Mr. C. T. D. Bravo, having been introduced to him some months before by Mrs. Cox, an old friend of his father's family. In about a couple of months afterwards he proposed marriage, and I ultimately accepted him, and we were married on the 7th December, 1875.

"My income was then about £3,000 a year, and the house, horses, carriages, and everything at Balham were mine. He had nothing but a very small income of his own, and casual allowances from his father.

"He was also pressing me to put down my garden and my cobs—my two great hobbies—and turn away Mrs. Cox, to save. I was paying [her] a salary of only £100; but he thus hoped, as he said, from all these sources, to save £400 a year.

"I used to ask him, why was there the necessity of this retrenchment, as I had always been accustomed to live largely within my income. He told me that he had kept a woman before marriage at Maidenhead for four years, and I believe he continued her an annual payment after marriage, and owed her or her sister £500, which he had borrowed, of which last fact I was ignorant until after his death.

"He was a very passionate man and short-tempered to the last degree. He once struck me because his mother was interfering in my household arrangements, requiring me even to put down my maid. This was three or four weeks before the fatal Tuesday, as far as I can recollect. He had on that day received a letter from his mother. He always met the postman himself, and took and read my letters.

"This letter made us both very angry. Mr. Royes Bell, who had attended me in my miscarriage, had recommended me change of air, and he said it was a useless expense. When we got to bed that night he continued very angry, and at last jumped out of bed and threatened to cut his throat. He rushed into the dressing-room, and I went after him and got him back. His words were:

" 'Now I will go and cut my throat!'

"And he actually left the bedroom for the purpose.

"On Good Friday last I had just recovered from my second miscarriage. He was very restless. He got in an awful passion because I was very weak, and had only left my bed that day for ten days, and he did not like my asking to be left alone to rest, as was my habit after luncheon.

"He was always reading Shakespeare, and we had a happy three weeks before then, and I got quite to like him and forgot his meanness, which had previously disgusted me.

"A compact between us before marriage was that Dr. Gully's name should never be mentioned, as I had told him, and requested him to tell his family, of my attachment to him.

"This attachment was quite innocent, and nothing improper had ever passed between us. But, although I never saw, heard of or from, or spoke of Dr. Gully after our marriage, he was continually, morning, noon, and night, speaking of him, always abusing him, calling him 'that wretch', and upbraiding me for my former acquaintance with him.

"On Saturday, Sunday, and Monday I observed nothing unusual in him. On Tuesday Mrs. Cox went to Worthing to choose a house for me, as recommended by Dr. Bell. I accompanied him to London, at his request, to pay bills, etc. Passing Dr. Gully's house (near mine), he said:

" 'Do you see anybody?'

"I said: 'No, I did not look.'

"He went on quarrelling about him, and said he thought I had better go to Worthing for a few days without him, which I refused to do. I then said I thought it a very cruel thing his always bringing up that name.

" 'I am not always talking to you about that woman.'

"And he admitted his error and asked me to make it up and kiss him. I said in a pet:

" 'No, I won't!'

"And then he said:

" 'You will see what I will do when I get home!'

"He looked at me in a very determined way, and I became frightened, and then I kissed him, and he said it was very wrong of him. I was always right."

Then Florence described what they did together in London before she left him in Jermyn Street, her own subsequent shopping, his return home and his unexpected ride on Cremorne.

"He went out, and was absent nearly two hours. He said the pony had bolted with him twice, and he was quite exhausted. I helped him out of his chair, he was so weak, and I recommended him a hot bath and, I think, also a glass of burgundy. I think he took the wine, and I went up to him to the bath, being anxious about him. I never saw him look so ill."

Speaking of the dinner, she mentioned his receiving the letter from his stepfather and being very upset about it. "His face worked the whole dinner—such a strange yellow look. I thought he would go mad every minute, and if I tried to turn the subject he always returned to it."

She described what happened when Charles came up to bed:

"He came in and wished me good night as I was going into my bedroom. Being so exhausted with my first long day in town, I fell asleep almost directly. The next thing I remember was being awoke by the housemaid (Mary Ann Keeber), I having discharged my maid whom I had been accustomed to from childhood. She said he was ill. I got up immediately and went to my husband. He was lying by the window unconscious in the spare room. . . . Not a word was said about poison by anyone until Sir William Gull came, but then not to me, or in my hearing; but I said loudly to Mary Ann and Mrs. Cox 'I am afraid he has been poisoned'—he was so sick. . . .

"He recovered consciousness, as far as I can recollect, about three or four o'clock on Wednesday morning: I was by his side, Mrs. Cox and four doctors being also present. . . . On the same day he said to me:

" 'You must marry again, but not a word of the past.'

"I thought he might get well. I had never heard of poison. . . . He did not tell me he had killed himself, nor did he charge anyone with having killed him. He kissed me several times, and repeatedly asked his mother to be kind to his darling wife.

"When we first married he thought I took too much sherry, and I gave it up to please him, for which he thanked me. He was sensible on Wednesday and Thursday. On Wednesday he said: 'You will take care of Katie,' meaning a child of his former mistress. He made no inquiry as to what caused his illness."

2 *Mrs. Cox's Statement*

In the very beginning of her Treasury statement Mrs. Cox dramatically amplified an item of the evidence that she had given at the inquest. There she had reported Charles as saying, when she first went into his room on the Tuesday night: "I have taken poison. Don't tell Florence." Now she too brought Dr. Gully into it. What she read to Mr. Stephenson was this:

"I was examined as a witness on the late Mr. Bravo, but from confusion, and from a mistaken idea of shielding, as I thought, the character of Mrs. Bravo, I did not tell the full particulars, which I am now anxious to state. There was no cause whatever or the slightest reason for his committing suicide for Dr. Gully, and therefore there was not the slightest reason why I should not have stated this before."

And then she gave her revised version of Charles's words:

" 'Mrs. Cox, I have taken poison for Dr. Gully. Don't tell Florence!' "

She went on:

"Beseechingly [sic] were the words he used when he first told me he had taken poison. The words 'Don't tell Florence' were used emphatically in a most imploring way.

"I said: 'How could you do such a thing?' He only screamed out as loud as he could three times for hot water."

Mrs. Cox outlined the treatment she had given Charles and then said:

"I did not tell him [Dr. Moore, the first doctor to arrive] about Gully. I thought it would cause such a scandal. I told Mr. Harrison, who was the regular attendant, directly he arrived, that he had taken chloroform. Here is a copy of Mr. Harrison's letter to me. I have the original. It is at Brighton, and I will send it up to you. I did not like to tell Dr. Moore, thinking suicide from such a cause a scandal. Mr. Bravo's temper was so violent. Had he recovered, as I thought he would if it was only chloroform, he would have been so angry.

"He had no reason to take poison, as she [Florence], I know, had not had any communication with Dr. Gully since her marriage, and their acquaintance before marriage was, though very imprudent, I conscientiously believed, entirely of an innocent character.

"On Good Friday, the first day she had come down after her illness, he was annoyed with her for lying down after luncheon, and not wishing him to remain in the room. He was so restless she could not rest. He got very angry and went out of the room and I put a match to his library fire, and he went and sat there.

"In the evening he said he despised himself for marrying her, said she was 'a selfish pig', that he had quite made up his mind not to live with her, and that he was going away, and that he wished he was dead.

"He was in a temper. I remained with him for some time, and I said:

" 'What do you think will become of Florence if you go away?'

"He said: 'Let her go to Gully,' or 'go back to Gully,' I can't remember exactly which he said.

"I told him it was very wrong of him; there was no reason— 'You know her every thought is for you. You know she does everything she possibly can to make you happy.'

"He was quite determined, however, he would go, and when he said he wished he was dead, I said it was wrong for him to say such wicked things, as God had given him life to do some good in.

" 'Pray go in to Florence and make it up with her.'

"He said 'Good night', but would not promise he would not go away. He seemed so determined I followed him upstairs. He went up and locked his bedroom door. I was so unhappy at thinking of his leaving the house, I knocked and told him I wanted to speak to him.

"He would not open it for some little time. I knocked again two or three times. He then opened it, and I begged him not to leave the house. He said that he had quite made up his mind to go; that he would not live with her any longer.

"I again reasoned with him for a long time, but he seemed quite determined, and shook hands, saying:

" 'You are a good little woman; I will always do what I can for you. Good night.' And he turned and kissed me on the cheek, and said 'Good night' again.

"He thanked me again, saying: 'You love Florence, and you do the best you can for me; I thank you for it.'

"I then went and told his wife she had better go to him, as

he was going to leave the house. She went, and I understood he was still very angry. He was determined to go. I could not rest all night. I thought he would go.

"The next morning he came up to my room and asked me if Florence had acknowledged she was sorry. I said she said she had done nothing wrong, only resting in the afternoon, and I begged him to go down to her.

"About ten minutes afterwards he told me he had seen her, and made it all right.

"Three or four weeks before that there was a quarrel between them, I believe through a letter from his home, and he was very violent, and he said he would go. This was about ten or eleven at night, they usually go to bed early, and he went, unbarred the front door, and went down the drive to leave the house.

"I followed him, and entreated him to come back. He would not for some time, and I said:

" 'Just fancy what a scandal it would be, and what will your mother say?'

"He said: 'Oh, my mother will only be too glad to have me back at any price.'

"He seemed determined to go. I said:

" 'Do you think you are doing your duty, as Florence's husband, to leave her?'

"And he repeated: 'My duty!' and he then consented and returned to the house. He went upstairs to his wife, and I re-bolted the door myself for fear the servants should know anything about it.

"He had often said how he hated Dr. Gully, how he wished him dead.

"I always tried to make peace between them [Charles and Florence]. These sudden passions seemed to overtake him, because at other times he was quite pleasant.

"The Coroner interrupted when I was about to say (reporting Charles's remark): 'Why did you tell them? Does Florence know I have poisoned myself? Don't tell her,' imploringly. I said I had not. 'What have you taken, Charlie?' He turned his head round, away from me, and said: 'I do not know.'

"I never said he took it medicinally. He was jealous of Dr. Gully, though he knew everything before marriage. He did not want to go to Worthing, and asked at dinner: 'Have you taken a house there?'

"He had a letter that morning from his mother objecting to Florence going, and he asked me whether he should show it to Florence. I told Mr. Royes Bell that he told me he had taken poison, and I repeated it to Dr. Johnson. That is all."

3 *The Law Takes Action*

It would have been interesting to see Mr. Stephenson's expression and hear his comments after he had shown Mrs. Cox and the wilting Florence out of his office that afternoon. That dry legal reserve that kept him poker-faced while he was taking down their statements must surely have broken down when the door closed behind them. For here was a startling addition to his dossier on the Bravo case, a series of revelations more significant than everything in the other thirty statements put together. The depositions of these ladies, the one so self-possessed, the other labouring under such distress, gave just the kind of intimate picture that the authorities wanted, and in their candid underlining of marital strife at The Priory provided for the first time a lead.

Jealousy, meanness, a passionate temper, here were emotions that could provoke suicide—or murder.

And now suddenly, a new name had come into the affair, a name which Mrs. Cox admitted having deliberately left out of her evidence at the inquest. Studying the two statements, Mr. Stephenson was convinced that in them, if anywhere, lay the vital clues to the mystery of how and why Charles Bravo had taken that massive and killing dose of antimony.

Poor Charles. Out of the mouths of his widow and Jane Cox he was now presented as an ogre. Suddenly the kindly, gay young man familiar to a host of friends around the law courts, the devoted and attentive husband as seen by visitors to The Priory, the happily married and considerate master as known by his servants, had turned into a vile-tempered and suicidal petty domestic tyrant. The man who before marriage had seemed to take Florence's lapse so lightly and been ready to forget and never to refer to it again was now shown as consumingly jealous of Dr. Gully, taunting Florence with him "morning, noon, and night", and unmercifully bullying her about him as they passed his house. It now transpired that it was actually on account of Gully that he had killed himself, having before that shown a suicidal tendency by threatening to cut his throat because of a dispute, fomented by his mother, about the expense of Florence's proposed holiday at Worthing. This meanness of his, indeed, was continually coming between them. First it was her maid she was to get rid of, then her cobs, then Mrs. Cox herself—and all to save a few hundred a year that she could well afford. There was, of course, a good deal of truth in this tale of Charles's desire for "retrenchment"; letters existed to show that his mother was influencing him in his attempts to get Florence to curb her "extravagance". But it now seemed that Mrs. Joseph Bravo was only too anxious to split up the marriage and get Charles back under her wing. And then there was his ungovernable temper, so surprisingly revealed by both ladies—that senseless outburst on Good Friday about Florence wanting to rest, and that earlier one when only the intervention of Mrs. Cox had stopped his walking out in the middle of the night. And once, it appeared, in a quarrel caused by his mother's interference, he had even struck Florence. Quick-tempered he may have been, but no one who knew him would have imagined him using physical violence towards his wife.

Mr. Stephenson did not know Charles, and this recital of his shortcomings, substantially the same in both statements, may not have sounded strange to him as he took it down and read it over at the Treasury. But it would have caused many other people to raise their eyebrows. It would have surprised, for instance, Ann Maria Bell, Royes's sister, to whom Florence had declared, as they talked in the garden together during Charles's illness: "We've been very happy, and Charles has said he's never been so happy in all his life. We've never had a word together." The whole picture of Charles and his conduct towards Florence, as now presented by Mrs. Cox and Florence herself, was so oddly different from that which so many people had known. But then it was a picture that none could controvert, because it was not the public one. Only Charles could have confirmed or denied it, and he was dead. Still, it was very queer that no echo of this jealousy and rancour seemed to have penetrated to the servants' hall, that sure and sensitive sounding-board for domestic discord.

How Florence must have shrunk from dragging Dr. Gully's name into the story. But how could she help it if she wanted to give substance to her tale of Charles's unbalanced and devouring jealousy—and offer a convincing motive for his suicide? And in any case here was Jane Cox, in her account, introducing the doctor's name in a way that ought to clinch once and for all the supposition that Charles had killed himself. Thus did Florence Bravo, aided and abetted by her good friend Mrs. Cox, obstinately and desperately try to put beyond all doubt her cherished theory of Charles's death. But did she not see that the entry of Gully's name into the affair gave a motive for murder as well as suicide?

If she did not, the Home Office authorities, to whom Mr. Stephenson sent the dossier with his report, did; in fact they took a very serious view of the matter indeed, and quickly decided on a drastic course of action. They passed the papers to the Attorney-General, Sir John Holker. And Sir John, equally struck by the sinister implications of the two ladies' statements —and not least by Mrs. Cox's acknowledged perjury in omitting Dr. Gully's name at the inquest—set the law in motion. On 19th June he applied to the Court of Queen's Bench for a writ to bring up the Coroner's Inquisition, in order that it might be quashed, and for a rule nisi calling upon the Coroner to show why a fresh inquiry should not be held before him or before commissioners to be appointed by the Court.

In opening his case before the Lord Chief Justice, Sir Alexander Cockburn, and his learned colleagues on the Bench, Mr. Justice Mellor and Mr. Justice Field, Sir John read over and compared the testimony given in the Coroner's official deposition and the notes of Mr. Reid. Then he read an affidavit made by Dr. Johnson.

This was largely a recapitulation of what Dr. Johnson had reported in the *Lancet*, and it emphasised the doctor's belief that Charles had not committed suicide. It mentioned Mrs. Cox's statement to him that Charles had said: "I've taken some of that poison," and Charles's firm denial when taxed with this: "I don't remember having spoken of poison." It also quoted Charles's admission that he had rubbed laudanum on his gums and that he may have swallowed some of it, and that whatever he had taken had been taken by himself. "My decided belief and impression is," wrote Dr. Johnson, "that he had not knowingly taken antimony or any poison other than laudanum."

He went on to report Mr. Campbell's visit to him before the resumed inquest and his curious assertion that he could get a suicide verdict in five minutes by repeating Sir William Gull's opinion; and also Mr. Carter's refusal to allow him to give evidence. Dr. Johnson finished by stating:

"I may add that in the course of the first night I was speaking to Mrs. Cox in the presence of Mrs. C. Bravo. I referred to what the patient had said about taking poison. Mrs. C. Bravo, hearing it apparently as far as I know for the first time, said: 'Did he say that he had taken poison?' Her manner appeared to manifest much less surprise than I should have expected under the circumstances. I never in my experience met with a case of suicide from antimony."

"Now, my Lords," said the Attorney-General in solemn and impressive tones, "here we have witnesses who could certainly have carried the inquiry further. It was clear that Mr. Bravo stated what practically amounted to a denial of suicide. The evidence on this important point was offered, and was not received. The Coroner refused to receive important evidence, and his doing so amounts to misconduct, which misconduct renders necessary the reopening of the inquiry."

The Lord Chief Justice here interposed with some remarks, and Sir John Holker, pressing his case, went on:

"I hope to show your Lordships that I make this application in the interest of public justice and from a desire of ascertaining some facts which will enable the Crown to make a charge against someone; but I think that if we had a fresh inquiry, with the opportunity of cross-examining witnesses, some important evidence might be obtained.

"I think it is very much for the interest of Mrs. Bravo and her family that there should be such further inquiry, and perhaps for the family of Mr. Campbell. They have come forward and said they were anxious to make statements, and, acting on the advice of the Law Officers, the Treasury Solicitor heard these statements. From these statements there was, it appears, some reason for Mr. Bravo committing suicide. There had been quarrels between himself and Mrs. Bravo and other evidence in favour of this statement, which might possibly satisfy a jury that it was a case of suicide.

"If the Coroner had examined Dr. Johnson, his view as to the suicide would no doubt have been shaken. He might have come to the conclusion that it was not a case of suicide, but one of murder, and would have made an investigation as to what was partaken of at dinner.

"There was a bottle of burgundy, of which Mr. Bravo took three or four glasses, and no one else touched it, the ladies taking sherry, and we find that when Mr. Bravo went upstairs a glass of marsala was taken up to Mrs. Bravo's room.

"In fact, but for the views as to suicide entertained by the Coroner, a great deal of light might have been thrown on the matter.

"It appears to be most important that the servants living in the house should be examined and cross-examined, in order to elicit all that they know of the matter.

"It appears to me, therefore, that the interests of justice require that a fresh inquiry should be granted, and which [sic] might result in a charge being preferred against an individual.

"But," he went on, "even if the effect were only to be a verdict that Mr. Bravo did not commit suicide, the inquiry would, at all events, be complete."

And he finished up by producing his strongest argument in favour of a new inquest. "Then there is the statement of Mrs. Cox," he declared, "to which I am reluctant to refer; but it certainly appears that she withheld important information from the Coroner's jury."

Dryly the Lord Chief Justice now remarked: "There is no

use in shutting our eyes to the fact that in your view it is not a case of suicide."

Sir John replied: "If it turned out to be a murder, my Lord, as I suspect it was, I hope we should be able to elicit facts which would justify a charge against someone or other. What we desire is to have an opportunity of cross-examining the witnesses."

And here he picked up his trump card, Mrs. Cox's deposition, and said:

"Now, Mrs. Cox has made an important statement which refers to matters which one would be naturally anxious not to disclose. It is as follows:" and he cleared his throat and began to read the Treasury Solicitor's transcript of Mrs. Cox's statement. His reading was verbatim, except that he omitted the name of Dr. Gully. Coming to the passage where it appeared he merely said: "And here comes a name that I must not mention."

At the end of the statement he said: "You see, my Lords, from her own statement, that she deliberately kept this information from the jury."

The judges conferred together for a moment and then Sir Alexander Cockburn addressed the Attorney-General:

"I think you have shown sufficient grounds, Mr. Attorney-General, to warrant us in giving you a rule nisi."

"Thank you, my Lord." Sir John bowed to the Bench of judges. He had made out his case.

On the following Monday, a week later, the Attorney-General appeared again in the same Court to complete the procedure necessary for the ordering of a fresh inquest. Mr. Carter had been called upon to attend, but Mr. Serjeant Parry, who was representing him, announced that he was confined to his house by a severe attack of erysipelas and offered his apologies. At the same time he said that Mr. Carter deeply regretted that the inquiries had not ended satisfactorily, and was anxious to submit himself to the Court and to act in whatever way they might direct. No doubt Mr. Carter, who for nearly two months had been reaping the whirlwind of his abortive inquest and writhing under the attacks and criticisms of the Press, was not sorry to be saved the crowning embarrassment of appearing before this Bench of learned judges, even though laid low by such a distressing complaint.

After a long hearing of legal arguments the Lord Chief Justice made his pronouncement:

"We have made up our minds, Mr. Attorney, to make the rule absolute for quashing the inquisition, and directing the Coroner to hold a fresh inquiry with a fresh jury." Having explained certain considerations affecting this decision, he said: "It is true the summoning of a fresh jury and the holding of a fresh inquiry will involve the painful exposure of the body, but it appears to us, nevertheless, to be the best course we can adopt."

A fresh inquiry, the unhappy unedifying story to be dragged out and picked over again—this time with a far more relentless publicity: so much for Florence's efforts to keep things quiet and then, with Mrs. Cox, to paint Charles in such strangely unattractive colours; Mr. Carter's sketchy and semi-secret inquest; the whole of that unsatisfactory, evasive failure to look the facts and implications of Charles's death in the face: so much for the self-deception—or worse—of those who so strenuously maintained that Charles Bravo had committed suicide. They had forgotten, perhaps at their peril, the old saying that murder will out.

But it was one thing for the learned judges in the Court of Queen's Bench, Sir John Holker and the rest to presume murder: it was another to point to a single obvious suspect. Since Mr. Joseph Bravo, brooding over the manner of Charles's death, had first suspected murder—but for lack of discernible motive could not logically point to any particular killer—the plot had thickened bewilderingly. And what could these official advocates of the murder theory see now, in the startling but none too clarifying light of Florence's and Mrs. Cox's statements? A complex picture indeed: three possible murderers and four motives. For now that Dr. Gully had come into the story they could see Florence, with or without Gully's or Mrs. Cox's help or connivance, murdering Charles in order to be able to return to her former lover. Again, they could see her killing Charles after being goaded beyond endurance by his jealousy and temper. They could see Gully disposing of Charles—with inside help—to regain Florence. And they could see Mrs. Cox, having learnt of Charles's intention to get rid of her, murdering him in order to keep her snug position with Florence. For those who believed that murder had been done there was an *embarras de richesse*. The authorities could be sure at least that someone in The Priory had given Charles the lethal dose, and they could be pretty certain that he had taken it some time after dinner.

Florence, Mrs. Cox—and Dr. Gully too—had plenty of time to reflect on all these matters as the late June and early July days passed and the date of the second inquest on the death of Charles Bravo drew nearer. And the public? Their appetite had already been whetted, but before them lay a feast of scandal and sensation more succulent than they could have imagined.

PART TWO

TRIAL BY INQUEST

CHAPTER 10

MR. JOSEPH BRAVO

THE SECOND INQUEST on Charles Bravo was arranged for 11th July at the Bedford Hotel, Balham; it was strange how, ever and again, this tavern came back into the picture.

After about a month of quiet at Buscot, Florence had recovered somewhat from the sorry state in which her mother had found her at Brighton; but she was still far from well. There was no real respite from worry and apprehension while the ordeal of this full-dress inquiry was hanging over her. Did she—despite the fact that she had her nearest and dearest around her—miss Jane Cox? Or did she, as the days of their separation lengthened, feel a growing sense of relief at being free from an association that was beginning to get oppressive? For better or worse, Mrs. Cox was away at Birmingham, and she saw her but once before the inquest. At the beginning of July they met in London, at the rooms in Holles Street which had been taken by the Campbells, where there was a conference at which Mr. Orr, Mrs. Campbell and brother William were present, doubtless to discuss the forthcoming proceedings. And if Florence was on edge at the thought of what was to come, Mrs. Cox was none too happy herself. She was still going over in her mind the events in the sick-room when Charles had first been taken ill; and now it was the matter of a stomach-pump that bothered her. Again it was Mr. Harrison to whom she turned for help; and on 15th June she wrote to him from 48 Villa Road, Handsworth:

Dear Mr. Harrison,—I am much obliged by your kind note. [Whether she was only now acknowledging his letter of 20th May or a later one is uncertain.] I wanted you to tell me about the stomach-pump. Mrs. C. Bravo has told me several times that she thought, had the stomach-pump been used, Mr. C. Bravo's life might have been saved. I told her you told me afterwards it was impossible to use it, and I know, long before Dr. Moore arrived—we could not get the strong coffee down—his teeth were clenched.

Mrs. C. Bravo said that Sir William Gull said it might have been used, but I told her Sir William Gull could not know, as you and Dr. Moore did, the state that Mr. C. Bravo was in. Of course this has grieved me dreadfully, and I should feel so much obliged if you would kindly write me on the subject and give me your own opinion.

I remain, dear Mr. Harrison, yours very truly, JANE C. COX

I hope you will kindly excuse me giving you so much trouble.

Busy Mr. Harrison must have found Mrs. Cox a nuisance with her doubts and queries and requests for reassurance, but whether he answered her this time is unknown: at any rate no reply has been preserved.

Meanwhile preparations were going ahead for the inquest. All the parties chiefly concerned—Florence, Mrs. Cox, the Campbells, the Bravos, Dr. Gully—realised that this second investigation into the circumstances of Charles's death, in itself an almost unprecedented proceeding, would leave unexplored nothing of conceivable relevance. They knew that the authorities were seeking a verdict of murder. And by this time there was no hiding the fact that Mr. Joseph Bravo was out for one too. So with the clash of family interests there flared up the bitter family feud whose all too public arena was to be the billiards-room of the Bedford Hotel, Balham: the Campbells *versus* the Bravos: suicide *versus* murder. And murder, it was understood, would almost certainly involve Florence, whoever else was involved too.

From that day in December, 1874, when Florence had first appeared at Palace Green, an undeniably eligible young widow, Mrs. Bravo had never liked her. She was not prepared to like any woman who was a potential wife for her adored Charles: and in her eyes Florence in particular, with her phaeton, her cobs and her showy ways, would have been the worst possible match for him. And when some ten months later Charles informed her he wished to marry Florence, the early coolness had turned to positive hostility. Mrs. Bravo's hope, expressed on the occasion of her absence from the wedding, that she might be able to look more kindly on Florence in time had left no doubt of her aversion then; and, alas, that aversion had never been overcome. Indeed, it had grown with the knowledge of Florence's extravagances (real or fancied) at The Priory. Poor Charles on his death-bed may have been satisfied by his mother's unenthusiastic promise to be kind to Florence; but even if truly meant at the time it could hardly remain so when Joseph Bravo, in grief at the loss of his stepson and repudiation of the suicide suggestion, began to suspect the worst after looking round the drug-cluttered medicine cupboards of The Priory. With his new-found suspicions he fed the animosity in his wife that was only too ready to burst into hatred; and as the day of the inquest approached the Bravos were united in their bitter ill-will towards Florence and her family.

The Campbells in their turn were ranged against the Bravos, and loyally bent on establishing Charles's suicide. Mr. Campbell's preliminary soundings of Dr. Johnson and Joseph Bravo himself during the week of the first inquest and his urgent advice to Florence to insert the advertisement in the news-papers, and to Florence and Mrs. Cox to make their statements to Mr. Stephenson, showed clearly enough the way his mind was working.

Both families realised that the inquest would be a crucial encounter in which one side or the other would be vindicated according to the verdict; and both expected some hard give-and-take during the course of it. It was lucky that both were wealthy and had no need to spare expense in the matter of legal representation. To watch Florence's interests Mr. Campbell retained Sir Henry James, Q.C. (who had been both Solicitor-General and Attorney-General and was to become Lord James of Hereford) and Mr. Robert Biron, Q.C.; on behalf of the Bravo family Mr. Joseph engaged no barrister, but the astute and forceful George Lewis (afterwards Sir George), junior member of the well-known firm of solicitors, Lewis and Lewis of Ely Place; Mr. Murphy, Q.C., was engaged on behalf of Mrs. Cox; and the Crown instructed Mr. John Gorst, Q.C. (afterwards Sir John) and Mr. Harry Poland (afterwards Sir Harry), while later on in the case the Attorney-General himself was to appear, as was Mr. Serjeant Parry (notable as the defender of the poisoners, Dr. Smethurst and Christina Edwards) on behalf of Dr. Gully. Mr. Carter may well have been intimidated at the thought of presiding over this glitter-ing parade of legal talent, but this time the authorities were seeing that he was not alone in his responsibilities, for they appointed to assist him as legal assessor Mr. Burleigh Muir, barrister-at-law.

What a contrast inquest Number Two was to be to that first inquiry of eleven weeks earlier. Then a few people had slipped discreetly into a secluded private house to hear the business rushed through almost under a seal of secrecy, a conspiracy of silence. Now, in the impersonal setting of a suburban tavern, the full glare of publicity was ready to be trained on an investigation that would relentlessly uncover every detail of the events leading to Charles's death; and every word would this time be taken down by sensation-seeking reporters and broadcast to millions of readers already primed by weeks of newspaper speculation and rumour for a drama of unparalleled "human interest". For Florence, who before had shrunk from even the mild official probings at The Priory, it was a horrifying prospect, and it was hardly less so for her family, and Mrs. Cox.

The Bedford Hotel, Balham, still stands (though entirely rebuilt) on its corner just next to the railway bridge that adjoins Balham Station. Electric trains now rattle past its windows which in the 1870s were begrimed by soot and smoke from steam engines. In those days, passing under the bridge from the hotel one came in a minute or so to Dr. Gully's house at the bottom left-hand corner of comparatively rural Bedford Hill Road, and a few hundreds yards farther on, to The Priory. The billiards-room was chosen as the court-room: it was much larger than the dining-room of The Priory, and had need to be. "The accommodation presented by the Bedford Hotel at Balham," said a contemporary broadsheet, "for holding the Second Inquiry into the cause of Mr. C. Bravo's decease is unusually ample. Not only is the inquest room of much larger dimensions than one might expect to find in so comparatively quiet a locality, but the hotel also affords the additional advantage of a series of rooms for separately locating the various classes of witnesses summoned to give evidence, as well as others for the accommodation of the jury and the numerous members of the legal profession who are engaged in this remarkable inquiry. From the moment that Mr. Broadbridge, the Coroner's official officer, announced to Mr. Charles Willis, the proprietor of the Bedford Hotel, that it was decided there to hold the second inquest, no pains were spared by that gentleman to make every possible provision for the general comfort of all who had to take part in what, from the outset, promised to be an unusually protracted inquiry."

As Mr. Carter made his way through the crowds outside the hotel (for the case was eagerly looked forward to by the public and scores had to be turned away from the doors) on the opening day of the inquest and passed up to the billiards-room with Mr. Muir, he was feeling a little apprehensive. This elderly, grey-whiskered and slightly pompous official knew that he had a lot to live down in connection with the name of Bravo and that this new inquest, a far more formidable affair than the first, would not be made any easier for him on that account. The limelight was on him now with a vengeance. And taking his seat at Mr. Willis's covered-over billiards-table, his back to the mirrored mantelpiece, he looked around the room.

It was packed to the doors with jurymen, officials, reporters, members of the public, relatives and friends of Charles and Florence and, at the table with him, an array of eminent lawyers such as had not appeared in any court-room of his before. It was unusual to see these Queen's Counsel in court without their formal costume. As the same broadsheet previously quoted remarked: "To the general public, who are accustomed only to look upon members of the legal profession in our respective law courts in the 'full dress' of coif and wig, of bands and gown, the personal appearance of most of the gentlemen in the 'undress' observed at an inquest may appear somewhat novel and strange. Sir John Holker, the Attorney-General [he did not appear on the first days of the inquest], presents the semblance of an English gentleman-farmer who has thriven upon the consumption of oxen and sheep bred and reared upon his well-managed estate. Then Sir Henry James might be taken either for a descendant of Ignatius Loyola or

Machiavelli, and Mr. Poland could 'get up' well as 'Mephisto' for a fancy ball of the 'Devil's Own', or an Inns of Court masquerade. Our simile might be carried still further by asserting a certain facial resemblance which exists between Mr. George Lewis, jun., and Jacques Offenbach."

After the opening formalities and the appointment of a Mr. Mark Cattley (who presented "the appearance of a shrewd intellectual member of the middle class") as foreman of the seventeen-strong jury, the Coroner addressed the jurymen. He said:

"It would be a great affectation on my part if I did not assume that you are well aware, from reading or from conversation, of the nature of the present case; but it is my duty to ask you to try and banish from your minds, as far as possible, all that you have heard or read, and to remind you that you will have to judge of how this gentleman came by his death only from the evidence which is placed before you. We shall have to go from here to Lower Norwood, where everything is prepared for us, and on our return here we shall have to enter into the evidence. . . ."

The court was then adjourned while the Coroner, the jury and other officials proceeded by train to Norwood to view the remains of Charles Bravo at Lower Norwood Cemetery. As Mr. Carter had said, everything was ready for them. Early that morning a little group of men, headed by Mr. J. Mold, the undertaker who had buried Charles, had arrived at Charles's grave armed with spades and other gear to dig him up under an exhumation order from the Home Secretary. The coffin had been raised and placed on blocks of timber, while above it a weatherproof screen had been erected. In order that the jury could go through the grim legal formality of "viewing the body" Mr. Mold and his colleagues had had to cut an opening in the coffin-lid—not an easy job, for the lead casing resisted their efforts for nearly an hour. Then into the aperture they had inserted a pane of glass.

"The morning had been exceedingly sultry," to quote from the same broadsheet as before, "and the closeness of the atmosphere was rendered still more oppressive by the pungent odour of the disinfectants used in order to enable the Coroner and jury to perform their sad task with comparative immunity. It was a remarkable fact that while the oak coffin and its ormolu handles presented to the eye, when raised from the vault, all the freshness of polish and lustre of their pristine condition, the head of the deceased gentleman exhibited every sign of the most rapid decay. The face had acquired the dark hue of a mummy, and the teeth were almost entirely black. This rapidity of decay was much remarked upon by those who were present, and one gentleman suggested that it had arisen not from any single instance of accidental or intentional poisoning, but from a gradual saturation of the system of the deceased."

(This theory of slow poisoning is suggestive; but the swift putrefaction of the body of Charles Bravo contrasts oddly with the remarkable preservation of two known victims of slow antimonial poisoning, both murdered by the poisoner Severino Klosowski in London some twenty-five years later. The first, Mary Chapman, died in December, 1897, and when she was exhumed in December, 1902, her "face and head were those of a woman who might have been coffined that day". The other was Bessie Taylor, whose body was exhumed in November, 1902, twenty-one months after her death, and "showed no putrefaction and no odour".)

Mr. Carter and his seventeen jurymen arrived at the gates of Norwood Cemetery about noon, split up into small parties and walked up the main avenue towards Charles's grave, taking the right fork at "the sumptuous Gothic mausoleum erected to the memory of the late Mr. J. W. Gilbart, the principal founder of the London and Westminster Bank". When they were all gathered round the coffin Mr. Carter made a formal inquiry of the undertaker and then explained to the jurors that they would each have to pass in front of and glance at the remains of the deceased gentleman displayed through the extempore window of the coffin. So, with the Coroner and Mr. Mold standing by, the jurymen filed solemnly past the raised coffin, with tall hats doffed, in the distasteful ritual of "viewing the remains". It is not surprising that, combining with the heaviness of the day and the mingled odours, the sight of the blackened mask of the late Charles Bravo grinning up from its oak and ormolu sarcophagus turned more than one of them queasy.

After this they all returned to the Bedford Hotel to resume the proceedings; and the first witness called was Mr. Mold, who identified the body just seen by the jury as that of Charles Bravo. Then Mr. Joseph Bravo was called.

As Mr. Bravo took his stand at the big table, facing many of the lawyers on the opposite side and with the Coroner at right-angles to him on his left, one of the chief figures in the drama was revealed to the Press and public for the first time.

They saw a man in his sixties, bald except for the darkish hair clustering round the temples of an unusually high forehead, with scanty eyebrows, brown, intense, rather sunken eyes and a long nose distinctly fleshy at the tip. His grizzled whiskers and moustaches, grown all-in-one, recalled an old-style military officer, and he affected a foreign-looking little imperial. Most noteworthy of all, in Mr. Bravo's swarthy complexion and the cast of his features there was no mistaking his West Indian Creole origin.

A good judge of character might have said that here was a passionate, temperamental man, a man, perhaps, of strong views and violent prejudices; and certainly not one to cross.

The court settled down attentively. The Bravo case had really begun.

Questioned by the Coroner in the course of his evidence as to events in the sick-room on and after Wednesday, Mr. Bravo said that Charles had never accounted for his condition other than by admitting that he had taken laudanum. And now came a significant intervention from Sir Henry James. He rose, bowed to the Coroner, and suggested that the time had arrived when an arrangement should be made for questioning the witnesses. He understood that his learned friends, Mr. Gorst and Mr. Poland, were appearing for the Crown and Mr. George Lewis for the friends of the deceased. It had been thought right that Mrs. Charles Bravo, as the widow and executrix, and a forthcoming witness, should be represented on this inquiry, and she was so represented by himself and Mr. Biron. He requested that he should be permitted to ask any questions which might appear to him to be necessary. As Sir Henry sat down Mr. Gorst rose and respectfully seconded this request, asking at the same time that those who represented interests should be allowed to cross-examine the witnesses. To this well-concerted plea the Coroner agreed; and so the lawyers' tactics were revealed and the way was clear for the ruthless handling of the other side's witnesses—on the principle that attack is the best form of defence—that made this inquiry look before it had finished more like a trial than an inquest.

Now it was Mr. Lewis's turn. In his early forties, he was the youngest of the leading lawyers in that court-room and, with his whiskered aristocratic features (reminiscent of the "swells" of the period depicted in *Punch*) adorned by a monocle, one of the most distinguished-looking. He was also to prove one of the deadliest and most ruthless. His immediate aim was simple: to get Joseph Bravo to rebut the idea of Charles's suicide as tellingly as possible; and Mr. Bravo informed the court:

"Up to the time of his death he was on terms of great affection with me, and the greatest love existed between him and his mother. Knowing him thus intimately, I can say that he was not a man likely to commit suicide. The fact was the reverse of that. He was a very courageous man. He was certainly not in any pecuniary difficulty. At the time of his marriage I made a settlement of £20,000, to take effect after the death of the survivor of his parents. I allowed him whatever he desired to have. Between December and April I had given him £1,100. From communications I had made to him he knew he had only to apply to me for money to have it at once. He had the first life interest in the settlement, and his wife the second, he having the power to dispose of the capital by will. The deceased kept an account at the London and Westminster Bank, and I told the manager of that establishment never to let the deceased's account at his credit go down to under £100."

Mr. Bravo added that his stepson took great interest in surgical matters and occasionally attended operations at one of the hospitals.

Mr. Lewis then read three of Charles's letters to his parents, written within nine days of his illness: all were chatty, affectionate and cheerful. And to emphasise the happy temperament of the dead man, he got Mr. Bravo to declare that Charles was always high-spirited and took an interest in everything. He also elicited from the witness that his stepson was "a man of great truth", who certainly would not have lied to Sir William Gull in his denial of taking anything but laudanum.

And then came two interesting admissions from Mr. Bravo. The first related to Mrs. Cox. He said:

"After [the marriage] my son discussed with me the expense which Mrs. Cox was to the establishment—a matter, he said, of £300 to £400 a year. I agreed with him that it was not a wise thing to have a charge of that kind, and about two months after the marriage I advised Mrs. Cox to return to Jamaica. She said she should not return."

So (in confirmation of Florence's statement to the Treasury Solicitor) the dead man was thinking of getting rid of his wife's companion! And she had refused his stepfather's advice to leave the country. It was the court's first sensation, the first hint of a possible reason someone might have for wanting to kill Charles.

Quickly on top of this came the second surprise.

Mr. Lewis: "Did your son either by speech or manner ever indicate that he had any feeling of jealousy towards anyone?"

Mr. Bravo: "Never, neither by speech nor manner has he indicated any such feeling."

Mr. Lewis: "Did your son ever mention to you the name of a doctor—a Dr. Gully?"

So it had come out, thus early: jealousy—another man—perhaps the third figure in a classic, time-worn situation, whose presence would explain everything. No matter that the witness denied that his stepson had ever shown the faintest sign of this ugly emotion, the seed of speculation was sown among the jury—and if Mr. Lewis could demonstrate to them later on that it was a red herring, introduced by someone to obscure the real issue, then perhaps their minds would veer all the more strongly away from suicide. No matter that Mr. Bravo denied too ever having heard Charles mention Dr. Gully; this man's name, produced now as a prelude to a tale of immorality and illicit love that would later be put before the court, would help the Bravo family to blacken the widow's character and even produce a pretext for Charles's murder.

So that when Mr. Bravo, expressing ignorance of Dr. Gully's name, went on: "I never saw any evidence of jealousy between the deceased and his wife. They were always most affectionate to each other when I saw them," Mr. Lewis was satisfied: he had achieved his purpose.

Speaking of Florence's demeanour in the sick-room, the witness said: "She did not appear much grieved in any way at the state of affairs." The jury may have taken this statement at its face value—but was it in reality an expression of the new feeling that Mr. Bravo had for Florence, a feeling that allowed him to think worse of her than she really deserved?

Mr. Lewis referred to the attack that Charles had had one morning in March, when he had reached Palace Green almost in a state of collapse. Mr. Bravo told the court the story of that peculiar incident, and said that before Charles's marriage he had never suffered from nausea, nor even sea-sickness on his various voyages to Jamaica.

Charles's money affairs then came up. Mr. Lewis read those three letters of Florence's to Mr. Bravo, written in early May from Brighton. And fastening on to Florence's allegation in the second letter that Charles had been pressed for money "by that dreadful woman", he asked:

"Now, had the deceased at this time securities at his stock-brokers'?"

Mr. Bravo: "Yes, he had £500 in securities; and other amounts were paid over after, making £1,100 paid in to us."

And to a juryman inquiring about these alleged financial demands Mr. Bravo answered:

"There is no truth in the suggestion that the deceased was pressed for money in any way. As to any 'horrible woman', I do not know that any so pressed him."

Now Sir Henry James (for Florence) rose to cross-examine Mr. Bravo. He took him through the events of Charles's illness, asked him more about "that horrid woman" and inquired about Charles's financial position.

Mr. Bravo: "The deceased was not in want of money. Of

the £1,100 he had had since his marriage from me I had given him £100 in January. In February he asked me for £500. In April he had £500 which I had to pay him. As he had told his wife, he got about £200 a year from his profession, and £800 a year from me, making about £1,000 a year."

Sir Henry asked about Charles's disposition.

Mr. Bravo: "He was quick in temper. I never told anyone he had a 'horrible temper'. I have said he had a rough edge to his tongue when put out."

Of Charles's medical knowledge the witness said: "I say my son had a general knowledge of medicine, and he had a liking for surgery, but as distinguished from surgery his medical knowledge was only general."

Mr. Gorst, for the Crown, now took over. He was interested in that attack of Charles's referred to earlier. Would witness tell them a little more about it? So Mr. Bravo went over it again in greater detail. It would not be Mr. Gorst's or Mr. Lewis's fault if the jury overlooked its possible significance now.

The question of Charles's means cropped up again. Mr. Bravo answered Mr. Lewis that if Charles had been pressed to return or pay £500, or even £1,000, to anyone, he could have had it without trouble. But Sir Henry James was not quite satisfied. Where would the money have come from?

Mr. Bravo: "From deceased's own resources, for he had £1,100 at his stockbrokers' when he died, and he could have got £1,000 more at once for the asking for it."

Apart from a few other minor questions, that was the end of the first day's proceedings. The evidence had not been insignificant. The court had heard Mr. Joseph Bravo, under the sure handling of Mr. George Lewis junior, describe his dead stepson as a truthful man, not in the least suicidal, not jealous, not pressed for a ready £1,000, quick-tempered when put out, but no more. And what the public would be likely to think of the meanness of a man of Charles's resources in planning to dismiss his wife's companion to save a mere £400 a year was immaterial so long as it suggested a motive for his murder. As for the newly-introduced Dr. Gully, he was as yet an unknown factor in the case, but before the jury finally filed out of Mr. Carter's court-room to consider their verdict his relationship with Florence was to be ruthlessly, even brutally, exploited by Mr. Lewis in his client's favour, and his name was to ring through the country as something worse than the seducer of a pretty woman patient.

CHAPTER 11

DOCTORS, SERVANTS AND OTHERS

1   *The Doctors*

AT THE END OF THE FIRST DAY Mr. Lewis had not quite
done with Charles's money dealings with his ex-mistress's
family. He wanted to make the position perfectly clear. So
as a start to the second day's proceedings he read some corres-
pondence that had passed between Charles and the sister of
"that horrid woman":

> *Junior Carlton Club, March 20th,* 1876
>
> My dear,—If I repay you the £500 you lent me you will
> not get more than £30 a year for it. I will, if you like, keep
> your money for another year, or repay you in June. Perhaps,
> unless you doubt my ability or will to pay, you will be wise
> to leave the money with me—you get more interest, and your
> capital is not very unsafe. I am afraid you thought me unkind
> when I met you yesterday. I assure you I do not intend to
> be so. Give my kind love to —, and believe me ever to be
> yours truly,   C—

> *Wednesday, March 22nd,* 1876
>
> My dear Charlie,—Until after I got home yesterday I did
> not quite understand what you meant about . . . [letter torn]
> . . . of course it is—further use to you, and you do not want
> to be bothered with it any longer, and as I shall be sorry to
> give you the slightest trouble on my account, you can send

it to me, and I will do the best I can with it myself, although I do not know what at present. Believe me, yours truly, —

March 22nd, 1876

My dear Charlie,—You can keep the money as long as you wish. What made me write, I fancied it troubled you to keep it. I know you give me more interest than I could get elsewhere, but with all I should be very sorry to bother you. God knows every £5 is a consideration to so small an income as mine is. Trusting you and your wife are well, believe me, yours ever, —

It must be admitted that the little transaction by which Charles withheld the repayment of a £500 loan to the sister of his ex-mistress, even while undertaking to pay her a generous interest, showed him in a shabby light. What was he doing in the first place, a man who apparently could get all the money he wanted from his stepfather, borrowing from a relative of the woman he was supposed to be keeping? Why did he want it? And why, when she had asked for it back, did he not immediately return it instead of persuading her to let him keep it by making magnanimous promises about the interest? But of course all this, however mean and grasping it made Charles look, did not affect the point that Mr. Lewis wished to emphasise: that Charles was not being pressed for money. (Incidentally, it was obvious from the woman's letters that she bore Charles no ill-will.)

For the rest of these next three days the court heard what the doctors had to say. Dr. Moore, Mr. Harrison, Royes Bell, Dr. Johnson, Sir William Gull, all gave their version of events in the sick-room; and although there were few highlights in their evidence it was listened to—and read next day—with that particular fascinated interest always accorded to the doctor on the witness-stand.

And when they had all been heard, one or two significant conclusions emerged from their stories. None except Sir William Gull thought that Charles had committed suicide—and in any case the others were almost unanimous in saying that they had never heard of suicide by antimony. Again, all but Sir William were favourably impressed by the dying man's earnestness in denying that he had taken anything but laudanum. The oft-repeated account of those anxious sick-room hours, though it may have differed in various particulars, seemed to the listeners in the court-room to have running through it one dominant monotonous theme:

Doctors: "You've taken something else besides laudanum. Tell us what it is."

Charles: "No, I've taken nothing else but laudanum."

Still there were some interesting individual touches. Dr. Moore and Royes Bell, for instance, noted that Charles had treated Florence throughout with every sign of affection. Sir Henry James seized on one implication of this attitude and questioned Dr. Moore:

"Is it your opinion that if he had entertained suspicions that he had been treated foully he was in a condition to state that suspicion?"

Dr. Moore: "Certainly."

And he went on to say that Florence had told him that her husband had been worried about some stocks and that he need not have worried.

Mr. Harrison, following, made a point that would certainly have cheered Mrs. Cox:

"My opinion is that if we had used a stomach-pump it would certainly have killed him."

Less happy for her was the surgeon's denial, once more repeated, that she had reported to him Charles's alleged statement about taking poison. As Mrs. Cox had feared when she had decided to write to him about it in May, this discrepancy was clearly going to be a major issue in the case. What Mr. Harrison said about it now was:

"She did not tell me that he had taken poison, but I understood her to mean that Mr. Bravo had taken chloroform in a poisonous dose, so as to produce poisonous effects."

The court heard Royes Bell amplify this chloroform reference of Mrs. Cox's when he gave evidence. Mentioning her announcement to him of Charles's confession that he had taken poison, Royes spoke of hearing Mrs. Cox reply rather vaguely to Dr. Johnson, when Johnson asked her what Charles had said he had taken, that it was chloroform. But the jury cannot have made much of this: to drag chloroform into the story on top of laudanum, when it was known that it was antimony that had killed Charles, must have seemed to them to be merely fogging the issue, if not deliberately introducing a false scent.

Mrs. Cox's statement came up again in Dr. Johnson's evidence, but he produced a queer little sequel to it which switched the court's interest momentarily to Florence:

"While talking in the presence of Mrs. Bravo I unintentionally referred to Mrs. Cox's statement that he had taken poison, and Mrs. Bravo, turning to Mrs. Cox, asked her: 'Did he say that he had taken poison?' Mrs. Cox replied: 'Yes, he did.'

"My first feeling was one of regret that I had mentioned it in her presence. I was rather astonished that Mrs. Bravo did not display more feeling than she did display when this was mentioned."

Dr. Johnson had something rather startling to say about the amount of antimony that Charles had taken—he estimated between thirty and forty grains. (A normal lethal dose would have been about ten grains.) He thought that if Charles had swallowed this in the early part of dinner he would have been ill before he left the table. He also believed that such a quantity of antimony would make burgundy so turbid that a connoisseur would notice it at once.

He spoke for all his colleagues who had preceded him as witnesses when he said of Charles:

"We were all struck by his earnestness."

But Sir William Gull, he admitted, had not seemed so impressed. Charles, it seemed, had sensed that Sir William disbelieved his denials about what he had taken; and when he had called him back to the sick-room he said, according to Dr. Johnson, that he was afraid Sir William did not think he had spoken the truth.

Mr. George Lewis had not missed the significance of all this. As Mr. Harrison, Drs. Moore, Bell and Johnson disbelieved in Charles's suicide he had had no reason to cross swords with them. But here was Sir William Gull maintaining that Charles had lied and had in fact deliberately taken poison: had not Mr. Campbell spoken of ensuring a suicide verdict at the first inquest by bringing forward this view, and Florence invoked it in one of her letters to Joseph Bravo in May? *Ergo*, Sir William was inimical to the Bravos' case and must be attacked, august leader of his profession though he was.

Sir William Gull was called, and he looked an impressive, oracular figure as he calmly stood now with his back to the door of the crowded court-room, his hands resting on the table, his head erect, his gaze firm and level. The court prepared to hear him with respectful attention.

He started his story with the receiving of the note from Florence, adding: "Mrs. Cox made no statement to me regarding Mr. Bravo." Mr. Lewis let him continue until he got to his interrogation of Charles in the sick-room. Then he questioned him sharply.

Sir William reddened. "I do not remember his saying anything about telling the whole truth. I will not swear he did not say so."

And then as Mr. Lewis, fixing his monocle more firmly in his eye, pressed the matter with another probing question Sir William became rattled and almost lost his temper. Glaring at the solicitor across the table he rapped out:

"I do not come here to equivocate! I think your questions unbecoming!"

The atmosphere in the court was tense at this little outburst —the first clash in an inquiry that before its end was to become notorious for scenes that would not have been tolerated at any normal inquest.

Sir William, his composure regained, went on:

"It would be surprising to me if I were to tell a man he was dying from poison, and he was not surprised; it would induce me almost to think he knew it."

And he made one or two other interesting points:

"I was sent for to see him for disease. . . ."

"The want or absence of expression of surprise may have resulted from one of two causes—either from indifference due to exhaustion induced from the poison, or because the sick man, being conscious of all, could not be surprised by my statement. . . ."

"I don't think it possible for a man to take forty grains of antimony without tasting it."

And finally: "I think if Mrs. Bravo had the slightest conception that her husband was dying of poison she would hardly have written to me as she did."

Sir William stood down. He had not had it all his own way, but there was no doubt that he had impressed the jury—by his personality if by nothing else.

Professor Redwood, who followed him, introduced a little light relief. After testifying to the results of the analysis and explaining some of the actions of antimony he gave a practical demonstration. Producing a large phial containing forty grains of antimony and four ounces of water he observed that a small quantity of the mixture might be held in the mouth for a short time without any taste being perceived. To illustrate this he put a small quantity in his own mouth, and Sir Henry James and a few jurymen followed his example.

Several jurors said that they could not detect any taste. The professor warned them nevertheless not to swallow any of the solution, which was a strong one; whereupon one of them loudly declared:

"Well, I have swallowed some, but I feel nothing wrong in the throat!"

A burst of laughter followed, and on this light-hearted note the Coroner adjourned the court.

2 *The Servants*

Now came the servants' turn. For the next three days Rowe, Mary Ann, Parton the coachman, the footman and the groom were to stand up in the court-room of the Bedford Hotel and tear away one more veil from the intimacies of life at The Priory. The doctors had had their say; it was time for the domestic revelations, the private inside picture, drawn in by the privileged observers from below stairs or the stable yard. And as the inquest got into its stride, with witness following witness, the popular appetite grew by what it fed on and the Balham Mystery became the talk of every club, public-house and railway carriage; and Mr. Mark Cattley and his sixteen fellow-jurors to the left of the door in the Bedford Hotel court-room were reinforced by millions of unofficial jurymen all over the country giving their uninformed and prejudiced verdicts on the Bravo affair.

What were Rowe and his fellow-servants able to add to the story?

One or two interesting and highly illuminating points, and some versions of incidents that conflicted strangely with the versions given, or to be given, by other witnesses.

Frederick Rowe, tall, quietly dressed, clean-shaven except for discreet mutton-chop whiskers, looked the perfect butler as he stood giving his evidence in low polite tones. (He had actually at this time left Florence's service.) But when he had finished he left another little mystery for the jury to puzzle over. What had happened to the burgundy that Charles had left undrunk in the decanter at Tuesday night's dinner? For the life of him Rowe could not say. For dinner that night he had decanted two bottles of sherry, one of marsala and one of burgundy. He thought Charles had drunk about three glasses of the burgundy.

"Whatever was left," he said, "was placed in the cellaret in that room [dining-room] by myself."

Later on, replying to Mr. Lewis, he admitted:

"I cannot swear whether I did or did not see the remainder of that bottle of burgundy after that night."

But a moment or two later he said:

"As to the burgundy left from that bottle, I think I placed it out when Mr. Royes Bell came, knowing he took burgundy."

All this was extremely vague and reference to his cellar-book, which he now produced, did not help him. It was evident in fact that poor Rowe was in a thorough muddle with his records of wine consumed: he admitted as much. But this carelessness was perhaps excusable in the turmoil which had followed Charles's seizure, and the general impression of the court was that Rowe himself was hiding no sinister secret. In any case, medical opinion had already suggested that antimony in the burgundy would have caused noticeable cloudiness.

Charles would hardly have missed this, as Rowe was able to point out:

"On the night he was dying he sent back a bottle of moselle for the best champagne, the one having been sent up by mistake for the other. If there had been anything wrong about the taste of the burgundy I think he would have noticed it."

If Rowe's cellar-book could not help solve the little enigma of the missing burgundy at least it opened the eyes of the stolid jurors and the public to what was habitually drunk at The Priory. It revealed that in fifty-two days ending 18th April Charles, Florence and Mrs. Cox had drunk between them 134 bottles, of which seventy-nine were sherry and marsala, favourite wines of Florence and Mrs. Cox—an average altogether of some two-and-a-half bottles a day! (It was stalwart drinking for three people, but Sir Henry James hastened to correct any bad impression by suggesting that guests were not infrequent at The Priory.)

But Florence's counsel had a more important task—to kill the damaging surmises about her relations with Gully which George Lewis must assuredly have started by bringing in the doctor's name on the first day. He asked Rowe if he had ever heard of him.

"I have never heard the name of Dr. Gully. I have never to my knowledge seen the person of that name. Since I went into the service, in November, I never knew of his coming to The Priory, and I never knew of Mrs. Bravo seeing him."

This was reassuring for the Campbells; and now Mr. Murphy broke in on behalf of Mrs. Cox, to remove any impression of strained relations that Joseph Bravo might have created in mentioning Charles's intentions regarding her. He extracted this answer from Rowe:

"Mrs. Cox was treated with consideration by Mrs. Ricardo before her marriage, and the same consideration was shown both by Mr. and Mrs. Bravo after the marriage. . . . I saw no difference in the demeanour of deceased towards Mrs. Cox during his illness to what it had been before."

Before Rowe stood down Mr. Gorst asked him:

"Now tell us, do you think the deceased was poisoned, then, before dinner?"

Rowe hesitated and said: "I cannot tell." Then he added:

"I think there was something wrong with deceased's stomach at the dinner. I put it down to the horse accident at the time."

Trim in a dark shawl and draped bonnet, Mary Ann Keeber followed Rowe and was allowed to be seated while giving evidence. She had first entered Florence's service over two years before at Streatham and could claim to know her and Mrs. Cox pretty well. From her the court got a clear, straightforward story of Charles's illness and her part in the crisis. Dealing with Charles being sick she made a point of possible significance:

"Mrs. Cox told me to take the vomit away, and I threw it down the sink in the housemaid's room and washed the basin out."

Hearing this, the jurors and others may well have thought that Mrs. Cox, in view of her admitted knowledge that Charles had taken poison, had acted suspiciously in not keeping the vomit for the doctors to examine.

Inevitably the name of Dr. Gully came up again: Mr. Lewis saw to that.

"A week or two after we had been at The Priory," said Mary Ann, "I knew of his coming. He was in the habit of coming there very frequently.

"He never came when Mrs. Ricardo became Mrs. Bravo. I never saw or heard of his coming then."

Mary Ann of course was in an excellent position to note how

Charles and Florence got on together, and she was able to tell the court:

"I used to wait upon the newly-married couple in their bedroom, and had seen them together constantly. I never heard Dr. Gully's name mentioned by either. I never saw any indication of jealousy in the deceased towards his wife. He always treated her with the greatest affection and consideration, and I never heard him speak to her except in an affectionate way."

This sounded a pretty convincing indication of a placid married life, for no husband and wife could hope to conceal *all* their little tiffs and differences—let alone more serious quarrels—from a trusted maid like Mary Ann, intimate with both and admitted without question to the privacy of their bedroom. And later on, when the jury heard Florence's Treasury statement read, they were to remember these remarks of Mary Ann's—and wonder. The two pictures were so very different.

It was clear how Mary Ann and her fellow-servants regarded Charles himself when she said:

"He was always a man who had a kind word for everybody, and he always tried to save trouble. Everyone in the house among the servants was very fond of him."

In what liquid had Charles taken the poison? Many people were unconvinced, from what had been written in the *Lancet* and elsewhere, and what Rowe had said, about the burgundy. And now Mary Ann produced a startling new possibility.

"I used to fill the deceased's water bottle after breakfast. . . . He was in the habit of going upstairs frequently when he was at home to clean his teeth, and I filled up the bottle on Tuesday evening after he came down to dinner."

The water bottle. Why not? It was an intriguing idea, even though Mary Ann had to admit that she had not noticed the state of the bottle on the Tuesday night but recalled filling it the next morning. The possibilities struck Sir Henry and others so forcibly that when Mary Ann resumed her evidence next morning she was confronted with a small water bottle and tumbler brought from The Priory. Sir Henry questioned her on them and she replied:

"The water bottle and tumbler produced are those which were in Mr. Bravo's room. Mr. Bravo was in the habit of cleaning his teeth frequently, using about a tumblerful each time. I had no opportunity of knowing whether he used water for that purpose at night when he went to bed, but I do know that he washed his teeth before dinner on the 18th April."

It did not need much imagination on the part of Mr. Cattley and his brother-jurors to see the point of all this. Could the tartar emetic have been put in the bottle some time after dinner on that Tuesday night and drunk by Charles on coming up to bed? Mary Ann had already said that there was generally only a little water left in his bottle in the morning, which implied that he drank some at least when he went to bed. It was a more plausible theory than the burgundy one in several ways. For one thing, it accounted much better for the precise time at which Charles had first been sick: poison in the burgundy, it was generally agreed, would have brought on the vomiting a good deal earlier.

Before Mary Ann had resumed her evidence on the seventh day of the inquest the jury and all the lawyers engaged in the case had viewed The Priory in order to get a mental picture which would enable them to follow the evidence better. Into the quiet house (now occupied by Florence and her mother, but no longer by Mrs. Cox, who was staying in apartments at Manchester Street) they trooped, looking into the rooms that had been the setting to the queer drama that they were now trying to solve—the dining-room in its ponderous dignity, the feminine fussiness of the morning-room, the library, the drawing-room. Then upstairs, past the variegated religious prints, to the first-floor landing, where, facing them slightly to the left was the door to Charles's room, the door which Mary Ann had seen so suddenly open on that Tuesday night to show Charles gasping in distress and shouting for Florence and hot water. They went in, and there, just inside on the left, they saw the widish single bed with its brass-knobbed rails at head and foot (was the bedstead French or Arabian?) where Charles had died. Beyond it was the window that they had heard so much about, the window from which he had vomited; and peering out they could see, just below, the leads from which the servant had collected the vomit into a jar on the orders of Sir William Gull. The story of those tragic fifty hours in which doctors and relatives had stood helpless round the bed and waited for Charles to die from the effects of the then unknown poison suddenly became much more real to them: they could visualise how things had happened and see how the incidents fitted in. Quietly they filed out, turning to the left along the short landing to the next bedroom with its double doors (the outer one baize-covered) which Florence had been occupying with Mrs. Cox on and for some days before the tragic Tuesday. Through this green door they could imagine Mary Ann pushing, to rouse Florence after Charles's repeated cry; and perhaps they wondered how it was that neither Florence nor Mrs. Cox had seemed to hear these loud shouts coming from just outside their door. Beyond this bedroom, along a right-angled bend in the passage, they saw the two dressing-rooms, in one of which Florence and Mrs. Cox had prepared for the night while Charles was down in the morning-room and Mary Ann at her supper. It was into this room, they recalled, that Charles had walked to reproach Florence for taking too much wine, while Mary Ann had tactfully concealed herself with the marsala in Florence's bedroom until he should have passed by to bed.

Their round of the house completed, they briefly viewed the stables and grounds and then returned to the Bedford Hotel—but not before they had seen, at the bottom of Bedford Hill Road on the right, the villa called Orwell Lodge, home of the Dr. Gully who looked like figuring so prominently in the case. It had been a worth-while tour.

Next at the witness-stand, after Mary Ann Keeber had finished, was Charles Parton the coachman. He had been with the Bravos only since 3rd February, a month after Griffith had left. Parton described the events of Tuesday as he had seen them; from the drive to London with Florence and Charles to the appearance of Charles in the stableyard after his unfortunate ride on Cremorne.

Now, Mr. Lewis was aware of Florence's statement at the Treasury which referred to a violent dispute between her and Charles on the way to town that Tuesday, so he now questioned Parton on this point.

Parton: "On the drive to town I heard no quarrelling or high words, or anything in the nature of a quarrel between Mr. and Mrs. Bravo."

Sir Henry James put a question about Dr. Gully.

Parton: "I was a stranger to the neighbourhood before I came to The Priory in February. I did not know Dr. Gully by sight, and I never knew him come to The Priory. I know where he lives, or is said to live."

And then he added:

"On the way to London, on the 18th, we had to pass by Dr. Gully's house. After passing his house, nothing was said and nothing occurred."

No quarrel, nothing said outside Dr. Gully's house . . . this again was to contrast so radically with another version that the jury were to hear later on. The conflicting material was piling up, even though the conflicts might not yet be apparent.

Mr. Gorst asked about antimony.

Parton: "I do not use antimony to my horses. . . . Nothing of the sort was left in the stable when I went to The Priory."

And he added that no rat poison had been in the stable while he had been there, though the gardener had told him that he had previously had rat poison.

Young Edward Smith, the footman, had nothing much of value to impart. He had accompanied the Bravos to town with Parton on the Tuesday and had waited at dinner that night. He had noted, however, that when he opened the carriage door for his master and mistress to get in, Mr. Bravo was showing his usual happy and cheerful manner; and that he appeared to be in his accustomed spirits at dinner. Like others of the staff he had never seen Dr. Gully at The Priory, he was not even quite sure that he knew the doctor's house, though he admitted it had been pointed out to him. Nor could the groom, George Younger, be any more helpful. He had seen Charles only briefly that day, and, like Edward Smith, he knew nothing of Dr. Gully. In reply to Mr. Gorst he said he had never seen antimony in the stables at The Priory.

The Attorney-General, going over the stories of these five servants, may have thought that little had come out of them to advance his case. If nothing had emerged to suggest suicide, there was equally nothing to point directly to murder. Rowe's and Mary Ann's testimony had shown Charles as a kind and well-liked master, happily married to a loving wife. Of course, Sir John Holker still had up his sleeve Florence's and Mrs. Cox's Treasury statements, which would want a lot of reconciling with what Mary Ann—seemingly an observant and truthful girl—had said. Further, there was the little matter of the missing burgundy, highly suspicious until Mary Ann had come out with her story of the bedroom drinking-water. To Sir John, and to everyone else who believed Charles might have been murdered, it began to look now as if the hand holding the antimony crystals had hovered not over the cut-glass decanter in the dining-room but the water bottle in Charles's bedroom.

3   *Amelia and Miss Bell*

"One of Mr. Bravo's sisters is deaf and dumb, and none of his family is afflicted with epileptic fits!"

The reply to Sir Henry James rang out on the next (eighth) day of the inquest in the homely indignant accents of Amelia Bushell, to nail an imputation by Sir Henry that Charles might have been mentally unstable.

It was a gambit that Florence and Sir Henry were almost bound to use in their efforts to establish Charles's suicide. But it was not a very successful one. A deaf-mute sister (Alice) there might be, but epilepsy in the family, no. Amelia's forthright answer showed the Campbells that they could not hope to justify Florence's tales of Charles's violent temper and over-riding jealousy by dragging in some hereditary mental taint.

Sir Henry did not pursue the matter. Perhaps his convenient place next to the extempore jury-box enabled him to know when a line of attack appealed to the jury or otherwise.

Amelia Bushell was more than just lady's-maid to Mrs. Joseph—who, most unfortunately for the Bravo cause, was lying seriously ill at Palace Green and would be unable to testify—she was a devoted and trusted family retainer, who had known Charles for fifteen years. He had been the apple of her eye; and when examined by Mr. Lewis she not surprisingly portrayed him as cheerful, high-spirited, truthful, and the very last person to commit suicide.

But in her account of the happenings in the sick-room after her arrival on the Wednesday, Amelia was certainly not hostile to Florence. She declared that Charles was always very pleased to see his wife, and that Florence had appeared very distressed at the time the Bravo party arrived, and pale and weak as if from exhaustion. She mentioned Florence's attempt to account for Charles's illness by the lunch at St. James's Hall, and that she herself had had not the slightest suspicion that "poison had been given" to Charles up to the time she was examined at the Treasury.

Much of Amelia Bushell's evidence dealt with Sir William Gull's visit and the fruitless questioning of Charles: as did that of Ann Maria Bell, Royes's sister, who followed her at the witness-stand. But now suddenly the story came vividly to life. Miss Bell, staring straight ahead of her as she spoke, seemed to be re-living the tense bedside drama of suffering, of suggestion-and-denial, of Charles's despairing plea to be believed when he swore he had taken only laudanum; and in re-living it she was able to convey the scene to everyone in court with a new and convincing clarity.

Again came the rejection of suicide, the ignorance of the name of Gully, the assertion of Charles's kind and cheerful disposition, of a happy marriage, of his show of affection to Florence in the last days. Charles, Ann Maria declared, was fond of his profession and ambitious to rise in it. "He was a particularly courageous man."

A laudanum bottle had been mentioned. Mr. Lewis now questioned her on it.

Ann Maria: "I remember the bottle of laudanum being spoken of. When my cousin said he had only used laudanum, his wife said: 'And where did you get it from?' He said: 'From your bottle, Florence; you know, your bottle.' I could not recognise or identify the bottle."

How did Ann Maria Bell feel towards Florence, the woman who had married, and in whose house had died, her fondly loved cousin Charles? Had she before his death shared her aunt's antipathy to her? And did she now, in her firm repudiation of the notion of Charles's suicide, believe that Florence had been concerned in his death? Close as Ann was to her uncle and aunt, there is no reading between the lines of her impartial-sounding evidence to suggest any deadly grudge against Florence.

And yet—two remarks of Florence's that Ann Maria thought worth including in her evidence leave one wondering. Was it Florence's genuine bafflement in the face of sudden mysterious disaster that this quiet self-controlled woman was stressing, or was it an ignorance, or innocence, too good to be true?

The first remark was uttered during that little talk that they had had in the conservatory soon after Ann Maria's arrival on the Thursday afternoon. After Florence had declared that she and Charles had been very happy, and had never had a word together, Ann Maria had "conversed with her, and she never suggested that Mr. Bravo had been jealous, or had cause to be jealous of her, nor that he had committed suicide, or any cause why he should have committed suicide. She spoke of the deceased very affectionately. She said nothing accounting for his illness."

Did the jury recall that Amelia Bushell had just told them of the suggestion that Florence had made to her on the Wednesday about the "coppery pan"?

The second remark had been made on the morning of Charles's death, while they had all been downstairs blindly speculating on the cause. It was almost trivial enough to have gone unremembered. But Ann Maria had remembered it— and now she gave it to the court:

"It was on the morning of my cousin's death that the cause was said by Mrs. Bravo to be a mystery and would remain so."

CHAPTER 12

PROPHET OF DOOM

AFTER Ann Maria Bell, George Griffith: after a model of clear, precise evidence, a rigmarole so vague, so contradictory and garbled as to be almost unintelligible in places. And yet Griffith's testimony contained the most sensational and suggestive piece of information produced since the start of the inquest.

It must have seemed strange to this prophet of Charles's doom to be recalled from Lady Prescott's stables at Herne Bay to the Bedford Hotel to play his part in unravelling the mystery of the death that he had here foretold. Clean-shaven, horsey-looking George Griffith was no scholar, and to his inarticulateness were added a wildly erratic memory and a certain shiftiness that inevitably made a bad impression on the jury. But there was no denying the importance of what he had to tell.

"I am coachman," he began, "in the family of Lady Prescott, Stroud Park, Herne Bay, Kent. I was coachman to Mrs. Ricardo at the time she married Mr. Bravo. I left her service on the 3rd January of this year. I had been in her service since the previous May. She kept three horses then—a brougham horse and a pair of cobs."

And then came his bombshell:

"I was in the habit of giving the horses tartar emetic—antimony. I kept it in the stables."

A low buzz of excitement filled the court-room. Antimony! In the stables of The Priory! At last the case was getting somewhere.

Griffith went on:

"It was the white tartar emetic, not the 'black antimony' or the 'liver antimony'. I bought some at Balham, some at Streatham, some in London. I have bought it of Mr. Robinson, chemist, at Streatham, and of Mr. Smith, at Balham. It is four years since I bought it at Streatham.

"I was in Mrs. Ricardo's service about four years ago, and left. I used the tartar emetic between May and January last as a lotion in sores for Mrs. Ricardo's horses.

"I bought it in powder and made the lotion myself. I bought a quarter of an ounce of Mr. Smith at Balham—he would not let me have more. I signed no book. I paid fourpence or fivepence for the quarter of an ounce.

"My mistress dealt at that shop, and they knew me . . . I made a lotion of a pint and a half bottle of the quarter of an ounce I got from Mr. Smith, and kept it locked up in a cupboard in the stable.

"It did for forty or fifty applications. A quarter of an ounce will go as far as that, and the bottle it was in was labelled 'Poison'. I broke the bottle a day or two before I left there, having poured the lotion down a sink in the stable yard.

"I left nothing of the sort in the yard.

". . . I do not remember signing for the antimony which I bought at Streatham. Mrs. Ricardo then lived at Leigham Court Road, Streatham. I had two horses then under me. I gave one of them as much antimony as would go on a three-penny piece [about five grains] in a bran mash.

"I kept that antimony in the saddle-room, locked up. I was in her service about nine months then. I don't know the month or year I left the service then—it is about five years ago; and when I left I took away the tartar emetic I had not used to use in my next service."

Now Griffith established his connection with Florence from her Malvern days:

"When I first went into Mrs. Ricardo's service she lived at Great Malvern, at the Priory House there, and I came with her to Streatham.

"I only bought the two quarter ounces I have mentioned while I was in Mrs. Ricardo's service."

Next he obligingly fitted into its place another piece of the picture:

"Dr. Gully recommended me to Mrs. Ricardo.

"I had been in his service eight years at Great Malvern. He kept sometimes one, sometimes two, and sometimes three horses. He retired from business and sold all off, and that was the cause of my leaving his service.

"When he left Great Malvern he came to live nearly opposite Mrs. Ricardo's, in the Leigham Court Road, Streatham. He visited Mrs. Ricardo's house in the Leigham Court Road.

"I don't know whether he knew I used tartar emetic to Mrs. Ricardo's horses.

"When I first entered Mrs. Ricardo's service, Captain Ricardo was not there. I left Mrs. Ricardo's service the first time because I was going to be married to Mrs. Ricardo's lady's maid, Fanny Plascott.

"When I came back to Mrs. Ricardo's service I found Dr. Gully lived as near to The Priory, or nearer, as he had lived to Mrs. Ricardo's house in the Leigham Court Road.

"I 'physicked' the doctor's horses when I was in his service. I got the antimony at all the chemist's shops. They did not make me sign for it. I never bought more than a quarter of an ounce at once, though I have asked for more. Dr. Gully never knew that I gave tartar emetic to the horses. I never got tartar emetic by Dr. Gully's orders. I know Clark's at Great Malvern. I never signed for it there."

Mr. Gorst now intervened, holding up a small ledger.

"Now, take that book into your hand, and look at 'George Griffith' signed there. Is that your handwriting?"

Griffith: "Yes; that is my handwriting."

Mr. Gorst addressed the court: "This book is a registry under the Sale of Poisons Act kept by Mr. Clark, chemist, of Great Malvern. This is the entry:

July 11th, 1869

Name of Purchaser—Dr. Gully
Name and quantity of poison sold—2 oz. emetic tartar
Purpose for which required—Horse medicine
Signature of purchaser—G. Griffith
Signature of person introducing purchaser—R. Bridges."

Griffith, a little deflated, continued:

"As to that purchase, I remember that now. I told Mr. Clark where I came from. I suppose what I did not use of that I threw away. I kept my poison at Dr. Gully's in my own portmanteau. I am not sure that Dr. Gully knew of it." And here poor George Griffith began to get confused under Mr. Gorst's relentless probing: "I will not undertake to say that I did not take a note from Dr. Gully to get that poison. I think I will undertake to say that I used the whole of that antimony or threw it away before I went to Mrs. Ricardo's service."

Mr. Gorst: "You have told us that a quarter of an ounce would serve for fifty horses, or make fifty applications. What could you want with a quantity which would make four hundred applications or doses, you having only two horses in your care?"

Griffith: "Well, I wanted to have it to use as I wanted it—a store to last for years . . . I don't know who first put it into my head to use antimony to horses. . . . Antimony is good for

175

worms and the 'black bots' in horses. One of Dr. Gully's horses suffered from 'black bots', and Mrs. Ricardo's suffered from worms.

"I never bought tartar emetic between the time I left Mrs. Ricardo's service in Leigham Court Road and when I returned to her service in May last; nor except when in the service of Dr. Gully and Mrs. Ricardo. I have had no occasion to use it since I have been in Lady Prescott's service. I am sure I have none now. I am sure I bought none in London."

The counsel around the big table had been listening to this with growing bewilderment. Now there was a whispered consultation between them as they referred to their notes; and they all agreed that Griffith had earlier said that he had in fact bought some tartar emetic in London and that he still had some in Lady Prescott's stables.

Here Mr. Gorst tried to extract from this muddled witness a clear statement as to his periods of service in his various places, and had to give up in despair. The best he could get was that Griffith was aged thirty-six, had gone to Dr. Gully when he was twenty-nine, stayed there eight years, and that five years had elapsed between his first and second service with Florence —which made arithmetical nonsense. No doubt the jury took note and evaluated the rest of his evidence with due caution.

Mr. Lewis rose to cross-examine on how Griffith came to leave The Priory.

Griffith: "Mrs. Ricardo gave me notice to leave; and for her reason said it was the wish of Mr. Bravo that I should leave, he saying I was not careful enough to drive in London."

Then he added resentfully: "I should have been there now if it had not been his wish that I should leave! I had driven him and her before they were married in and out of London, in the landau."

Mr. Lewis: "How long before you drove him had you driven Dr. Gully in the same landau with Mrs. Ricardo?"

Griffith: "Well, from four to six weeks. I had driven them out together two or three times a week. I used to pick him [Dr. Gully] up on the road, sometimes near his own house. I do not think he ever got in at The Priory. I have driven them up to London sometimes, and about the country . . . I have put him down at his own gates. . . . Up to the last two or three months Dr. Gully was in the habit of driving out with Mrs. Ricardo. He used to call Mrs. Ricardo 'Florrie', and Mrs. Cox by her name 'Mrs. Cox'. Mrs. Ricardo called him 'Dr. Gully'. It was about eight weeks after I drove Dr. Gully and Mrs. Ricardo together that I heard of her intended marriage with Mr. Bravo. During those eight weeks I saw Dr. Gully every day—up and down the road, going on to the Common, and so on.

"The doctor never spoke to me about my leaving, but I spoke to him about my character, thinking I should not get one from Mr. Bravo. Dr. Gully said it was a pity I was going to leave, and he hoped 'she would be happy'.

"I did not know the name of Mr. Bravo until they were married and had come from Brighton after the marriage. I did not see him after he was married.

"I have lately met Dr. Gully in London. I went to his house last Sunday to dine with his butler.

"When I went into Dr. Gully's service I had antimony in my possession—about half or a quarter of an ounce. I did not use much antimony to Dr. Gully's horses. They did not require it —not much. During seven of the years I was there I only bought what I had at Mr. Clark's, Great Malvern." And here he got confused again at Mr. Lewis's jabbing questions. "I cannot swear that I did not buy that for Dr. Gully. I will swear that he did not tell me to buy it—if he did, I have forgotten.

I don't believe he ever did tell me to buy it. I can't swear that I did not tell Mr. Clark that Dr. Gully had sent me for it."

The wretched coachman was now floundering hopelessly. He could only continue: "When I swore that I had only bought antimony in quarter ounces, and only two of these, I had forgotten this." And looking hopelessly towards the jury, he exclaimed: "The jury may do as they like about believing me!"

Mr. Lewis changed the subject:

"Do you know about the late Captain Ricardo being taken ill at Great Malvern?"

Griffith: "I heard about it—it was talked about at the time. I don't know what were his symptoms."

This seemed fruitless, so Mr. Lewis switched back to antimony.

Griffith: "At the time I bought the antimony none of Dr. Gully's horses were ill. They were never ill. The antimony would keep them from being ill. I cannot name anybody who saw me give tartar emetic to horses at any time . . . I don't believe I was sent by Dr. Gully for the antimony at Great Malvern. I may have been sent for it by him, and I may have delivered it over to him. It was labelled 'Poison', 'Tartar Emetic', and it had the name of the chemist. I cannot remember one way or the other if Dr. Gully's name was or was not on it as well.

". . . I went into Mrs. Ricardo's service in Captain Ricardo's lifetime, but he had left her.

"She was living at the Priory House, Great Malvern, Dr. Gully's house. I had seen Captain Ricardo there once at dinner. He was a patient before that under Dr. Gully—that was before the Captain left his wife."

So with this baffling hotch-potch of assertion and contradiction to reflect on, the wearied court rose at the end of the eighth day. The jury could be forgiven if they were bemused by George Griffith's rambling and random evidence. He was an appalling witness, admittedly—but was there anyone in that court-room who did not feel that somewhere in the coachman's garbled tale of chemists' shops and stable yards, that ranged over the years from Great Malvern to The Priory, was the key to the mystery? For through it ran, from first to last, the crystalline connecting thread of antimony.

Not only that. For the first time it brought in, no longer as a shadowy character that nobody seemed to have met or heard of but now as a chief actor in the drama, Dr. Gully. The doctor had been expecting this and had prepared for it. At the resumption of proceedings on the ninth day, therefore, Mr. Archibald Smith, barrister, rose and addressed the Coroner, saying that in conjunction with his learned friend, Mr. Serjeant Parry, he had been instructed to watch the case on behalf of Dr. Gully, and that Mr. Serjeant Parry would attend in the course of the day. Now the thrusts that would assuredly be vicariously aimed at him by Mr. Lewis and Mr. Gorst in their pointed, probing questions to Griffith and others would be countered.

The court had not finished with George Griffith. Mr. Lewis took over first, and asked him about Charles Bravo's death.

Griffith: "I read the newspapers from time to time a little. I saw the death of Mr. Bravo was attributed to tartar emetic. It did not then pass through my mind that I had been in possession of tartar emetic."

But he was soon in deep water again when Mr. Lewis returned to the matter of the antimony and its purchase at Malvern—refuting and qualifying his statements of the previous day until the jury must have wondered whether they could believe anything he said at all. But he ended up with a significant little grumble that they could accept as a true indication of his feelings:

"I went back to Mrs. Ricardo's service in May last. The occasion of my going back was that she had written to me to come back. It is my impression that I should have been in Mrs. Bravo's service now but for Mr. Bravo, the deceased!"

It was now Sir Henry James's turn. He alluded to the comparatively minute amounts of antimony that had been registered as sold to other customers of Mr. Clark at Malvern; and a juryman quickly took the point, remarking that the book showed no quantity as large as two ounces as having been sold to anyone except Griffith.

Soon afterwards witness spoke of antimony at The Priory:

"I kept the tartar emetic in a cupboard at The Priory stables. I never gave any of it to anyone in the house, and no one had any. Mrs. Ricardo did not know of it, and never knew of it. She never went to the cupboard where it was kept. I had none when I left. I threw it away before I left—I poured it down the drain in the yard, and as to what I did with 'the bottle', I broke one or two of them, and may have left one there, but there was nothing in it, I know.

"Mrs. Ricardo came to the stables sometimes, but she never looked in the cupboard—that I know. I had no powder or liquid emetic when I left."

This urgent disclaimer sounded sincere enough—and perhaps it was. It was as if Griffith, aware that he had already got himself mixed up quite dangerously enough with this business of the antimony, was now determined at all costs not to be connected with the lethal dose—nor with anyone at The Priory who might have been in a position to administer it. It was as if he was saying "I know nothing about anything, and at least it was not *my* antimony that the poisoner used".

The jury, of course, had to decide how much he was to be believed in the light of the rest of his performance at the witness-stand.

Griffith continued: "I had a collision shortly before I had notice—on Lord Mayor's Show day. I was driving Mrs. Cox and Mrs. Ricardo then, in Bond Street, and I ran into a wine cart. It was said I was careless. I had a month's notice. The people who owned the cart said I was in the wrong when I ran into them. I said I wasn't."

Mr. Archibald Smith now intervened for the first time and got these answers from Griffith:

"I don't know if I went to Dr. Gully in 1862. I had had the management of horses before I went into Dr. Gully's service. I did not use tartar emetic at first, but I learnt it out of a book, *The Pocket Farrier*, and from Clement Baldwin, the coachman where I was groom.

"When I have wanted tartar emetic, I have gone to chemists for it, and I have constantly used it, except when in Ireland, for some fifteen or sixteen years . . . I don't think I told Mr. Clark I wanted it for anything else than horses. I don't recollect one way or other whether Dr. Gully sent me to purchase tartar emetic. I don't recollect telling my master that I used it. . . ."

Mr. Gorst challenged him on something he had said the previous day.

Griffith: "I remember saying yesterday that I had some [antimony] in my present stables at Herne Bay. . . . It was not true . . . I tried to buy it in London, but could not . . . I may have had some of the two ounces I bought at Malvern when I bought a quarter of an ounce at Streatham, at Robinson's, opposite the White Lion.

"What became of that I don't know. I think my wife threw it in the fire when the children ran about . . . I think I said the cupboard in which the poison was kept at The Priory was locked, but I meant the tartar emetic was locked in the stables. The cupboard was not always locked; it was generally un-locked. I think it was sometimes locked. The bottle was always labelled 'Poison'. I got the label off the paper the poison was in." And here the rattled Griffith took refuge in sarcasm. "If anybody liked to drink a stuff labelled 'Poison' they could, but it was open to them!"

A few minutes later, as Griffith was being sent off under police escort—in a welcome release for himself and the long-suffering jury—to Herne Bay to fetch the copy of *The Pocket Farrier* from which he had said that he had first learnt how to use tartar emetic, Mr. Lewis, with a neat touch of drama, produced Griffith's second bombshell. His voice rang through the court:

"Stay! I want to ask another question or two!"

The tired jury looked up with a new interest.

"You remember hearing talk about Mrs. Ricardo's marriage with Mr. Bravo?"

Griffith nodded.

"Did you ever then express an opinion that he would not live long?"

There was a murmur in the packed and stifling court-room. Griffith looked first surprised, then confused, then plainly uneasy.

"I—I don't remember. I can't swear that I did not."

Mr. Lewis, in slow, emphatic tones: "Now, just reflect, and tell me if you did not say, 'Poor fellow!' in relation to Mr. Bravo's marriage with the then Mrs. Ricardo, 'he will not live long'?"

Griffith was helpless under the lawyer's attack. He saw there was no evasion.

"I—er—I might have said so." And then with a little more heat: "I said all I could about him when he got me out of my home at The Priory!'"

"Did you say Mr. Bravo would not live four months after his marriage?"

"No, I did not say that."

Mr. Lewis beckoned to the court's summoning officer and said:

"Call Mr. Stringer."

Mr. Stringer (who will be remembered as the manager of the Bedford Hotel) appeared and was directed to stand beside Griffith at the table.

Mr. Lewis turned to Griffith:

"Do you know Mr. Stringer?"

Griffith nodded.

"Now will you say that you did not use this expression in relation to the late Mr. Bravo, 'Poor fellow, he won't live four months?'" Mr. Lewis's voice was challenging. "Answer that question standing face to face with Mr. Stringer!"

What could the wretched Griffith say? There was hardly room now for even the feeblest prevarication; yet he still held out against the inevitable admission:

"I don't know that I said four months. I may have said five or six months."

And then he added, pushed further still by the relentless Mr. Lewis:

"I don't think I have also expressed that same opinion at Lady Prescott's before some of the household."

Mr. Lewis left that point—it was immaterial.

"Now tell me what you meant by it."

Griffith was now quite unnerved. He stammered out:

"I did it in aggravation—nothing else. I had only seen the gentleman on two occasions, but I looked on him as having got me out of my place!"

"But why should he die?"

"Well, it did not matter to me if he was dead or alive."

Mr. Lewis dangled his monocle:

"And how long did you give him to live?"

"Six months, I think. I didn't care whether he lived or died."

"Was he in good health then?"

"Well, he had been bitten by a dog."

"Did you mean he might die of that?"

"Well, yes." Griffith grasped at the straw. "Perhaps I thought he could die of the bite. I am not sure I expressed that opinion to anyone. I think I have mentioned the dog bite." He was obviously thinking out the pros and cons of having mentioned the bite as he went along. "I don't know that I mentioned it to Mr. Stringer at the time I spoke."

The matter of the dog bite was dropped for the moment and Mr. Lewis put some queries about Dr. Gully. Then came a curious question:

"Did Dr. Gully tell you that he would send a letter which would not make them 'very comfortable' after the marriage?"

Interest in the court-room livened up again: was another little bombshell coming?

The listeners were disappointed at Griffith's emphatic reply:

"No—that I swear positive!"

Mr. Lewis had almost finished with him now; just two more questions on Charles Bravo's death:

"When you read the account of Mr. Bravo's death you were not surprised to see that he did not live for more than four months and a fortnight?"

"Well, I was surprised."

"Did it surprise you to find that Mr. Bravo had died by tartar emetic?"

To this George Griffith gave a cryptic and—considering its implications for himself—damaging answer:

"No, it did not."

However, Mr. Lewis did not take it up, and after a few more questions from Mr. Archibald Smith and the jury, Griffith stood down. In his place came Charles James Stringer, to fill in the dtails of his little conversation with the coachman in this very hotel. He wound up by saying:

"He gave no reason for what he said, and I asked no questions. He said nothing about the dog biting Mr. Bravo, or of leaving in consequence of the marriage.

"I took the words to arise from the spleen of the man at being about to leave his situation through the marriage."

Alas for poor Griffith! Charles Stringer had been able to confirm Mr. Lewis's submission that the coachman had given Charles Bravo "four months"—not five or six—to live, thus making his prophecy accurate to within a fortnight. And that was not all: his tale of getting tartar emetic in Streatham and Balham chemists' shops was now blown sky-high. The two chemists in question, Charles Robinson of Streatham Hill and Percy Smith of Balham, now produced their poison registers to show that they had never sold him any antimony. Only Henry Clark of Malvern, with his record of the sale of two ounces to him in July, 1869, could substantiate his statement. And Mr. Clark, in his testimony, said one or two significant things:

"I have never known so large a quantity sold across the counter as two ounces except to medical men or to veterinary surgeons. I should have let a man like Dr. Gully have it, and I should have sent it on his order. I believe I had Dr. Gully's letter through my hands at the time. It is not probable that a man would have two ounces of tartar emetic supplied without some letter."

He also said: "The tartar emetic will keep its power for any reasonable number of years."

That was the end of the ninth day's evidence, and after the adjournment George Griffith and his escort caught their train to Herne Bay. The court had not quite heard the last of him, but now its members could—even if still a little bemused—attempt to sift the grain from the chaff and assess what his evidence was really worth.

First and foremost, to him had been traced the antimony which it seemed overwhelmingly probable had caused the death of Charles Bravo. The jury could hardly dismiss the extreme likelihood that it was from the two ounces bought by him at Malvern—whether or not on Dr. Gully's orders—in July, 1869, that the lethal dose had eventually come. The firm denials of the chemists at Streatham and Balham ruled out his possessing any other supply of tartar emetic. Some of that original Malvern stock seemed undoubtedly to have been preserved down to 1875-6 and to have been used by him on Florence's horses during his last period of service at The Priory. And all along it seemed highly doubtful that he had kept any proper control over this lethal drug. At Dr. Gully's he had, so he said, kept it in his portmanteau; at Leigham Court Road it was admittedly locked in a cupboard, but at The Priory it was in an open cupboard, in stables which were generally, but could not be always, locked. Equally dubious was Griffith's assertion that he had thrown away the surplus on leaving Leigham Court Road. If so, what antimony was he using on the horses at The Priory? In the light of this, his statement that he had got rid of all remaining antimony on quitting The Priory could not be relied on. The jury could hardly avoid the conclusion that an ill-disposed occupant of The Priory might have slipped into the stables at any time up to 3rd January, while Griffith was still there, and taken what was wanted from the bottle invitingly marked "Poison". Or, for that matter, the undiscarded poison might have been equally accessible between 3rd January and the beginning of February, while there was no coachman at The Priory. Again, taking a wider view, the jury might visualise any of the people who came into the story from the Malvern days of 1869 or 1870 right down to 1876 taking and secreting the antimony at any time during this period: Dr. Gully, Florence, Mrs. Cox—and of course the newest suspect of all—George Griffith himself.* And could they pin a motive on Griffith, as they could, or would soon be able to, on the others? Why, certainly. There was Griffith's burning resentment at being sacked by Charles for so-called careless driving.

And now, to add to all this, there was the sting in the tail of Griffith's evidence, the extraordinary story of his little conversation with Mr. Stringer in the Bedford Hotel on the Bravos' wedding day. What were the jury to make of that? It might of course have been mere talk due, as Mr. Stringer had suggested, to "the spleen of the man"; but dare they ignore it on this account, when it was clear that George Griffith had both the motive and the means?

It was a lot for Mr. Cattley and his fellow-jurors to take in and think about, and perhaps they missed another deeper implication in George Griffith's prophecy—the suggestion, not that he himself was going to kill Charles Bravo at or about a certain time, but that he knew that someone else was likely to.

---

* Griffith implied that he made a lotion of all antimony he bought, thereby disposing at once of the crystals. But as, according to him, a quarter-ounce of antimony made a pint and a half of lotion, the two ounces he bought at Malvern would have produced a gallon and a half—a huge quantity of poisonous liquid to store. It is far likelier that he mixed small amounts of lotion as required and kept in his stables the unused residue of crystals—a handy uncontrolled poison readily available to himself and anyone else with access to the stables.

CHAPTER 13

MRS. CAMPBELL AND OTHERS

"I CANNOT CONCEIVE IT POSSIBLE that Mr. Bravo could have retained, for two hours, the burgundy if it had contained antimony. If he had taken antimony in water in his bedroom, when he was going to bed, it is possible that he would have become sick in about a quarter of an hour.

". . . A large quantity might, I should think, produce an effect in about five or six minutes."

These were perhaps the most significant remarks of Dr. Joseph Payne, who opened the tenth day's proceedings by giving evidence on his post-mortem examination of Charles Bravo and its results. Also interesting from the same point of view was a reply of his to Mr. Lewis:

"As to the appearance of the stomach, this indicated that the poison was taken in a highly dilute form."

Between them, these pronouncements seemed to dispose pretty thoroughly of the burgundy theory: it now appeared virtually certain that Charles had taken the poison in a drink from his bedside water bottle, that same carafe that Mary Ann had filled on the Tuesday evening after he had gone down to dinner. The missing burgundy, then, looked like a red herring, perhaps introduced by someone to lay a false scent.

Then, after two chemists' assistants had followed Dr. Payne with evidence about the sale of antimony, Griffith himself reappeared at the witness-stand, fresh from Herne Bay, with *The Pocket Farrier* and another book on the same subject. He had no more revelations now and the standard of his evidence may be judged from his still maintaining, in the face of the chemists' statements to the contrary, that he had bought tartar emetic from Mr. Smith of Balham and Mr. Robinson of Streatham. There can have been nobody in the court-room who was not thankful to see him stand down.

John Pritchard, Dr. Gully's butler for twenty years, who came next, had nothing startling to tell. The highlight of his appearance was an acrid dispute that flared up between several of the counsel. Pritchard was telling of a call paid by Mrs. Cox to Dr. Gully's house (for a reason that was to become apparent later in the inquest):

"She asked for Dr. Gully. She said: 'Is the doctor in, Pritchard?' I said: 'Yes.' I was sorry afterwards that I had said yes, because I had orders from the doctor never to let either Mrs. Cox or Mrs. Bravo into the house."

There was loud laughter in the court. Mr. Serjeant Parry, sensitive to a slight against his client, Dr. Gully, protested vigorously to the Coroner, objecting particularly that Mr. Gorst had joined in the hilarity.

Mr. Gorst: "I plead guilty to having smiled. . . . If evidence is given which is amusing, I shall smile, for I shall not attempt to go through a case with a wooden face!"

Through the hearty applause cut the hammering of the Coroner's gavel and his threats to have the court cleared if the interruptions continued. But Mr. Serjeant Parry had not finished:

"This is a case in which two learned gentlemen of experience are representing the Crown, and they are here in reality for the purpose of fixing guilt upon three individuals. All their questions are directed to that object, and not as to ascertaining what is the cause of this unfortunate young man's death."

Clearly Mr. Gorst's smile had been the last straw for Mr.

Serjeant Parry: the Serjeant's resentment must have been piling up for some little time to produce this outburst. And one of the counsel at least thought he had gone too far.

Mr. Lewis: "I cannot help saying that this is rather an unjust observation on the part of Mr. Serjeant Parry to charge anything of that kind to Mr. Gorst. Mr. Gorst has acted most impartially on the part of the Crown, and has fairly brought out evidence telling in both ways."

Mr. Gorst now took up his own case:

"If the remarks which Mr. Serjeant Parry has made about the mode in which I have conducted this investigation be true, I have not properly carried out my instructions. I am instructed to come here to do my best to endeavour to lay before the Coroner and jury all the evidence which can throw any light on the death of this unfortunate young man. I do not suppose it will be possible for me to conduct my case in a manner pleasing to my learned friends, but I shall carry it out to the best of my ability in accordance with my instructions. I emphatically say again that these instructions are not to bring any charge against any person."

It was fantastic, deplorable. All the dignity due to Her Majesty's courts of law had flown clean out of the windows of the Bedford Hotel's converted billiards-room. The Coroner was helpless, the rest of those assembled struck dumb with amazement at this unseemly squabble between learned and eminent counsel. The thing was more like some stage farce than a solemn process of the law. However, the fracas did serve to clear the air and reduce the tension that at times in the last few days had been clearly noticeable around the big table.

In a calmer atmosphere Mr. Lewis resumed his examination of Pritchard.

The gist of the butler's evidence was that he had been aware of a great attachment between Dr. Gully and Florence, but had not seen her at the doctor's house since the previous November, nor did he know of any communication between them since then. Alluding to Mrs. Cox's visit again, Pritchard said that Dr. Gully had reluctantly agreed to see her, that he (Pritchard) showed her into his study but had no idea what was said there. Soon afterwards he saw her leave, going towards The Priory.

Did Pritchard know that Dr. Gully had been seeing Mrs. Cox by appointment? The question came from one of the jury and roused a flicker of new interest. But Pritchard said:

"I am not aware of Dr. Gully meeting Mrs. Cox by appointment. He has told me that he met her once at the station. He did tell me he had met her twice; it may have been three times —I don't know whether by appointment or not.

"I told him I thought it was very unwise for him to speak to her. I told him that because I thought he had done with her. I don't know what he said to this advice. I told him so because I had had quite enough trouble before when he had to do with them, and I did not want my master to be bothered any more with them."

There was mild comedy in the picture of this trusted, forthright old manservant speaking his mind to his master on the subject of his master's lady friends. But less amusing was the other picture which the butler conjured up—that of Mrs. Cox hobnobbing with the doctor when all communication between them was supposed to have ceased. Pritchard's words, as he stood down at the end of the inquest's tenth day, left many people in the court-room wondering.

Day number eleven, and George Griffith back at the witness-stand—but only briefly, to give entirely inconclusive testimony about entries in his expense book that might or might not have referred to tartar emetic.

Dr. George Johnson was next called, and there was a serious and resolute look about the Senior Physician to King's College

Hospital as he stood up to give evidence for the second time. He was in fact there to impugn the testimony of the great Sir William Gull on a vital point. Sir William had declared emphatically that he had been sent for to see Charles Bravo for disease. Now Dr. Johnson said:

"When Sir William Gull drove down with me, I told him the whole history of the case. I described the symptoms. Sir William Gull said: 'That looks like poisoning.' I said: 'There can be no question as to that: it is clearly a case of poisoning. There are only two doubtful points—first, what is the exact nature of the poison, and, secondly, how did it get into the patient's stomach?'

". . . I repeated to Sir William the conversations I had had with Mrs. Cox, and subsequently with the patient, as to the latter's denial of taking anything but laudanum.

"I cannot conceive that Sir William could have been under the idea that he was going to see a case of disease, unless he forgot what I said or disbelieved me."

Had the famous Sir William Gull been nodding? Could he perhaps have saved Charles Bravo if he had appreciated what Dr. Johnson was now so forcibly declaring that he had told him on the drive down to Balham? It was a startling thought, and might so very well weaken the confidence that the jury had in this out-and-out advocate of the theory of Charles's suicide.

But Dr. Johnson had something else rather disturbing to say. This involved Florence:

"The fact of the poisoning of Mr. Bravo was mentioned to Mrs. Bravo on the Wednesday"—the day before she wrote to Sir William Gull.

Now he had the jury speculating on that note which Florence, so desperate to save Charles's life, had sent Sir William on Thursday morning with not a word about poisoning in it. It was a strange omission to make at such a critical moment.

Dr. Johnson showed what he thought of the note and Sir William's conduct in apparently acting on it, in a devastating parting shot:

"It seems to me, if he thought he was going to see a case of disease, that Sir William placed more reliance upon a lady's note than upon what I had told him!"

Now three of Charles's barrister friends gave evidence, Frederick MacCalmont, Edward Hope and Edward Willoughby. Cheerful, happily married, courageous, unlikely to commit suicide—this was their unanimous verdict on Charles. MacCalmont denied hearing Charles ever mention Gully. (Here at least was proof from one intimate that Charles was a man of his word.) Something Edward Hope said threw an interesting light on Charles's attitude to Mrs. Cox:

"I saw him on 11th of April in the Exchequer Court. He had a pen in his hand as if calculating something, and he said: 'After all, Mrs. Cox must be costing us £300 a year.'

"When he was setting up his household he remarked upon the clothes women wanted, an expense which 'has hampered us', he said, and that he had had to go to his stepfather for a cheque to pay for something in regard to the wedding, and got a cheque at once for £500.

"He was not a man fond of money, but he liked to talk of investments."

"Not fond of money" . . . The jury were to hear a different slant on Charles's character from the next witness, Florence's mother.

"The deceased had a 'money mania'—he was always speaking of the cost of things, the cost of carriages and such-like," she said; and added that Florence considered him "penurious and saving".

For these ten days the Campbells had been sitting by, watching things going not at all according to their hopes. Nobody but Sir William Gull had spoken up for suicide—and now he looked slightly discredited—while the general view on Charles was that he was a fine fellow with none but trivial defects of character, and a good husband. It seemed, therefore, that Mrs. Campbell, as the first witness from the anti-Bravo camp, had a lot of leeway to make up. And yet when she stood down at the end of the twelfth day the picture that she had left of Charles was by no means that of a suicidal villain: while of course she did everything to uphold Florence she did not go out of her way to blacken her daughter's husband.

"I saw no trace of jealousy or bad feeling towards his wife," she said. "I have no personal knowledge how this poison was administered—I wish I had. From my knowledge of my son-in-law I should not say he was a likely man to commit suicide."

But when she said later: "I never supposed such a thing as murder," she left it very doubtful as to how in her opinion Charles had died.

Was it fancy to suppose that the evidence of Mrs. Campbell betrayed, if anything, a bias against Mrs. Cox? By nuances and undertones it seemed to hint that all this shocking trouble that Florence had got into was somehow due to her companion, that if there was anything discreditable in the affair the blame was Mrs. Cox's. It even appeared that Mrs. Campbell was trying to dissociate the two women, to show above all that they were not in league.

She spoke of her arrival at The Priory on the Thursday:

"When I got to Balham, from what Mrs. Cox told me, and from her manner, I was impressed with the idea that she thought the deceased had taken poison.

"Shortly after that I saw my daughter, and she suggested that the cooking-vessels at St. James's Hall had caused it."

This was not the first time that Mrs. Campbell had, in her evidence, linked Mrs. Cox's name with the word poison:

"When I first saw Mr. Royes Bell I said to him: 'I hear from Mrs. Cox that Charlie has taken poison.'"

Did this fond mother believe in her heart of hearts that Charles *had* been murdered by Mrs. Cox—with or without her daughter's connivance? If she did she was faced with the almost impossible task of bringing it home to Mrs. Cox without involving Florence too.

An ample, commanding figure in black, with a matronly and much-beribboned bonnet tied under her chin with a bow, Mrs. Campbell felt the heat a little (and no wonder, in that stifling court-room) and fanned herself gently as she gave her evidence. Her story began with Florence's first marriage and came down to her stay with Mrs. Cox at Brighton.

She spoke of her daughter's friendship with Dr. Gully: "That intimacy met with our entire disapproval. I had remonstrated with her on the subject, and it was in consequence of that intimacy that we saw nothing of my daughter those years she was at Streatham and Balham." She went on to tell of the family reconciliation when Florence gave the doctor up, Charles Bravo's appearance and Florence's engagement to him, and her own vain attempts to get Charles to tell his parents of Florence's past.

After four letters from Charles and Florence to Mrs. Campbell had been read (two from Charles dated January, 1876, and two from Florence dated April) to show how happily married the pair seemed to be, Mrs. Campbell came to Charles's illness and death. Then followed a surprise about certain meetings of Mrs. Cox with Dr. Gully and a curious story about a bottle of "laurel water". Mrs. Campbell said:

"The sitz-baths and spinal washes mentioned in the letter read yesterday [from Florence, describing the treatment she was having after her miscarriage] were prescribed for her by Dr. Gully." (Sensation in court.)

"Mrs. Cox told me that she met Dr. Gully going to the station, and he asked how Mrs. Charles Bravo was [knowing from a previous meeting with Mrs. Cox that Florence was ill]. Mrs. Cox told him she was very poorly and could not get sleep, and he said: 'Tell her to use sitz-baths and spinal washings, and I will send you a bottle of laurel water, of which she is to take thirty drops until she gets sleep.'

"This communication was made perfectly openly. Mrs. Cox told me in the presence of Mrs. Bravo the Saturday after the death.

"I do not know what became of the laurel water, which was not, as I heard, taken by my daughter for the purpose for which it was prescribed, as she got sleep without it."

This was sensational: no one in the court-room could fail to see the significance of a bottle of alleged sleeping-mixture being sent to Florence by her old friend a fortnight before her husband's death by poisoning. Mr. Lewis was up in a flash, cross-examining the witness about the bottle.

Mrs. Campbell answered:

"As to this bottle of 'laurel water', I heard my daughter say to Mrs. Cox: 'You need not keep it; take it out of the house.'

"I heard from Mrs. Cox that Dr. Gully said to her: 'I'm going to London, and I will leave it at your house.' The house was in Lancaster Road, Notting Hill. The 'laurel water' was made up at Smith's—not at Brixton, but at Balham.

"The reason it was to be taken from Balham to Notting Hill to come back to Balham was that Dr. Gully was going in that direction; but Mrs. Cox gave me no reason why it should not have been sent from Mr. Smith's, at Balham, to The Priory, at Balham.

"Her account to me was that he was to take it to Notting

Hill, and that she was to go there to fetch it—she going every day to let her house."

The matter was now left, as Mr. Lewis went on to question Mrs. Campbell on other points; but it came up again when Mr. Murphy examined her.

"The way it 'came out' about the laurel water," she said, "was, that Mrs. Cox went to the cupboard and said: 'Here is this bottle of laurel water.' My daughter said: 'You need not keep it. I shall not want it any more; you had better take it away.'"

Now a new counsel stood up to interpose for the first time—the Attorney-General himself, "sleepy Jack Holker", that brilliant advocate with the persuasive manner, whose nickname belied his penetrating shrewdness:

"Where was this?"

"This was in Mrs. Cox's bedroom—where she was at the time, and where my daughter was in bed at the time. Mrs. Cox was preparing the things to go away to Brighton."

Mrs. Campbell continued a little later:

"It struck me that it was strange that she [Florence] was receiving things from Dr. Gully, and that it would have been better if it had not been—but it struck me, too, that Dr. Gully had done it in kindness.

"I forgot to mention about this laurel water in my statement before the Solicitor to the Treasury, it had made so little impression on my mind. My daughter told me a few days since that Mrs. Cox had thrown the bottle of laurel water away. She told me a week ago, since my statement at the Treasury, that someone had been making inquiries about it."

It was unfortunate that Mrs. Campbell had forgotten to mention the bottle to Mr. Stephenson—the only effect was to bring it into greater prominence now. It was a pity also that it had not been kept, to allay the doubts about it so suddenly bred

in the minds of the jury and counter the suspicious questionings of Mr. Lewis and the Attorney-General. Now there could
only be damaging speculation about its contents.

There was bound to be surmise too about these meetings of
Mrs. Cox's with the doctor; but all that Mrs. Campbell could
say in answer to Sir John Holker was:

"I heard that Mrs. Cox had seen Dr. Gully going to the
station several times since my daughter's marriage with Mr.
Bravo, that she had asked him for some remedies for Jamaica
fever, and that she had had some prescriptions given her by
him. It was no affair of mine how often she had seen him."

No; but as Mrs. Campbell told the attentive court-room
about it now, she was ensuring that it would be very much the
affair of the Crown and Mr. George Lewis—when Mrs. Cox
took the witness-stand. But did she not realise that each time
she pointed the oblique finger of suspicion against Mrs. Cox
she also pointed it at her own daughter?

Her dilemma was obvious even in expressing, as she was
asked to do by Sir Henry James, the state of Florence's feelings
for Mrs. Cox. If she said that they were extremely close she
was throwing them together in a way that might make them
appear confederates in the eyes of counsel, who were waiting
for just such an admission, and of the jury; while if she said
that the two were no longer friendly she would imply a sudden
rupture that might be given an equally sinister meaning. So
taking the safe middle course, she replied:

"She is on quite good terms with my daughter."

And what did Mrs. Campbell have to answer Sir Henry on
her daughter's relations with Dr. Gully?

"I was under the firm impression in November, 1875, that,
much as I disapproved the acquaintance of my daughter with
Dr. Gully, no impropriety had occurred between them, and
I think so still." What mother worth her salt could say other-

wise when asked in open court about her daughter's virtue?
She went on:

"Mr. Bravo never pointed in his conversation to that
intimacy being a criminal one in his knowledge. It never struck
me that he thought the intimacy was of a criminal character,
and I don't think he thought it was; he looked upon it as 'an
extraordinary infatuation', as I had regarded it."

But a little later she replied to Mr. Murphy:

"With regard to the dislike for Dr. Gully, I heard the
deceased say that he wished he could annihilate Dr. Gully."

Mrs. Campbell might have asked herself why Charles wanted
to annihilate the doctor if he thought Florence's intimacy with
him not of a "criminal" character!

Where did the Campbells think Charles had got the poison?
Mr. Gorst asked Mrs. Campbell the question. She had already
explained to Mr. Lewis that the whole family and Mrs. Cox
had discussed the suicide theory at Brighton, and now she told
Mr. Gorst:

"There was a great deal of conversation as to where this
poison was obtained. My daughter suggested that he might
have helped himself to it from his father's stables—Mr. J. Bravo
having told my husband that he always kept it in his stables."

This explanation had an ingenious and ironic touch. Here,
on the one hand, was Mr. Joseph Bravo, going around saying
that The Priory was full of poisons and even visiting the police
to voice his misgivings at the discovery of antimony in Charles's
body; and here, on the other hand, was Florence, dismayed at
Mr. Bravo's sinister suspicions and bitterly resentful at his
"tampering" with Charles's drawers at the Temple, planting
the antimony on Joseph Bravo himself! But the validity of the
suggestion was another matter—and the court was to hear
about this next day.

Mrs. Campbell had mentioned Mrs. Cox's meetings with

Dr. Gully; she further intrigued the court by telling, in answer to a question from Mr. Lewis, of an approach by Florence herself to the doctor during Charles's illness:

"I heard from my daughter on the Thursday evening that she had sent Mrs. Cox to Dr. Gully for his advice, as to whether anything could be done for the deceased."

Later on, Sir Henry James elicited a little more from her:

"I am given to understand that the remedies suggested on the Thursday [a spinal mustard plaster, cold water applications to the stomach and minute doses of arsenicum] were suggested when the medical men had given up all hopes of the deceased, and some of the medicines were administered. I was told that they were suggested by 'a friend', and Dr. Gully's name, it would be likely, would not be mentioned in the family."

Did it seem significant to the jury, even while they could admire Florence's refusal to neglect any chance of saving Charles, that Dr. Gully's name kept cropping up in the story right up to Charles's death, despite the fact that relations between The Priory and Orwell Lodge were supposed to have been broken off months earlier? They were bound to ask themselves just what part the doctor, with his seemingly clandestine communications with Mrs. Cox, his prescription of laurel water, his recommendation of arsenicum and the rest in defiance of ordinary medical etiquette, was playing in the affair.

During her cross-examination by Mr. Lewis, Mrs. Campbell had to divulge a good deal about Florence's unhappy years with her first husband, Captain Ricardo, as well as details of her life with Dr. Gully which Florence had hoped and prayed would never be raked up again. The shadow of a past that might or might not have any bearing on the death of Charles Bravo was beginning to loom over the proceedings in the court-room of the Bedford Hotel in a way that would have been quite inadmissible in any ordinary inquest; and there was nothing that Florence could do about it. The net, it seemed, was deliberately being cast so wide that even if Florence escaped the charge of murder, she would never evade the shame—almost as bad in Victorian times—of being branded an immoral woman.

The court had heard much, while Joseph Bravo was giving evidence, about Charles's money affairs: now Mrs. Campbell threw a little light on Florence's. She told Mr. Lewis:

"Captain Ricardo settled £40,000 upon my daughter. Some of that was expectant upon the death of his mother, and upon her death that portion so expectant fell in. The interest of that money makes a portion of the £3,000 or £4,000 of my daughter's income.

"Mr. Bravo senior, on the second marriage, gave his bond to pay the interest on £20,000 to the trustees of the last marriage settlement. Florence had £200 or £300 a year, too, from her grandfather."

And to a question of Sir Henry James she replied:

"The settlement of the £20,000 will come to Mrs. Bravo after the death of Mr. and Mrs. [Joseph] Bravo."

What of Florence's suggestion that Charles had obtained the antimony from his stepfather's stables? Next morning—the thirteenth day of the inquest—the court saw Mr. Joseph Bravo standing once more at the table, called by Mr. Lewis to refute it categorically:

"I never kept tartar emetic, and it is not an accurate statement that I ever told anybody that I did. I never knew of antimony being applied to my horses."

Surely Joseph Bravo, uttering his words so forcibly, his long dark face so earnest in denial, could not be lying? And if it was not from his stables that the tartar emetic had come, Florence's wish must have been father to the thought and the quest for the source of the lethal dose was still on.

But before he stood down Mr. Bravo had something else to tell the court—something not very helpful to the cause of Mrs. Cox:

"I had a conversation about her returning to Jamaica. It was about two months after the marriage of my son that she called upon me at my office and informed me of the serious illness of Mrs. Margaret Cox [a relative in Jamaica]. Mrs. Jane Cox told me that it was the wish of Mrs. Margaret Cox that she should at once proceed to the island, and she called to ask my advice.

"I expressed a strong opinion as to the propriety of her going at once to the island. She urged that it would be inconvenient —that she knew not what to do with her boys. I told her it was for the boys' future welfare that she should go; that it was a duty she owed to her boys as well as to her relative to go at once.

"I urged in every way the propriety of her going, but all in vain. I think this occurred in the early part of March. It is not within my knowledge that she received a more pressing letter to go in April."

Mr. Bravo had prefaced these remarks by a modest recital of the help he had given Mrs. Cox in placing her boys at school and advancing her money when the rents of her Lancaster Road house were unpaid; and he had finished by pointedly saying: "I believed Mrs. Cox to be a very respectable woman."

Could anything be clearer than that Jane Cox had now lost her respectability in the eyes of her benefactor? But piqued though Mr. Bravo might be at her refusal to follow his advice, it seemed a little hard on her to be so roundly condemned for this alone. Was there something else that had caused her to forfeit his regard? At any rate, the jury could take note that Mrs. Cox was determined, even to the extent of flouting Mr. Bravo's advice, to stay at The Priory.

Mr. Lewis now read four letters from Charles to Mr. and

Mrs. Bravo, dated March and April of that year. In the one to his stepfather was a passage relating to money affairs:

"As the day on which we promised to repay you the £500 is only a week off, I may just as well ask if you approve the plan of deducting the amount from my allowance."

This was odd, for Mr. Joseph Bravo had not previously spoken of a *loan* of £500. He now therefore told Mr. Lewis:

"I gave the deceased £100 on his wedding day, and in addition the deceased had £1,100 from me between the 1st of January and the time of his death. Of this, £500 was a loan on the joint acknowledgment of his wife and himself, £100 was a gift from myself in January, and £500 was the proceeds of a security that was realised and the amount placed to his credit in the books of the firm. I sent him a cheque for the amount early in April. I did not apply the money which had come into my hands in payment of his loan, but sent the amount on.

"Since the death the sum of £1,166 had come into my hands arising from the sale of my son's securities, and out of this sum has been paid the £500 he borrowed. When deceased on the 26th of March wrote to me [passage quoted above] about the £500 loan from me to him I said, 'Let it lie'."

In not making clear in his first evidence that £500 of the £1,100 that he had handed Charles was a loan, Joseph Bravo was less frank than he ought to have been. And the revised explanation shows him as less generous than he had wanted to appear. But still there was no question of Charles being financially embarrassed.

Mr. Jepson Atkinson, a barrister friend of Charles's, who was called next, suddenly switched the interest from these background affairs to the forefront of the mystery. As he told of his intimacy with Charles at Oxford, where they had shared rooms, and later in communal chambers in the Temple, the court had no idea what he was leading up to. Then he said:

"I noticed that he before going to bed always took a deep draught of cold water; he used to drink it from the water bottle in his or my room, or wherever he was, without using a tumbler. This was an inveterate habit with him."

"He very often used my water bottle, that is, when we have been together. He was in the habit of coming into my room while I was in bed to read what he had written during the day, and so I noticed it. I visited his father's house up to about two or three years ago and often slept there when they lived at Lancaster Gate. Thus I had opportunities of observing that the same habit was with him then, and I also observed it when we went to Paris together two years ago."

Like a piece of a jig-saw puzzle it locked into the picture whose possibilities Mary Ann Keeber had opened up with her account of the daily filling of the water bottle in Charles's room; it fitted, too, the theory of Dr. Johnson that water drunk in the bedroom, and not burgundy at dinner, was the vehicle of the poison. How better could the killer's work be carried out—if killer there was—than by taking advantage of this long-standing habit? Considering Mr. Jepson Atkinson's pregnant words the jury, the lawyers, and everyone else in the court-room could have had little further doubt how the poison was administered.

The witness had something more to declare:

"He was, I can say, the last man in the world likely to commit suicide, and I should like to say why I think so: he was the best man I know, as a barrister, acquainted with medical juris-prudence. He was a very clear-headed man, with a great deal of common sense and very little sentiment—and no feeling for any woman would make him take painful and uncertain poison with the effect of which he was thoroughly acquainted."

It was a neat little character sketch, adding a few more facets to the impression of Charles Bravo that bit by bit the witnesses had been building up; and somehow it was convincing. Mr. Jepson Atkinson, in his brief testimony, had advanced the case for murder and tellingly confirmed belief in the likeliest way it could have been done.

Evidence from Charles's stockbroker, Mr. J. Meredith Meredith Brown, followed which showed him never to have been short of money, but anxious about Florence's securities, deeply interested in financial questions, careful, and likely to be worried by losses. And then there was the biggest stir in court that had occurred in all these thirteen days, when Mr. Burleigh Muir said: "Call Mrs. Cox!"

CHAPTER 14

MRS. COX

"CALL Mrs. Cox!" With that cry, on the afternoon of the thirteenth day, the atmosphere of the inquest changed. A chapter had ended and a new one was about to begin. Hitherto the witnesses, except for that very queer customer George Griffith, had been on the side of the angels—or at least of the authorities; essentially outsiders who through their knowledge of Charles and his background, affairs at The Priory, events in the sick-room, could help to set the scene in which Charles had lived and died and direct suspicion's still wavering finger. Now came the deeply involved, the principals—Mrs. Cox, Florence and Dr. Gully. The Crown might look on them as suspects, but wicked popular prejudice was already calling them guilty. And with the appearance of Mrs. Cox the inquiry in the billiards-room of the Bedford Hotel ceased, to all intents and purposes, to be an inquest; it became a trial: the place for witnesses at the big table became a dock, while at least some of the counsel ranged themselves into a prosecution and defence.

Demurely and with downcast eyes Mrs. Cox entered and took her place in answer to the call. She wore deepest black even to the bows on her skirt and the shawl that covered her stuff dress. These funereal tones were relieved only by the frilly kerchief in some lighter tint that was around her throat, and the curiously flowered and feathered bonnet that crowned her sallow spectacled features and jet drawn-back hair. If this long-awaited appearance was an ordeal to her, she did not show it; but then Jane Cox was not accustomed to parade her feelings. In fact, under that impassive, seemingly indestructible composure of hers was much less confidence than might appear. For in these last few weeks fate had dealt hardly with her; she was no longer in Florence's employ. The four-year friendship and partnership between them was over, and now it was not she but Mrs. Campbell who was installed at The Priory to listen to Florence's confidences, comfort and advise her. It had all come about as part of Mrs. Campbell's plan—formed as she had perceived the perils of her daughter's continued intimacy with her equivocally-placed companion—to separate and divide them. Mrs. Campbell had taken full advantage of the weeks at Buscot after their departure from Brighton to wean Florence away from Mrs. Cox's influence; and perhaps after all Florence had not needed much persuasion. For she too must have seen the risks of appearing to be too much hand-in-glove with her companion, who already looked like being in trouble over Charles's alleged admission that he had taken poison. Not that there had been any drastic break that could be commented on; as Mrs. Campbell had said in her evidence, they were on quite good terms. But Mrs. Cox was now on her own, in rooms in Manchester Street, Manchester Square, to which she had come after leaving Handsworth. And that was not all; she had been deserted by another friend. Mr. Joseph Bravo had made it clear that she was no longer *persona grata* with him— and only the two of them knew whether her refusal to take his advice about returning to Jamaica was the sole reason for this.

So Mrs. Cox, as she faced the packed and hostile court-room on the 27th of July, faced it alone. But at least there could be no doubt now what her course of action would be: first and foremost she was going to look after herself—no matter what might happen to anyone else.

In answer to questions by Mr. Murphy she began by telling

something of her past and her life with Florence, and was just describing her meeting with Charles when Mr. Lewis interrupted, to draw attention to her low, almost inaudible voice.

Mr. Murphy offered to repeat her answers for his benefit, and Mr. Lewis replied curtly that he preferred to hear the answers given, adding in that sharp sarcastic tone of his the barbed remark:

"A lady who can speak across the dinner-table can surely speak loud enough to be heard!"

At this some of the crowd at the back of the room stamped their feet and beat their umbrellas on the floor in vigorous applause.

"This is monstrous!" exclaimed Sir Henry James. Mr. Serjeant Parry threw up his hands in horror.

"Applause in a Court of Justice!" he protested. "It is terrible, it is fearful. There is a sort of reign of terror in reference to everybody who is called!"

Order was somehow restored and, louder now, Mrs. Cox continued her outline, mentioning Charles's refusal to let his mother know about Florence's acquaintance with Dr. Gully, Charles's and Florence's decision to keep her on, the anonymous letter. Charles, who had thought it was from Dr. Gully, had told Florence furiously:

"If you had not told me of the acquaintance with Dr. Gully before our marriage, I should have been upon the sea to-night!"

On this little note of Charles's jealousy the court adjourned; and next day Mrs. Cox opened with something on which everyone had been speculating since hearing of them from Mrs. Campbell—those meetings of hers with Dr. Gully:

"Some time in the month of March I was going to the Army and Navy Stores in Victoria Street, and I accidentally happened to meet Dr. Gully. Dr. Gully said: 'Will you ask Mrs. C.

Bravo to let me have the book with the newspaper cuttings, as they can be of no use to her now?' The book contained cuttings from newspapers which Dr. Gully had written. I had forgotten to return it.

"The next time I had any communication was very shortly after. I met him on my way to the Balham station, by accident, certainly not by appointment. I told him Mrs. Bravo had returned the book, and that she was very much annoyed at his sending anonymous letters. He denied having sent any, positively.

"I asked him if he would kindly let me have the treatment for Jamaica fever, which he had promised me some time before, as I was probably going out there soon.

"I had letters from my aunt wishing me to go to Jamaica when I told Dr. Gully I should probably be soon going there.

"Nothing was arranged about his sending me the treatment for fever. Some short time after this conversation I received a treatment from him when I was going to the station."

And here followed an odd story of Charles's behaviour which, if true, showed unpardonable conduct:

"On my way to the station Mr. C. Bravo met me, and gave me two letters, one he said was in Dr. Gully's handwriting, and he asked me to open it before him. Those were letters which he had from the postman, whom he met a short distance from The Priory.

"The letters were addressed to me. I told him I could not do it, as I was in such a hurry to catch the train. He insisted on my opening the letters. I was annoyed. . . . He said I could open them going along, which I did. One letter was from my son, and the other from Dr. Gully about the treatment, and filled three pages. Mr. Charles Bravo looked them through.

"He gave them back to me. He made some remark, but I don't remember what it was. When I arrived at my friend's house [Mrs. Fowke] I told her of his insisting upon opening the letter, and I remarked upon his jealousy in doing so.

"The next occasion (the third time) of my having any communication with Dr. Gully was outside the Balham station, when he was looking at the time-table. . . . He asked me how Mrs. Bravo was. The date of the meeting was after the miscarriage of Mrs. Bravo on 6th April, but I cannot give the exact date. I told Dr. Gully of her miscarriage, of the intense pain she was suffering in her back and of her want of sleep.

"I believe I asked him if sponging her back with cold water would not do her good. He said: 'Spinal washes and cold sitz-baths morning and evening.' I asked him what she could do to get sleep, and he said he would let me know what was best for her.

"I told him I was going to my house in Lancaster Road. I was at my house on the following Monday, the 10th April, and found the treatment."

Now came the explanation about the mysterious laurel water:

"I found also a small bottle of 'cerasee'; I know it is so spelt in Jamaica. The name of Smith, chemist, Balham, was upon it, and a label with the word 'Poison'.

"Having got the bottle and the treatment I told Mrs. C. Bravo what had occurred between Dr. Gully and myself. Mrs. Bravo did not want the cerasee. . . . She asked me to put it away in my room."

Juryman: "Is laurel water and cerasee the same thing?"

Mr. Murphy: "I think it is. Mr. Smith can tell us."

Mrs. Cox: "I took it away as she told me, and I put it in the medicine cupboard in my room. It was a small white bottle with a glass stopper."

It seemed plausible; but still it was a thousand pities that the bottle had been thrown away, and that the jury had only Mrs. Cox's and Mrs. Campbell's word for its contents.

Earlier Mrs. Cox had mentioned a letter from her aunt pressing her to go out to Jamaica. Now Mr. Murphy produced a second letter, dated from Jamaica the 23rd March, 1876, and received by Mrs. Cox on the 11th of April. He read from it this passage:

"Both Mrs. Margaret Cox and I [the writer was Dora Fox, Mrs. Margaret Cox's companion] think it would be better for you to be here. Could you not leave the boys and come over for a few months? Mrs. Cox thinks it would be for your interest to be here, as you understand business so well. Decide quickly."

Mrs. Cox now said that on receiving the letter she had read it to Florence, who had then sent for Charles. Mrs. Cox read the letter to him, and he said:

"It seems that you are obliged to go. I will take care of the boys while you are away, and I shall be very glad to see you here when you return."

So Charles was not thinking of dismissing Mrs. Cox after all! Here was a sensation: Mr. Murphy had shrewdly produced testimony from her that (besides showing Charles in a generous light) seemed to remove any motive she might have for killing him. On the face of it, the Crown's chief case against Florence's companion had broken down.

Having made his point Mr. Murphy switched back to the meetings with Dr. Gully; and Mrs. Cox went on:

"I met Dr. Gully on one other occasion besides those I have mentioned—when I was getting into the train at Balham station. It was subsequent to Monday the 10th April. I got into a railway carriage, and he got in after me. He asked me how Mrs. C. Bravo was, and I told him she was better. That meeting was also quite accidental."

Four meetings with Dr. Gully, apparently unplanned, apparently innocent, one in London, the other three at or near Balham station. What were the jury to make of them? Was Mrs. Cox trying to get Dr. Gully involved in the affairs of The Priory for some reason of her own? Was she trying to revive his interest in Florence—or make it *look* as if his interest were reviving? If there was nothing sinister here there was plainly a monstrous unwisdom.

Charles's jealousy and bad temper—this was the theme of Mrs. Cox's next disclosure. It all came out much as in her Treasury statement; but now here it was, broadcast at first hand to a fascinated audience, and sometimes in a voice so low as to be barely audible—the tale of Charles's marching down the drive at eleven o'clock at night, determined to leave Florence, of his flying off into a paddy when the convalescent Florence, wanting to lie down, had objected to his restlessness. And at each outburst it was Mrs. Cox who had been the mediator, skilfully manœuvring between the two of them and apparently retaining the affection of both.

Then came her detailed story of Tuesday's happenings and Charles's illness—and with it her bombshell, repeated from her Treasury statement:

"Charles said: 'Mrs. Cox, I've taken poison for Dr. Gully. Don't tell Florence.' "

But this was not all. She now capped her Treasury statement by adding something entirely new:

"We were alone together once on Wednesday, Mr. Royes asking me to stay in the room a little with Charlie. As soon as Mr. Royes Bell was out of the room, the deceased turned round and said: 'Why did you tell them? Does Florence know I poisoned myself?'

"Then I said: 'What have you taken, Charlie?' He turned his head round and said, impatiently: 'I don't know.'

"Immediately after that his wife came into the room, before I had time to make any observation to that. In answer to his question: 'Why did you tell them?' I had said: 'I was obliged to tell them—I could not let you die.'

"I did not mention this conversation to the surgeons or to anybody and I did not because I thought he did not wish me."

So, step by step, Mrs. Cox had built up her extraordinary story. First it was just Charles's admission of having taken poison, next it was Dr. Gully for whom he said he had taken it, and now there was Charles's reproachful question: "Why did you tell them?"

Each new version of the tale, each fresh trimming, underlined more strongly one of two things—either that Charles *had* committed suicide, or that Mrs. Cox wished people to believe he had. Forthcoming evidence might suggest which: meanwhile it was the puzzle at the very heart of the mystery.

It was Mrs. Cox's third day of evidence, and still she was in the hands of her own counsel, Mr. Murphy. She now told of her fifth and last meeting with Dr. Gully, on the Thursday of Charles's illness:

"Before our breakfast on the morning of Thursday, about nine o'clock, Mrs. Charles Bravo asked me to go to Dr. Gully to ask him if he could prescribe anything; that the doctors had given her husband up and had 'no hope'. We were alone. She said she should never be happy if every means were not taken to save him. I replied: 'It would be better not to send to Dr. Gully;' and she said she knew where he had saved one patient's life who had been quite given up by other doctors.

"I had said it would be better not, because I knew Mr. Bravo would not like it. I went out of the garden gate, down the road, and knocked at Dr. Gully's door. After some conversation with Pritchard, I went in Dr. Gully's library.

"When I saw Dr. Gully I told him that Mr. Bravo had told

me he had taken poison, and that he was not expected to live; that he was very ill indeed, and that Mrs. Bravo was anxious to know if anything could be prescribed for him.

"Dr. Gully asked me how he was suffering, and I told him of the sickness and of the agony Mr. Bravo was in; and Dr. Gully said that he thought that the condition was amenable to homœopathic treatment. He told me to give him two drops of arsenicum in a dessertspoonful of water—I don't remember now how often—to have a mustard plaster down the spine, and a compress over the belly. I went directly home to Mrs. Bravo and told her.

"I was present when Mrs. Bravo told the doctors about this treatment, and she said: 'They have had their way, and I, as his wife, will have mine.' She then told them what Dr. Gully had ordered; but his name was not mentioned. It would not have been a pleasant name to mention there. Mrs. Joseph Bravo gave the arsenicum herself."

Incidentally, Mrs. Cox provided the arsenicum from her own medicine chest. It was a pity that she had not been so forthcoming about Charles having taken poison when she had called on Sir William Gull later the same day.

Soon afterwards came Mr. Murphy's inevitable question about her addition of the words "for Dr. Gully". Mrs. Cox replied:

"It is a fact that then [at the first inquest] I did not give the words that Mr. Bravo had taken the poison 'for Dr. Gully'. My reason for omitting it is that, as far as I knew, there was no reason for his taking poison 'for Dr. Gully'; and I thought it would be such an injury to her (Mrs. Bravo's) reputation to make such a statement.

"I saw no harm in keeping back those words. At a subsequent period, when I had reflected upon the matter, I made a statement to the Treasury in which I mentioned those words.

"I had mentioned these words before I spoke of them to the Treasury. The first day of the inquest was on the 25th of April, and I went to Brighton the next day to look for lodgings, and told Dr. Dill then. There were reasons why I should tell Dr. Dill, and they are that he knew all the circumstances of the acquaintance of Mrs. Ricardo and Dr. Gully."

Friendly Mr. Murphy, Q.C., had finished with her; now it was the Attorney-General's turn, and "sleepy Jack Holker" was less amicable.

He began straight away by impugning her truthfulness. He read part of her testimony at the first inquest which Mrs. Cox had sworn to as the "whole truth".

Mrs. Cox: "That is what I said then."

Attorney-General: "Then! Now you say that there is a good deal in that which is not true?"

Mrs. Cox was silent and seemed to be in deep reflection, at the same time tracing imaginary patterns with her gloved finger on the table in front of her.

Finally she replied, after Sir John had repeated the question:

"I will not say that it is not true; but I own that I did not use the words that he took the poison 'for Dr. Gully'. I did say before the Coroner that the deceased did not explain to me why he had taken the poison."

Sir John: "Then you did not tell the whole truth?"

The point being made, the Attorney-General passed on to the main business of his cross-examination—and the court very soon learnt what that was:

Sir John: "Now, Mrs. Cox, you saw a good deal of Mrs. Ricardo and Dr. Gully; now, what do you suppose was the nature of their acquaintance?"

Mrs. Cox: "I thought he was very much interested in her."

Sir John: "Now, Mrs. Cox, will you tell us if you looked upon him merely as her friend or as her lover?"

Again Mrs. Cox said nothing. She looked down at the table, which she was fingering abstractedly, as if assessing the quality of the cloth.

Sir John repeated the question, and at last she replied:

"I cannot say exactly."

Sir John, more sharply: "I put it to you again. Did you know that Dr. Gully was her lover—Mrs. Ricardo's lover?"

Silence from Mrs. Cox, and a long pause. Then Sir John spoke again:

"You lived with her for four years, and I ask you, did you not know sooner or later during that time that Dr. Gully was Mrs. Ricardo's lover?"

Lover . . . the word fell once more on the spellbound court. Silence again from Mrs. Cox; then finally a low faltering answer:

"Yes, I think I did."

Sir John: "When did you first know?—was it at Leigham Court Road?"

Mrs. Cox: "Yes, I concluded so from his coming there so often."

And so the polite persuasive inquisition went on, dragging out the story of those years of Florence's widowhood, until Kissingen was mentioned. Then Sir John said:

"Before they went, you knew that Dr. Gully had been visiting Mrs. Ricardo?"

Mrs. Cox: "I must have known that he had been coming to see her."

Sir John: "As her lover?" The jury was never going to be allowed to forget that word and all its implications.

Silence, while the court waited expectantly. The Attorney-General repeated his question. Still silence, while Mrs. Cox went on stroking the table-cloth with her gloved finger. But this silence was as eloquent as the loudest "Yes". And, satisfied,

Sir John now drew the Coroner's attention to the time and the court adjourned for lunch.

The afternoon brought Jane Cox no respite from Sir John's pressure. He started with Kissingen again:

"At the time they went did you not know that they were lovers?"

Mrs. Cox: "Well, I do not know exactly what you mean by 'lovers', and Dr. Gully as her 'lover'. I should like to know what you mean."

Sir John: "You know that he was fond of her, and that she was very fond of him; that they were more than 'mere friends?'"

Mrs. Cox: "Well, I knew she was fond of him. He was extremely clever."

Sir John: "You know she loved him?"

Mrs. Cox: "I know she was fond of him."

Sir John: "Will you not go further?"

Mrs. Cox: "No. Well, if Dr. Gully had not been married it might have been a match."

The trips together, the doctor's constant visits to The Priory, piece by piece the whole tale came out. The Rome visit was mentioned; and still Sir John relentlessly pressed his single theme:

"Now, what was the demeanour of these two people—did they not treat each other as lovers?"

For a time it looked as if Mrs. Cox was not going to answer. Then at last a hesitant reply came out:

"I think they were fond of each other; there is no doubt of that. They kissed each other."

Florence's Brighton meeting with Charles, and their engagement, were spoken of.

Sir John: "Now, did you tell Mr. Charles Bravo how fond she was of Dr. Gully?"

Mrs. Cox: "She did so herself."

Sir John: "Did you tell him that Dr. Gully was Mrs. Ricardo's lover—that they had been abroad together for weeks?"

Mrs. Cox: "I did not tell Mr. Bravo this because Mrs. Ricardo told me she had told him."

Sir John: "Do you think—and you know the manner of man Mr. Bravo was—that if he had known as much as you have told us now he would have married Mrs. Ricardo?"

Mrs. Cox: "I believe he would have married her. . . . Mrs. Bravo never told me she was afraid her husband would find out about her previous conduct with Dr. Gully. She had no reason to fear, as she had told him everything."

Before the court rose that day it had heard details of the couple's married life at The Priory, Charles's illness—including Mrs. Cox's statement that she had thought she had told Mr. Harrison that Charles had admitted taking poison—his death, and Florence's and Mrs. Cox's stay at Brighton. Mrs. Cox said she had told Dr. Dill of the "poison for Gully" remark because Florence had been under him and he had advised her to break with Dr. Gully.

Next morning—the sixteenth day—the Attorney-General wound up his cross-examination. What had he established above all in the minds of the jury? That Florence and Dr. Gully had been lovers? Yes—but what exactly did he and Mrs. Cox mean by lovers? Mr. George Lewis, rising now on behalf of the Bravos, was going to make sure that no shadow of ambiguity remained about this. Adopting shock tactics, he went straight into the attack:

"From those conversations that you had with Mr. Charles Bravo before his marriage, did you believe that Mr. Bravo knew that Mrs. Ricardo had had criminal intercourse with Dr. Gully?"

"Criminal intercourse" . . . in two words he had removed the last doubt, stripped the last shred of glamour and romance from the Attorney-General's euphemistic term. A low, excited murmur filled the court-room.

Mrs. Cox, her expression masked behind her glinting eye-glasses, looked down at the table and said quietly:

"I knew that she had told him everything before the engagement."

Mr. Lewis, his voice rising sharply: "Will you answer my question, madam? Do you believe he knew she had had criminal intercourse with Dr. Gully?"

Mrs. Cox: "Knew it on the 1st of November?" (This was the approximate day of the engagement.)

Mr. Lewis: "That is the time I am speaking about."

Mrs. Cox: "No, not then."

Mr. Lewis: "Was it your impression from his conversation that he believed her to be a perfectly chaste woman?" With a cruelly effective choice of words he was turning the knife in the wound.

Mrs. Cox: "I believe before the marriage he knew everything, but not at that time. . . . He believed her to be a chaste woman, and I did not create any suspicion that she was different from that. I left her to tell him what she liked. I did not keep anything back before the marriage. Well, I did; but let me fully understand what you mean."

Mr. Lewis: "You say that you kept something back before the marriage; what was it?"

Mrs. Cox: "I kept back from him what Mrs. Ricardo told me after giving up her acquaintance with Dr. Gully."

Mr. Lewis: "What was it she told you?"

Mrs. Cox: "Of her intimacy with Dr. Gully."

Mr. Lewis: "What do you mean by 'intimacy'?"

Mrs. Cox: "You may draw your own conclusions."

Mr. Lewis, angrily: "No; I decline to do that. Tell me now, madam, was it a criminal intimacy with Dr. Gully that she told you of?"

Mrs. Cox was silent, stroking the table-cloth in that way that had become habitual with her. The tense court-room hung on her answer. Then it came out, slowly, barely audible:

"Yes; a criminal intimacy."

The buzz that ran around the public benches was a measure of the shocked surprise, the gloating satisfaction, of the sensation-hungry listeners. There was full freedom now to condemn this flagrantly immoral pair for a murder with which they had not yet even been charged!

After a pause Mrs. Cox went on: "But you will remember that I had not an idea of that before she told me. I did not think the intimacy was of that character. She told me of it the day before her leaving Brighton—before her marriage; and I urged her to tell Mr. Bravo. I did not hear her tell him; but he spoke to me upon the subject afterwards."

Mr. Lewis: "Did he speak to you and let you know that he knew that his wife's intimacy with Dr. Gully had been of a criminal nature?"

Mrs. Cox: "Yes, at Palace Green he told me."

It had been a rough passage for Mrs. Cox; and no one could say that Mr. Lewis had extracted from her what he wanted without a struggle on her part. But he had another piece of ammunition ready:

"Did you say at the Treasury: 'He (Mr. Charles Bravo) had no reason to take poison, as she (Mrs. Bravo), I know, had not had any communication with Dr. Gully since her marriage, and their acquaintance before marriage was, though very imprudent, I conscientiously believed, entirely of an innocent character'?"

This would show that, at the time of her Treasury statement, she was lying to save Florence's character.

Mrs. Cox: "Yes, I stated that."

Mr. Lewis: "How came you to state there, in that deliberate statement, that you 'believed' — conscientiously believed — her acquaintance with Dr. Gully 'before marriage' to be 'entirely of an innocent character' when you knew to the contrary?"

But Mrs. Cox was ready for this.

"I did not say there 'I believe it to be of an entirely innocent character'; I said I 'believed' it so to be, and so I did before she told me to the contrary.

"I kept it back wilfully; I did not think it necessary to bring forward Mrs. Bravo's name more than there was any occasion for."

She had won that little skirmish: who could prove the Treasury Solicitor, in taking down her statement, had not made an error that was never noted?

For almost the rest of that day Mrs. Cox sat there patiently answering Mr. Lewis's thrusting, aggressive questions. In telling how she went into Charles's room on hearing of his seizure she said:

"He screamed out very loudly for the 'hot water' but he did not say very loudly what he said to me ['I have taken poison,' etc.]. I don't know that Mary Ann could hear his words to me."

Here Mr. Murphy interposed, and Mr. Lewis called upon the Coroner to prevent him interfering at a "grave moment" in the witness's cross-examination. Then, turning to the jury, he said he left them to draw their own conclusions from such interruptions at such moments.

Mrs. Cox continued: "I don't know if she could have heard or not what Mr. Bravo said about the poison if she was there, for Mr. Bravo did not speak in a loud voice."

Did the jury think it strange that Charles had had the

presence of mind, in the throes of his sickness, suddenly to modulate his voice from a shout to a murmur inaudible to the near-by Mary Ann?

It was remarkable how unmoved and self-possessed this meek, black-clad woman managed to remain throughout Mr. Lewis's deadly inquisition. But once she did give way a little to emotion.

"I still feel great affection for Mrs. Bravo. I don't consider I swore falsely because I did not mention certain words. I did not because they would have injured Mrs. Bravo's reputation. I did not consider it swearing falsely."

Mr. Lewis: "Would you have considered it very wicked to have sworn falsely?"

Mrs. Cox's voice trembled and she looked down as she answered: "I never thought of myself; I thought of Mrs. Bravo. It was thinking of her that I withheld the words 'for Dr. Gully' in my statement to the Coroner."

When Sir Henry James took over from Mr. Lewis for the short remainder of that day's hearing there was an easing of tension. But poor Florence's character suffered one more blow. Mrs. Cox said:

"I observed soon after living with her this sad habit of hers of taking too much wine. I learnt from her that she had acquired that habit from her first husband; that she had suffered wretchedly from him; that he had used violence towards her; that she sometimes left him on that account, and that he sometimes left her without any assigned reason. I also learnt from her about Captain Ricardo having attacks of delirium tremens and that it was in relation to him that she acquired this bad habit.

". . . I did what I could to check her and restrain her from this habit of drinking, but not with success."

So now, in the eyes of the world, Florence was a drinker as

well as a bad woman; and next day—the seventeenth of the inquest—the sordid unveiling went on:

"In November, 1873," said Mrs. Cox, "—it was after her return from Kissingen—she had an illness, and Dr. Gully attended her. I made an inquiry as to what the illness was, and was told by Mrs. Ricardo that it was an 'unusual natural illness'. Dr. Gully said the illness arose from 'a kind of tumour', which, he said, was removed.

"I gave at that time entire credence to the statements made to me."

A long recital of events followed, and then Mrs. Cox declared:

"Since I have given up my position with Mrs. Bravo I have no resources."

Sir Henry James next asked the question that sooner or later was bound to come:

"Now, Mrs. Cox, had you any antimony in your possession or did you know of any being in use at The Priory while you were there?"

Mrs. Cox: "I never saw any in my life."

Sir Henry: "From all you heard and all you saw, had you any reason to suppose that Mrs. Charles Bravo had any antimony in her possession, or that she has ever used it in any way."

Mrs. Cox: "I never did."

To Mr. Serjeant Parry, who followed Sir Henry, she stated:

"Upon the solemn oath I have taken, no word passed between myself and Dr. Gully about poison in those interviews, or about antimony."

At Mr. Gorst's suggestion, Mrs. Cox's statement to the Treasury was then read; and in answer to a juryman's question she said:

"It was not within my knowledge that Mr. Bravo habitually drank water before going to bed."

A final question came from Mr. Cattley, the foreman. Did not the witness think it very strange that the deceased should have called out for his wife, and then told the witness, when she came instead of his wife, that he had taken poison, and "Don't tell Florence?"

Mrs. Cox: "I didn't hear him call 'Florence'. He only called 'Hot water, hot water, hot water', while I was there."

So after the best part of five days—long nerve-racking days for her—they had done with Mrs. Cox. She had been badgered and bullied, but she had never lost her head even under the fiercest attacks of Mr. Lewis. It might be too much to say that she had given nothing away that she did not want to; but she had not worsened her own case, even though she had not improved it. For what, after all, did her evidence amount to? From her own point of view, she had not entirely explained away those meetings with Dr. Gully, and her story (now surprisingly added to) of Charles's "poison" admission was still gravely suspect. Then there was the dubious matter of the laurel water, and those tales (unsupported except by Florence) of Charles's astonishing jealousy and bad temper. Also, she had admitted perjury—but was not the effect of this against herself much less than the effect against Florence? For it appeared that she had withheld vital evidence for the sole purpose of shielding her friend—a motive with which the jury might even sympathise a little though they could not approve it. And it was hardly Mrs. Cox's fault that her continued efforts to protect Florence had broken down under the Attorney-General's and Mr. Lewis's assaults, and that she had had to admit Florence's "criminal intimacy" with Dr. Gully—thus putting her ex-employer beyond the Victorian pale! Nor perhaps was it her fault that Florence's good name had been further blackened by Mrs. Cox's disclosure of her drinking habits. All this suited Mr. Lewis and Mr. and Mrs. Joseph Bravo admirably, and it was not a bad thing for Mrs. Cox either. For it might deflect attention from her to Florence. No; on the whole, she felt, as she returned to her lonely rooms at Manchester Street that Wednesday evening, she had reason to be not dissatisfied with her five-day ordeal.

CHAPTER 15

FLORENCE AND THE DOCTOR

"How many persons are suffering from Bravo on the brain? How many slip nightly from the pages of the special *Evening Standard* into a slumber whereof the inevitable features are a little dinner, a young man suffering from poison in a bedroom, a death-bed scene, and a swarm of crows feasting on the dead body? The 'Balham Mystery' is still the engrossing topic of the hour."

This choice tit-bit from *The Penny Illustrated Paper* for 5th August, which reported briefly some of Florence's evidence, showed the kind of thing Florence was having to put up with as popular interest in the inquiry reached its climax. The same sheet described her as "a decidedly graceful and handsome blonde (her hair has been dyed a canary colour), blue-eyed, and with a very winning and amiable expression of countenance". If there was any doubt about her notoriety before Mrs. Cox's evidence there was none now. For the crowd of casual idlers, the scandal-hunters, the eminent and fashionable in search of drama and excitement (Mr. Henry Irving and other celebrities were among them) who packed the court tighter than ever that Thursday, Florence was the supreme draw of this most sensational case since the Tichborne trial. Incidentally, the authorities now made a concession to supposed feminine refinement by excluding women from the proceedings.

Faithful brother William had escorted Florence to the

Treasury Solicitor, and it was on his arm that she now entered the hushed and expectant court-room. Heavily veiled and in deepest mourning from head to foot—the black contrasted strikingly with her canary-tinted hair—she was clearly under some emotional strain. Her hand was trembling perceptibly as she took the book, but on being sworn she kissed it firmly and decisively. Then she threw up the crape veil to expose her pale, set features and took her seat, making an effort to compose herself. Sir Henry James began his examination, and spectators noted that a deep sigh escaped her as she answered her first question. Thereafter she gave her replies calmly and distinctly, hesitating momentarily only once or twice.

She went through her story from the days of her first marriage—the harrowing time with Alexander Ricardo, his death, her association with Dr. Gully, her meeting with Charles, her renunciation of the doctor, Charles's confession to her of his "establishment", her "communication" to him.

Sir Henry, whose aim was to steal the thunder of the Crown and Mr. Lewis by getting her to tell "the worst" straight away:

"I must ask you to state without reserve of what that communication consisted."

Florence: "I told him I had been in Dr. Gully's society constantly from the time of the Leigham Court Road residence; that I had been journeys with him at home and abroad; and that I went to Kissingen alone with him. I told him of visits to Devonshire and Southsea, and the others. I told him all.

"While I was staying at Mr. Brooks's house in 1871 I suffered from an illness—it was in April, 1871, and Dr. Frodsham, of Worcester, attended me.

"There is no truth in saying that that illness was in any way connected with miscarriage." (Sensation in court.) "In 1874 I had a similar illness, and Dr. Dill knew what that illness was.

"I state upon my oath that that illness of 1871"—and here

Florence's voice shook and she was near to tears—"was not in any way connected with miscarriage, and was in no way the result of improper intimacy with anyone.

"I have to state that there was at one time an improper intimacy between myself and Dr. Gully. There was——"

She could not go on. She buried her face in her hands and sobbed. If this was what the scandal-seekers agog in the public benches were waiting for, here it was. But shame must have touched all but the most callous at this unpretty spectacle of a woman forced into open confession of her sins. In dead silence William escorted her from the room.

But very soon she was back; and she forced herself to continue:

"The first occasion of that intimacy was in 1873, on the visit to Kissingen, and there were 'intimacies' on the occasion of that visit—more than one.

"On returning to England I went back to the Leigham Court Road. In the November of that year I suffered from illness, and I was then attended by Dr. Gully."

Sir Henry: "That illness was a miscarriage."

Florence: "It was, and I did my utmost to conceal the fact of that from everyone about me. So far as I know Mrs. Cox did not know what that illness was, and I did all I could to prevent her from knowing it.

"The improper intimacy with Dr. Gully ceased on our return from abroad. . . . I stated at the Treasury that that was an innocent intimacy. When I informed Mr. Charles Bravo of the intimacy which had occurred between Dr. Gully and myself in 1873, he made me take my solemn oath before God that I would not divulge it to any other human being."

So now the jury knew that not only Mrs. Cox but Florence too had perjured herself in her Treasury statement.

Florence added: "I had told Mrs. Cox previously, at

Brighton, before Mr. Bravo 'proposed' to me. That was the first time that Mrs. Cox knew of this."

Her story continued, down to her dispute with Charles about her marriage settlement and her sending for Dr. Gully to advise her what to do about it.

Mr. Lewis here interrupted: "The fact is that Mrs. Bravo's private fortune was settled upon herself; but Mr. Bravo demurred to having the furniture and everything about the house settled upon her as well."

Florence: "The particulars of the settlement I left to my father, and this was the one matter brought to my notice."

That night Florence had little rest. Again and again she saw herself in that court-room, confessing her disgrace to the world. But she felt none of the relief that might have been some compensation for unburdening herself of her secret. She had not in fact told the whole story. And, tossing sleeplessly, she determined next day to make good her omission. Was it not better to do this voluntarily than have it dragged out of her by the Attorney-General or that horrible Mr. Lewis? And the morning papers, stressing her account of her intimacy with Gully at Kissingen, confirmed her resolve: as did a word with her father and Sir Henry James.

So her first words when the court reassembled caused a stir:

"Since I gave my evidence here yesterday," she said in a trembling voice, "I have made to my friends some communications which I have not made before, and my attention has been particularly called to the reports in the newspapers of my statement that my first (and only) intimacy with Dr. Gully occurred at Kissingen, on the visit in August, 1873.

"I was, when I gave evidence, most anxious that I should not appear to have been the mistress of Dr. Gully through all the years of my acquaintance with him."

The court wondered what was coming next. Sir Henry looked at Florence and said slowly and emphatically:

"In begging you now to tell the whole truth, I will only ask you to answer 'Yes' or 'No' to the question whether you were not improperly acquainted with him before that visit to Kissingen."

In the tensely hushed court-room the only sound was of Florence's sobs. Finally the tearful low-voiced answer came:

"Yes."

There was the truth—the whole truth. Its telling was the ultimate degradation that had haunted Florence ever since she had seen at Brighton that her affair with Dr. Gully must come out.

Sir Henry: "Have you any correction to make as to your evidence regarding the period after the Kissingen visit—that there was no further 'improper intimacy'?"

All Florence's pent-up emotion was now released in her eager answer:

"I have no correction to make in that. Upon my oath, there was no improper intimacy after that time. I informed Mr. Charles Bravo of the intimacy on the Kissingen visit only. I was anxious to appear to him not to have been the mistress of Dr. Gully for any length of time."

Tears came again when Florence said that, as far as she knew, Mrs. Cox had no idea of the character of the intimacy, and that she had never been intimate with Dr. Gully during Alexander Ricardo's lifetime.

But now Sir Henry steered her back to the main story and she spoke of the anonymous letter and its effect on Charles:

"He became livid with rage, but was not angry with me, but with the fact of such comments being made upon him and upon me."

A letter of hers to Mrs. Cox, dated March 12th from Buscot, contained this passage:

"As Charles cannot come down I have resolved to come home, being miserable without him and you."

Soon afterwards Sir Henry asked:

"There were occasions when he was rather harsh to you?"

Florence was in tears again:

"I do not wish to say anything against him. He did strike me once, but he burst into tears immediately he did it.

"During the last six weeks we were as happy as the day was long; this was while his mother was away at St. Leonards."

Then the old jealousy theme crept in again: Charles's resentment, reiterated "morning, noon, and night", his wishing to give up The Priory because Gully lived so near. She described the events of the Tuesday, not forgetting the quarrel as they had passed Gully's house; and here she significantly added to her Treasury statement:

"He said, with regard to Dr. Gully: 'We shall never get over it, and we had better separate.' "

So the tale went on, covering Charles's seizure, illness and death. She caused a slight sensation by disclosing the pretext for holding the first inquest at The Priory:

"As to the letter sent to the summoning officer in regard to the holding of the inquest, Mr. J. Bravo said it would be more pleasant to have the inquest at The Priory."

Of her Treasury statement, which Sir Henry then read, she said:

"I was too ill to sign the statement—in fact it was the next day I had brain fever."

Before handing her over to the mercies of Mr. Lewis, Sir Henry prompted from her the following formal declaration:

"I never purchased antimony in my life. I never had it, and never heard of it as tartar emetic, and excepting from what I have heard from Mrs. Cox, and from what I know through this inquiry, I do not know how my husband came by his death."

Mr. Lewis opened with Florence much more mildly than he had with Mrs. Cox. There were no shock tactics this time, and the only little difference was as to when, in the light of Charles's letter to Florence dated October 22nd from the Temple, she had told him the whole story of her intimacy with Dr. Gully. This ended the day's hearing, and as the August Bank Holiday was to follow, it was decided to defer until Tuesday Florence's further examination on account of the holiday crowds that would undoubtedly be attracted to the Bedford Hotel. So on the Monday a number of other witnesses were questioned instead: Mrs. Harford, an old friend of Mrs. Cox's; Charles Maddox, chemist's assistant, of Smith's, Balham; Dr. Moore; Mr. Harrison; Ellen Stone, cook at The Priory; Mr. Brooks; and Mr. Henry Smith, F.R.C.S.

Most of their evidence was of minor importance. It was hoped that Dr. Moore and Mr. Harrison, now recalled, might answer the query: What was the state of the water bottle shortly after Charles's seizure? But unfortunately neither of them could help much here. When Mr. Harrison had poured himself out a drink at midnight the bottle was, he said, about three-quarters full; but of course it might have been replenished—or changed. Mr. Brooks, giving details of Florence's marriage settlement, added another facet to Charles's character:

"When Mr. Bravo called upon me for the first time on 15th November—I had heard he would call—I rose from my chair to shake hands with him and offer my congratulations upon his being about to marry an old friend of mine. He said: 'Damn your congratulations; I only want the money'. . . . I was annoyed at his manner, and referred him to my partner when he called again."

Mr. Henry Smith, the King's College surgeon and relative of Charles, who had visited the sick-bed with Dr. Johnson on the Thursday afternoon, made some interesting points.

"Mr. Bravo, I should apprehend," he said, "had some knowledge of medicine, certainly he had of surgery.

"It is a common thing for people to put tartar emetic—not a poisonous dose—into the wine of a person whom it is desired to cure of drinking habits. I have done so myself.

"There is nothing in the post-mortem inconsistent with the theory that he took laudanum himself, and then tartar emetic to get rid of that narcotic poison."

But here Mr. Lewis cut in—very sharply—to make Mr. Smith admit that equally there was nothing in the post-mortem which pointed to Charles's having taken laudanum and then tartar emetic!

The surgeon added:

"If a man had swallowed, or thought he had swallowed, laudanum, hot water would be the proper thing to call for to make him sick—it is a very common emetic.

"Mr. Bravo used to come to the hospital to see operations. He had no opportunity in his visits of obtaining any poison. The drugs are kept in a part of the hospital altogether apart from the operating-room, and he never went to any other part than the operating-room."

But he did make an admission to Sir Henry James bearing on that earlier suggestion of Sir Henry's to Amelia Bushell that there was an epileptic in Charles's family:

"One sister of the late Mr. Bravo is deaf and dumb, and the other is in a convent. I consider she is feeble in mind and body." So, belatedly, Sir Henry and the Campbells had made their point after all.

Refreshed by two quiet days at The Priory, Florence took her seat in the court-room on Tuesday morning and faced Mr.

Lewis with a little more confidence. Her first statement was a denial:

"I was not aware that my husband was in the habit of drinking water before going to bed." This amounted either to a downright lie or to a firm assurance that he did *not* drink water on retiring.

Mr. Lewis then read a number of letters from Charles to Florence written in February, March and April. Then he asked:

"After hearing these letters read, do you mean to say, and to tell the jury, that your late husband was always—'morning, noon, and night'—speaking in disparaging terms of Dr. Gully?"

Florence: "I do. I told others in his lifetime than Mrs. Cox. I told my mother. . . ."

Mr. Lewis switched back to the Malvern days. He was nearly ready to play a trump card. Answering his questions Florence said:

"I have pledged my oath that no criminal intimacy with Dr. Gully occurred in the lifetime of my first husband.

"At the time I was at Malvern there was nothing occurred between myself and Dr. Gully which I wished to keep and to be kept a secret, which I was ashamed of my servants speaking of, or that I desired anyone to keep secret.

"I had a maid at Malvern named Laundon."

Poor Florence. She had no idea what was coming.

He produced a letter in her handwriting, dated November 16th from Buscot but with no year (though internal evidence showed it to have been written in 1870). He read it:

Dear Laundon,—I am quite satisfied with your apology, and, as I told you before, that had it not been for Field (who is not worthy of you), you would never have been rude to me. Nobody regrets more than I do that circumstances compelled my parting with you, for I like you personally and you suit me in every way. I will do all I can to procure you a good situation, and hope you may soon succeed in getting one. I hope you will never allude in *any way* to *any one* of what passed at Malvern. Let it all be buried in the past, and if *anybody* questions you please refuse to answer *any inquiries*. I shall remain here till January, and then think of having a house at Clifton.

With kind remembrances to yourself, yours truly,

FLORENCE RICARDO

Burn this.

Florence went white to the lips and a murmur went round the court-room. Putting down the letter Mr. Lewis asked with biting clarity:

"What was it, Mrs. Bravo, that was never to be alluded to to anyone, and to be buried, and no inquiries answered?"

As if begging him to believe her, Florence burst out:

"It was to my attachment to Dr. Gully; but not to a criminal attachment then!" Tears ran down her cheeks and she bowed her head.

Suddenly she straightened up and brushed the tears away; and now her words came pouring out in a torrent of protest and revolt:

"That attachment to Dr. Gully has nothing to do with this case—of the death of Mr. Charles Bravo! As to that, I will answer any questions. I have been subjected to sufficient pain and humiliation already, and I appeal to the Coroner and to the jury, as men and as Britons, to protect me. I think it is a great shame that I should be thus questioned, and I will refuse to answer any further questions with regard to Dr. Gully!"

If Florence was acting, it was superb: the words, uttered with such tragic force, seemed to come straight from her over-burdened heart. The crowd in the public benches at least had no doubt of her sincerity, for they stamped their feet in a dumb show of approval. As for Mr. Carter and the jury, those particular Britons, embarrassed and perhaps sympathetic though they were, could not help her. Meanwhile Mr. Lewis stood impassive, his monocle glinting in his eye, waiting to go on.

When there was silence he said:

"You see the words wherein you express the hope that she will not allude to 'what passed at Malvern'. Now, Mrs. Bravo, what 'passed' at Malvern?"

Florence: "Why, she knew of my attachment to Dr. Gully; and"—heatedly—"it seems to me that you and such as you think it is impossible for a woman to love a man without what is wrong occurring! According to you, that must occur."

Mr. Lewis ignored this, and pressed the point:

"You use the terms, 'Not to say anything of what passed at Malvern'. What passed?"

Florence, obstinately: "I have explained it."

Mr. Lewis: "Did you mean your attachment to Dr. Gully by these words?"

Florence: "So I have told you."

Mr. Lewis, having scored his point, passed to other matters. But he soon tripped Florence up again.

Florence: "In 1874 and 1875 Dr. Gully did not profession-ally attend me nor prescribe for me, because he knew I could prescribe for myself."

Thereupon Mr. Lewis called for certain prescriptions made up for "Mrs. Ricardo" at Smith's the chemists and read:

"May 25, 1874. Oil of savin, thirty drops."

Florence, confused: "I had forgotten, because he prescribed homœopathy, and does not advocate allopathy."

How was it that Florence had thought Charles was pressed for money by his ex-mistress (or her sister) when this was not the case? To underline his question Mr. Lewis read those two letters from herself to Mr. Joseph Bravo, written in early May from Brighton. All Florence could say to this was:

"At that time I thought he was pressed for money by 'this woman'. I thought that was one of the causes [of his suicide], and I thought jealousy was another. I think that—even after hearing his letters read to-day.

How came Charles to commit suicide if two days before his illness he was—as she had described him in a letter to her mother—"as happy as a King"?

Florence: "It is my impression that two days before the seizure he was 'as happy as a King'."

A few more questions and Mr. Lewis's inquisition was over. But there was little relief for Florence: it was now Mr. Gorst's turn, for the Crown.

It was not long before he too caught her out. The separation between Florence and Ricardo was referred to.

Florence: "Dr. Gully was not one of the trustees in the separation deed on my behalf. Dr. Gully did not even know of the separation."

Mr. Gorst, holding up a parchment: "Why, here is the deed of separation, with your signature, and Dr. Gully's and Mr. Brooks's names as your trustees!"

Florence: "I had no recollection of it, Mr. Gorst."

For a time Mr. Gorst concentrated on the period before Florence's marriage to Charles. Speaking of her meeting with Dr. Gully at the lodge of The Priory he asked:

"Did Dr. Gully say anything about the time that Mr. Charles would be likely to live after marrying you?"

Florence: "Dr. Gully had never seen Mr. Bravo. . . . He reconciled me to Mr. Bravo in regard to his action on the settlements, and he reconciled me to surrender all my goods and chattels into Mr. Bravo's hands. I acted upon Dr. Gully's advice, and withdrew my objections to Mr. Charles Bravo's views."

Mr. Gorst, ironically: "So, in fact, it was Dr. Gully who made the match at last?"

Another question brought this answer from her:

"With regard to my statement at the Treasury, I did not know that it was to be made public, or I should not have disclosed the disputes I had had with my husband. I thought the only purpose of my statement was to throw some light upon this 'mystery'."

Later:

"I could not have told Mrs. Cox that I had acquired the habit of drinking more than was 'good for my health' during the lifetime of my late husband [Captain Ricardo]. I could not, for it would not have been true."

A cryptic matter was hinted at by another exchange:

"I do not know whether, just after my late husband's death, soon after I went to Brighton, I made a statement to Dr. Dill, making a grave charge against my late husband." She added an irrelevant remark, which Mr. Gorst dismissed impatiently.

"I don't mean that! But did you make a statement to Dr. Dill which involves a grave charge against your late husband?"

Florence: "I have answered you, and can say no more. I saw Inspector Clarke, of Scotland Yard, at Brighton, and knew that he was making inquiries about my late husband's death. I told him he might go to Dr. Dill."

Mr. Gorst: "Did you refer Inspector Clarke to Dr. Dill for the doctor to tell him particulars about the late Mr. Bravo which you could not, but which you had told the doctor?"

Florence was silent: and Mr. Gorst pressed her. She went as far as to own that she had sent Inspector Clarke to Dr. Dill to inquire about her health, and then burst out:

"I shall not answer on the subject you mean, and I will not—there!"

But Mr. Gorst persisted: "Did you not know that Clarke would hear a most serious charge against your husband from Dr. Dill—a charge made by you?"

Florence: "No, I did not. I did tell him that if he wanted to learn something he could go to Dr. Dill."

And that was all about this little mystery. What had Florence told Dr. Dill—and if it was something that would strengthen her rather shaky position now, why did she not divulge it?

Mr. Gorst had finished, and now Florence faced Mr. Serjeant Parry, who elicited from her that Dr. Gully had honourably stood by his pledge not to see her after her marriage. But when Mr. Murphy took over, something more interesting emerged—about her relations with Mrs. Cox.

Mr. Murphy: "And now, Mrs. Bravo, do you not feel towards Mrs. Cox the same kindly regard you always have felt?"

Florence was silent for a while, her eyes downturned. Then she said in a low voice and as if choosing her words very carefully:

"I think she might have spared me many of these painful inquiries to which I have been subjected."

It was perhaps the most pregnant sentence spoken in that court-room: an epitaph on a dead friendship: Florence's last word to Jane Cox: a message whose full meaning and depth of reproach only the ex-companion and intimate sharer of four years' confidences could appreciate. It signified the end between them.

A few more questions from Sir Henry James and Florence's ordeal-by-evidence was over. Her final answer to him was:

"I did make a will after I was married, and left all I had to Mr. Charles Bravo, even to my jewels. I trusted him thoroughly."

On the next day—the twenty-second of the inquest—only

three more witnesses remained to be examined—an under-housemaid at The Priory; George Griffith's wife Fanny, who told of throwing away some antimony of her husband's before they returned to The Priory in May, 1875; and Dr. Gully himself.

If it was the final humiliation for Florence to have her affair broadcast to an eager, gloating public, so it was for James Manby Gully, M.D. Day by day he had followed the evidence with growing misgivings and he knew now that, whatever happened, his reputation was ruined irretrievably. All his thirty years of work at Malvern, his career as a hydropathic pioneer, would go for nothing and his name be trailed in the mud, both by the public and the medical profession. And that was not the only thing he had to worry about: already in the popular mind he was not only a seducer—he was also being pointed at as a possible partner in murder. Oddly, he had not been subpœnaed to testify at the inquest; but well aware that his absence from it and his continued silence would increase the feeling against him he decided to appear voluntarily. So after the two minor witnesses had had their say his name was called and he took his place at the table, being allowed to remain seated as he had recently been ill. Poor Dr. Gully. Even this small concession was grudged him: churlish protests came from the public benches and from some of the jury too.

The doctor described himself and then explained his presence:

"I come here to be examined entirely at my own wish."

Mr. Serjeant Parry: "We have heard of your unfortunate intimacy with Mrs. Ricardo—now Mrs. Bravo."

Dr. Gully: "Too true, sir; too true. I have read Mrs. Bravo's statement as to that intimacy. I am sorry to say that statement is true and correct, and I feel my position most bitterly in having to stand here and say this.

"I have heard the rumours and suspicions which have been

aroused in this matter, and I upon my solemn oath declare that I had nothing whatever to do, directly or indirectly, with Mr. Charles Bravo's death.

"I have received many insulting and threatening letters."

He went on to deny having seen Florence since the previous November, and said he had never met Charles Bravo. He also denied ever having had any tartar emetic since going to Malvern in 1842, and refuted energetically the suggestion that he had given Griffith an order to the Malvern chemist for any tartar emetic. He then mentioned his meetings with Mrs. Cox and a casual encounter with Griffith a month back.

Mr. Lewis took over, and the court had to wait some little time for the rough handling of the doctor that everybody guessed was coming. The lawyer was choosing his moment. It arrived when the Malvern days came under review.

Mr. Lewis: "Was it during the period she was a patient of yours that the attachment between you commenced?"

Dr. Gully: "Well, it commenced after a fashion; it was a friendly understanding. She was alone a great deal, and she used to have tea with me at my house."

Mr. Lewis, brusquely: "That is no answer to my question! Did the 'attachment' commence then?"

Dr. Gully: "If you like to call it so—yes."

Mr. Lewis: "Do you know what passed at Malvern at that time that Mrs. Ricardo should desire her servant 'never to allude to' and 'to answer no inquiries' to 'anyone' about?"

Dr. Gully, slowly and after a little thought: "I cannot conceive what that was; there was nothing passed between us that need not be known. I knew she had discarded her family for me in the spring of 1871, when I returned from abroad."

Mr. Lewis was working up to his point: "You knew that she had given you her entire affections; given up for you her home, family and all—even to her good name?"

Dr. Gully: "I knew she had been given the chance of giving me up and had refused."

Mr. Lewis's voice rang through the court-room in a final challenge:

"You knew she had given up her name for you—her good name—her honour?"

Squarely the doctor faced his accuser; in his expression there was sorrow, weariness, almost resignation:

"Well, she had given up her home; but what do you mean by her honour?"

"Mr. Coroner, I really must protest!" It was Mr. Serjeant Parry, on his feet in angry defence of his client. "This inquiry is in regard to the death of Mr. Charles Bravo, and the questions which are being put are inflicting moral torture on the witness and are totally irrelevant to the inquiry! I would respectfully ask you, sir, to disallow this kind of questioning."

But again the sheepish Mr. Carter felt helpless to intervene. It would have needed a stronger man than he to check the aggressive, dominating Mr. George Lewis. So once more the witness had to answer—and Mr. Lewis won his point.

"There came a time when she sacrificed her honour for me." It was not a pleasant sight to see this eminent and ageing doctor, already disgraced, driven into this ultimate admission of un-chivalrousness.

More questions followed; and finally Dr. Gully was stung into revolt:

"I don't see the relevancy of these questions!"

Coroner: "You are a witness, sir, and not a judge of the relevancy of questions."

So the interrogation went on, tendentious, suggestive, provocative; and almost every thrust the doctor turned away with a denial. But what did that matter to Mr. Lewis? True or false, might not the implications shrewdly packed into his barrage of questions have their desired effect on the jury—soon to decide on their verdict?

Mr. Lewis gave place to Sir Henry James, and Sir Henry to Mr. Serjeant Parry, whose last question brought this reply:

"Captain Ricardo was never a patient of mine nor of my partner's."

One more question from the jury and it was over. Like Florence, her "ancient lover" (as the newspapers called him) had faced the music; and he came away stripped of whatever remnants of dignity, self-respect and honour he had not already parted with. But what had come out of his evidence? Was there any real indication that he was concerned in Charles's death—or that he and Florence were still so close that Florence might have killed Charles in order to return to him? Perhaps people forgot to ask themselves this. After all, they had something almost equally telling against him: in that court-room he had been virtually tried and found guilty of immoral conduct with a pretty woman.

And the same thing applied to Florence. She too had been on trial for immorality; but round her neck, like a millstone, had been something else besides her association with Dr. Gully; there had been her friendship—was it confederacy?—with Jane Cox. She might have won the crowd's sympathy in the "moral torture" to which she had been subjected, but her evidence covering the months of her marriage had not altered the impression that, if Mrs. Cox was suspect, she was suspect too.

At all events the last word of evidence had been heard and the die was cast. They could but wait now for the verdict. Did the chief actors in the drama think they knew what that verdict was going to be—Florence at The Priory with her mother and perhaps Mr. Campbell and William, Mrs. Cox alone in her rooms off Manchester Square, Dr. Gully at Orwell

Lodge with the faithful Pritchard, and Mr. Joseph Bravo at Palace Green, burdened now with the further worry of his gravely sick wife?

Was it to be a victory for the Campbells or for the Bravos?

CHAPTER 16

WILFUL MURDER

1 *The Jury Pronounces*

AFTER Dr. Gully had been heard the court was adjourned for a day to enable the Coroner and his assessor to prepare their summing up, and it assembled for the last time on the 12th August. The Coroner then addressed the jury.

It was a fair and comprehensive summing up, putting clearly the points at issue and the possible alternatives of suicide, accident and murder. Significantly, it was confined almost entirely to the few days before and during Charles's fatal illness. Never once did Mr. Carter mention the past; and in ignoring the painful events of Florence's widowed years he seemed to be showing what he really thought of the liberties—powerless to curb them though he had been at the time—that Mr. Gorst and Mr. Lewis had taken in order to stress the motive she might have had for murder. As he re-told the familiar story of the four days of Charles's seizure, illness and death, there came before the eyes of all in that court-room, for the last of many times in that prolonged inquiry, the vivid scenes of the dinner for three, Charles at his bedroom door calling for help, and on his death-bed in the throes of an unknown poison, the bewildered doctors vainly questioning him. And at the back of the whole picture were the two enigmas which Mr. Carter stressed to the jury: Mrs. Cox's disputed report to Mr. Harrison of Charles's admission about taking poison, and

Charles's steadfast denial of having taken anything but laudanum.

The jury were about to retire when one of them, Mr. Hunt, made a query. It referred to the question put to Florence by Mr. Gorst as to whether, on going to Brighton after the funeral, she had not made a grave charge against Charles's character to Dr. Dill. Mr. Hunt now said:

"You have directed us to inquire into the character and habits of this unfortunate young man, but I wish to refer you to the evidence of Dr. Payne of the post-mortem examination.

"I believe he there said there was no appearance of disease in the body, except what had been induced by the poison, and that it was in all other respects a perfectly healthy body. I take it, then, that remark was exceedingly comprehensive, and that there was no trace of disease whatever.

"I make that remark in consequence of the question asked about Dr. Dill."

There was an undertone of mystery about all this which Sir Henry James hardly removed when he hurriedly interposed:

"The jury will forgive me, but as a consequence of the remark just made by this gentleman, Mr. Hunt, I hope there will be no conjecture. With reference to this question, it was the duty of the Crown counsel to bring to your knowledge what they wished to convey. As they have not done so, it is no part of your duty to consider that point at all, and I believe, moreover, that this conjecture would prove to be erroneous."

Who can say what Florence, ill and overwrought from her recent tribulations, confided to Dr. Dill at Brighton? Was it perhaps that Charles himself had been administering antimony to her in an attempt to cure her of her drinking? (Such a treatment was known, as Mr. Henry Smith had testified.) Or was it—and here Mr. Hunt's veiled reference to disease seems to give a clue—that he had been suffering from some physical

taint, hardly to be mentioned in public, like venereal disease?
But whatever it was, the fact remained that Dr. Dill had not
been called as a witness and it was therefore, as Sir Henry told
the jury, no part of their duty to consider the point at all.

At half-past eleven the jury retired to consider their verdict.
Two and a half hours later they were still deliberating, and the
foreman sent out a request for writing materials. Then at
twelve minutes past three the door of the court-room opened
and, in a sudden hush, the sixteen jurymen filed in solemnly
and took their places. The Coroner called their names to see
that all were present and asked:

"Have you agreed upon a verdict, gentlemen?"

"We have," Mr. Cattley replied, "and we have it in writing."
And as he handed the Coroner a sheet of paper all the jury stood.
The silence, the tensely watching faces of counsel and public,
bespoke the almost intolerable suspense of this culminating
moment. Slowly and deliberately the Coroner opened the
paper and read it to himself. He turned to the jury and said:

"Are you unanimous in delivering this verdict? Have you
twelve jurors agreeing with it?"

Foreman: "We have more than twelve."

Coroner: "Then I will read the verdict of the majority."

Clearing his throat he read out in a loud voice:

"We find that Mr. Charles Delauney Turner Bravo did not
commit suicide; that he did not meet his death by misadventure; that he was wilfully murdered by the administration of
tartar emetic; but there is not sufficient evidence to fix the
guilt upon any person or persons."

Wilful murder. Publicly, officially, the words were out.
Immediately the crowd in the public benches started shouting,
stamping, beating their umbrellas on the floor. The verdict
was murder—but, for the ghoulish court-room crowd, murder
was not enough. What spoiled their Roman holiday, damped

their twenty-three days of mounting desire for blood with a woeful anti-climax was the fact that no killer had been named. They had been denied their victim (or victims): so in an orgy of frustration at the jury's pronouncement they crowned their uncouth behaviour of the last three weeks with this final contempt of court. When the Coroner's hammerings on the table had silenced them Mr. Cattley, on behalf of his fellow-jurors, made a request for some remuneration as a recompense for the personal inconvenience and loss that they had suffered, and the Coroner agreed to pass their request on: meanwhile, he said, he was only empowered to give them twelve shillings—the total sum to be shared between all the jury for their twenty-three sittings!

After an adjournment the jury returned to sign the inquisition form. To this formal document Mr. Mark Cattley and twelve colleagues put their names, the other three having dissented from the murder verdict. (The seventeenth member of the jury had retired through illness early in the case.) A few words of thanks from both sides and the Coroner discharged the sixteen. Their unenviable work was done: and as the door of the Bedford Hotel billiards-room closed on them and Mr. Carter and the last of the officials, there ended one of the most fabulous inquests in legal annals. In its twenty-three working days forty-three witnesses had been examined. Costs were something like £15,000, much of this being fees to the eminent lawyers engaged by the various interests. Sir Henry James had received, in addition to the heavy fee with his brief, a hundred guineas a day; Mr. Murphy, called on the 17th July, had received fifty guineas a day as well as his retainer; a similar sum went to Mr. Serjeant Parry, appearing on the 22nd; to the three juniors engaged went over twenty-five guineas a day each; and Mr. George Lewis took a flat thousand guineas.

And what had this inquiry achieved? A partial success for

the Crown, of course. A bitter reverse for the Campbells, who had fought so hard for that other verdict. And a victory for Mr. and Mrs. Joseph Bravo. But what a limited victory after all. "Not sufficient evidence to fix the guilt upon any person or persons." The world might point its finger and condemn, but what use was that to him and his wife if the law was powerless through lack of evidence to do the same—as the wording of the jury only too plainly hinted would be the case? "Her [Florence's] detractors stated that 'she dyed her hair', but they did not prove she poisoned her husband," as one writer put it.* And at what a price in legal dignity had this Pyrrhic victory been bought. "Public feeling has been revolted," said *The Times* next day, "by the manner in which the investigation has been conducted, and by the lengths to which it has been pushed." The *Daily Telegraph* declared: "The expressions of public opinion which have been heard in the court have been, to say the least, indecent. The altercations which have passed between the learned gentlemen engaged in the case have been far from seemly." Thus the *Saturday Review*: "It is hardly too much to say that the inquiry as to the death of Mr. Bravo is, in every way, one of the most digusting public exhibitions which have been witnessed in this generation."

The *World* had a special rebuke for the jury: "Nothing can excuse the offensive manner in which the jury conducted themselves when Dr. Gully appeared, noisily demanding, in reply to Mr. Serjeant Parry's request that he might be accommodated with a seat, that the aged if vigorous medico should stand." And many papers blamed the unhappy Mr. Carter for failing to control the proceedings better. But could anybody but a High Court Judge have handled that unruly pack of lawyers?

On another point the *World* wrote sound sense. "With

* *Recollections of Forty Years* by L. Forbes Winslow. (John Ousely, 1910.)

reference to the mode in which the cross-examinations were conducted," it said, "it is desirable to remember that the exceptional nature of the case rendered a certain amount of exceptional pertinacity inevitable. It should be borne in mind that this inquiry had about it a good deal of the nature of a family quarrel—and these quarrels are the bitterest of all—fought out in a public court. It was the object of Mr. Bravo's friends not only to find out how he died, but to clear his memory from a stain. The circumstances under which he married the lady who is now for the second time a widow were not particularly creditable to his character as a man. To vindicate his character it was necessary, if possible, to disprove the veracity of the two chief female witnesses; and when Mrs. Bravo excited admiration by 'turning round upon her persecutors' it must not be forgotten that a letter had just been read, of whose existence she was probably unaware, containing a sentence which at first sight seemed essentially to conflict with her oral testimony. These considerations may not justify 'the persecution', but they perhaps go some way towards explaining why questions, which naturally and rightly appear irrelevant, and which can have been little less than torture, were pressed with a relentless pertinacity."

The next move after the inquest verdict was up to the police. There was little that they could do. The Priory had been searched for poisons weeks ago, and the inquiry had produced no evidence that would justify an arrest being made. So on the 12th August the Commissioner of Police issued the following notice:

MURDER: £250 REWARD. Whereas, on the 21st of April, 1876, Charles Delauney Turner Bravo, of The Priory, Balham, died from the effects of tartar emetic, and a Coroner's jury has returned a verdict that the deceased was wilfully murdered, the above reward will be paid by Her Majesty's Government to any person who shall give such information and evidence as shall lead to the discovery and conviction of the murderer or murderers in this case, and the Secretary of State for the Home Department will advise the grant of Her Majesty's gracious pardon to any accomplice, not being the person who actually committed the murder, who shall give such evidence as shall lead to a like result. Information to be given to Superintendent Williamson, Detective Department, Great Scotland Yard, London—E. Y. W. HENDERSON, *Commissioner of Police of the Metropolis.**

2 *Pros and Cons*

And what of Florence, now that it was a police matter and there was no longer any refuge for her in the possibility of Charles's suicide? Shattered and stunned, she hid herself in The Priory to receive the consolations of her family, empty though these must have been, considering the implications of the verdict. With feverish interest she had read the papers and seen that they all agreed with the murder finding though some regretted that the jury could not go further and name the killer or killers. Was she still, in the face of all this, clinging to the suicide idea? If so, she was (apart from her loyal family, Mrs. Cox and the unrepentant Sir William Gull) a voice crying in the wilderness. And even if Charles had killed himself on some sudden irrational impulse, would he, with his knowledge of forensic medicine, have chosen antimony with its agonising effects?

* There was one claimant of the reward. In December a Mr. Raymond of Torquay wrote to the police at Scotland Yard saying that he had sent Charles Bravo six packets of 'Heyman's Remedy', his cure for dipsomania (presumably containing antimony). The police forwarded the letter to the Treasury Solicitor, who thought the claim a gross swindle and recommended no action.

There was another point: his complete indifference as to what had caused his illness, hailed by the suicide clique as proof that he knew what he had taken. They overlooked the opposite possibility that, if antimony had indeed been planted in his water bottle, he would, before rubbing his gums with laudanum, have swallowed his usual tasteless draught and later quite sincerely denied having taken any other drug than laudanum. In any case, was this apathy so unnatural to a man so ill and exhausted that he wanted only to die?

If suicide was a lost cause, so was misadventure. "Large doses of antimony," as Sir John Hall says, "are not left lying about accidentally." But though the jury summarily dismissed the misadventure possibilities eighty years ago, others have since built them up strongly. A recent book on the case* quotes a letter written in 1923 by Mr. Justice Channell, a retired Judge of the High Court and member of the Judicial Committee of the Privy Council, in which he said that he had known Charles Bravo well and also Mrs. Cox's counsel, Mr. Murphy, who had discussed the case with him. From knowledge of Charles and all the available facts Sir Arthur Channell was convinced that his death was an accident: that he had bought the tartar emetic to put into Florence's sherry as a cure for her drinking habit and that on the Tuesday night, having accidentally swallowed some laudanum, he took some of the antimony as an emetic— not knowing, despite his study of forensic medicine, its lethal properties. Hence his telling the doctors that he had taken no poison but laudanum. But would he not, at death's door and in the greatest agony, have mentioned *anything* that he had taken, even at the cost of revealing his discreditable though well-meant little plot? And Sir Arthur does not explain what happened to the container of the antimony and how it was that the doctors never found it. Further—and most important—

* *How Charles Bravo Died* by Yseult Bridges (Jarrolds, 1956).

how could Charles have administered tartar emetic to Florence without giving it also to Mrs. Cox, seeing that they *both* drank sherry and marsala at meals, from the same bottles or decanters? Finally, would Charles, while dosing Florence with scrupulous accuracy, have suddenly given himself—on this laudanum-swallowing pretext—enough 'emetic' to kill four people?

Also based on misadventure is the theory advanced by the author of the above-mentioned book. Charles is here made out to have swallowed tartar emetic (which he had procured for certain fell purposes of his own, and the later disappearance of whose container is accounted for) in mistake for a bedtime draught of Epsom salts. This theory is founded on the assumption that he had just drunk enough laudanum to confuse him into making the fatal error. (But Charles had forcibly maintained that he had merely rubbed his gums with the drug, though admittedly he may have swallowed a little.) The author further argues that the salts and antimony containers may have been disastrously alike—"perhaps he kept the tartar emetic in a similar box". What part did Epsom salts in fact play in that night's drama? Royes Bell had prescribed them for Charles and there was a packet of them in his room that night which Royes had removed to give to Professor Redwood for analysis. But the whereabouts of the salts in the bedroom may be significant. The author declares that the first two doctors actually found them on Charles's bedroom mantel-piece—their presence betokening habitual or intended use; but this does not seem to be confirmed by the doctors themselves. Four of them testified to finding on the mantelpiece only bottles of laudanum, chloroform and liniment (Royes adding Condy's Fluid). Were the salts found, not displayed among the regularly used medicaments, but relegated to a cupboard or drawer? And if so, did Epsom salts ever come into the picture at all? But whether they did or not, the laudanum problem persists. Suppose Charles *had*, while rubbing his gums, swallowed enough laudanum to confuse him: surely, to avoid washing the drug away at once, he would have done his gum-doctoring *after* and not *before* drinking any 'salts'.

But Florence in her worry was toying with no such convenient thoughts of death by accident. If Charles had been giving her small doses of tartar emetic to cure her of her drinking, and she was aware of it (it has been suggested that this was what she told Dr. Dill), why did she not rush to inform her father and Sir Henry James and ask that Dr. Dill be called to testify? It would have vitally altered appearances in her favour.

So with accident and suicide ruled out, there remained only murder—with the dreadful implication that, whether or not some outside accomplice or confederate were involved, it was murder by someone at The Priory. There could be no other explanation. And Florence knew what the cruel and vulgar public had been saying, even before the verdict was arrived at. It was crystallised in a wicked little poem that was going the rounds, parodying some lines of Goldsmith's:

> When lovely woman stoops to folly
> And finds her husband in the way,
> What charm can soothe her melancholy
> What art can turn him into clay?
>
> The only means her aims to cover
> And save herself from prison locks
> And repossess her ancient lover
> Are Burgundy and Mrs. Cox.

The immoral wife arranging the murder of her husband in order to get back to the arms of her "ancient lover"! It was a lovely solution for the man in the street; it took in everything so neatly, gave such a melodramatic fictional twist to the affair.

Of course it ignored the fact that the poison had almost certainly not been in the burgundy, but then burgundy fitted into the jingle much better than cold water. And it ignored so many others things. Was there a jot of evidence to show any desire by either Florence or the doctor to start the affair again? When they had parted the previous October their four-year romance had (certainly on her side) burnt itself out beyond reviving; it was dead of a natural inanition caused largely by the disparity in their ages. Their coming together had in any case been an emotional freak, the abnormal infatuation of a be-wildered, hurt and lonely young woman on the rebound of revulsion from a loathed and drunken husband, for an elderly man of compelling charm, virile beyond his years, who had no compunction in taking what was so readily offered him. (To do James Gully justice, he was prepared to give a good deal in return.) Not that the sexual motive was the only or even the dominant factor in their attachment. Bitterly disillusioned by a marriage which gave her neither physical satisfaction nor companionship, Florence found in James Gully just that mixture of lover and father-figure that she desperately needed. But the need was temporary; and when she was healed of her emotional wounds she was finished with Gully and ready to take up a more normal life; and Gully for his part acquiesced. The people who so blithely mouthed the little parody had forgotten to ask themselves why Florence, if she really had not done with Gully, should have bothered to part from the doctor, marry Charles Bravo and then poison him, all in a space of six months. As for Dr. Gully's continuing to live so near The Priory, that was natural enough considering that when he had moved into Orwell Lodge he had newly furnished it throughout and would have been put to considerable cost and trouble in moving again.

But if Florence could be absolved from murdering Charles, with Mrs. Cox's active aid, in order to return to Gully, Mr.

Lewis and the Crown counsel had built up far too formidable an edifice of suspicion against her to absolve her from murder altogether. This applied to Mrs. Cox too. And in those conjecture-ridden August days after the verdict, when the police at Great Scotland Yard were going over the evidence and considering their course of action, the Campbells too were totting up the reckoning against Florence, and even to this hard core of suicide advocates the result was frightening. Not more so, they had to admit, than the sum of evidence against Mrs. Cox. But this was small consolation; for, despite all Mrs. Campbell's efforts at the witness-table, it appeared that they must inevitably stand or fall together.

First, what did the Campbells—and the police—see against both of them jointly?

Chiefly their closely tallying stories, unsupported by anyone else, of Charles's jealousy and bad temper, which were the whole basis for the suicide suggestion. And then their extreme intimacy over the last four years, an intimacy of shared confidences and secrets—on Florence's side at least—which continued after Florence's marriage and looked like having been intensified in the fortnight before Charles's seizure when she and Mrs. Cox slept together and he was ousted to another bedroom. With such communion reigning, could one of them have had evil designs on Charles without the other knowing? As Sir John Hall says*: "If one be guilty the other could hardly be innocent." And, more concrete, there was the fact that they had had the bedroom landing to themselves for half an hour on the Tuesday evening before Charles had come up to bed: an ample opportunity to lay the poison. It was significant too that neither had appeared to hear Charles's anguished cry almost outside their door.

* *The Bravo Mystery and Other Cases* by Sir John Hall (John Lane, The Bodley Head, 1923).

These things—and possibly the highly suspicious nature of Charles's sickness in March—told equally against both. What did the record show against Florence alone?

There was her untrustworthiness—should it be called untruthfulness?—on specific points of evidence: for instance her denial that Dr. Gully knew of the deed of separation from Alexander, when in fact he was one of the trustees; and her denial that Dr. Gully had prescribed for her in 1874 or 1875, when in May, 1874, he had treated her with oil of savin. Small items—but how many other undiscovered inaccuracies were there? And if they were intentional, what was she trying to hide, and why? There was too her wavering, inconsistent attitude to the cause and manner of Charles's seizure. First, naturally enough, it was pure accident—the "coppery pan"; but when she stuck to this explanation even after Dr. Johnson had mentioned poison in her hearing, her conduct began to look odd. And when she wrote to Sir William Gull without referring to poison at all it looked suspicious. Yet, on another tack altogether, there was her talk with Royes's sister on the Thursday afternoon, when she could suggest no explanation whatever; and then her declaration on the Friday morning that the cause of Charles's death would always remain a mystery. Only later, in writing to Joseph Bravo from Brighton on the 6th May, had she eagerly taken up the suicide idea, advancing financial pressure from "that dreadful woman" as a factor; and from then on she had ever more eagerly championed suicide. The source of the poison? Perhaps from Mr. Joseph Bravo's own stable! Finally there was her belated bombshell of Charles's almost insane jealousy and vile temper. And if the police and the Campbells cared to look for vaguer pointers, there was her mercenary letter of 5th May to Joseph Bravo, in which she had, a mere fortnight after Charles's death, seemed to be haggling over what was due to her from his estate. As for motive: discounting any intention of Florence's to return to Dr. Gully, these assessors could still see one reason she might have had for killing Charles—a loathing engendered by his meanness and his ill-tempered and jealous goadings. But this very motive, of course, depended on the truth of her own and Mrs. Cox's highly suspect allegations about Charles.

Against Mrs. Cox one incriminating fact stood out head and shoulders above any that compromised Florence: her story of Charles's reputed admission about having taken poison. There was only her word that Charles had ever made the admission. Mary Ann, standing very near, had never heard it; and Mr. Harrison denied categorically that she had reported it to him. And then there were the queer variations to her tale. At the first inquest she said that Charles had told her: "I have taken poison. Don't tell Florence." To Dr. Johnson she gave another version: "I've taken some of that poison, but don't tell Florence." To the Treasury Solicitor, yet another version: "I have taken poison for Gully. Don't tell Florence." On top of all these came her trimming at the second inquest: Charles's words to her: "Why did you tell them?" If Charles *did* admit taking poison, why did she not immediately send for Dr. Moore, who lived near, instead of for Mr. Harrison? And why did she not send for a stomach-pump? Why, again, did she throw the vomit away, instead of keeping it for the doctors to examine? Her answer to this was that it did not occur to her that the doctors ought to see it, and that she wanted a clean basin in case Charles were sick again. Her reply to the query why she did not tell Dr. Moore about the alleged poison was that she believed Charles would recover from the effects of the "chloroform" and thought he would be "angry". But whatever the intentions and actions of Mrs. Cox on that Tuesday night, Charles died of forty grains of antimony, and the scandal of Dr. Gully—which she maintained she had been so anxious to conceal—came out in full. Yet if she had really been at one with Florence in wanting to bury the past would she have been so forthcoming at those four meetings with the doctor— accidental though they may have been—that culminated in the arrival of the bottle of laurel water at The Priory? These and other questions throwing grave doubt on the *bona fides* of Jane Cox the jury had answered with their verdict of wilful murder. If they had believed her they would have brought in suicide. And if a motive were sought there was the fear still gnawing at her heart—despite Charles's reassurances—that on her return from Jamaica she would be dismissed from her post, to face with her three growing boys a terrible insecurity. And yet—it left the unsolved conundrum: if neither Mrs. Cox nor Florence could have acted without the knowledge of the other, how had Florence stood by and allowed Charles to be murdered by her companion?

Pondering on all this in his Scotland Yard office, Super-intendent Williamson was baffled. But he had not yet covered all the possibilities: there was another approach to the problem. Who besides Florence and Mrs. Cox might have had a motive for killing Charles? In The Priory itself, nobody; but outside, the "ancient lover", for one. Suppose he had murdered to avenge himself on his supplanter? As a doctor, he could provide the antimony, and for an essential confederate within the house there was Mrs. Cox, with her own reason for wanting Charles dead. Their meetings before the 18th April could show that they were hand-in-glove; and though Jane Cox had herself volunteered to Mrs. Campbell that she had met the doctor, this could have been in order to disarm suspicion in case someone else mentioned the meetings. The mysterious bottle of "laurel water", whose contents nobody could prove, fitted in less easily. It could hardly have contained the antimony, for Mrs. Cox had offered it to Florence *before* the murder, and though

Florence had declined it and told Mrs. Cox to put it away, there was always the risk that she might have done otherwise. Still, the poison could easily have been conveyed in some other way. Toying with this theory, the Superintendent had to admit that it was possible—if Gully had really desired revenge on Charles. But there was not the slightest evidence that he had. And then again there was the problem of Florence's connivance.

Could Charles's discarded mistress have killed him, with inside help? The Maidenhead lady's name had not come out at the inquest and little was known of her, but it was clear from her sister's letters to him that she bore him no grudge; and as for Charles's debt to her, this would have been paid by Joseph Bravo as a point of honour. Nor had it even been suggested that she knew anyone at The Priory who might have administered the poison.

There remained George Griffith, disgruntled ex-coachman, foreteller of Charles's doom, and the inquest's most sensational witness. He had the motive; he almost certainly had the means (for his declaration that he had got rid of all the antimony was as untrustworthy as much of his other evidence); and his astoundingly accurate prophecy could not possibly be ignored. He had given Charles four months to live and Charles had overstepped the term by a mere fortnight! To strain a metaphor, George Griffith was the dark horse in the case. Persistently at Malvern, Leigham Court Road and The Priory he had appeared behind the scenes, perhaps the onlooker who saw most of the game. Dr. Gully, Alexander Ricardo, Florence, Mrs. Cox, Charles, he had known them all. He was the link, the common factor, in the whole mysterious story. But yet— he had been miles away at Herne Bay on Tuesday the 18th April, and there had been no whisper that he had had any confederate in The Priory.

This then was the enigma that faced Superintendent Williamson and his colleagues in August, 1876: a tangled web of multiple motive, conflicting evidence and dark conjecture, bedevilled by jealousy, hatred, illicit love, and begetting suspicion against at least four people. But suspicion was not enough: the vital, final clue to the puzzle of Charles Bravo's murder seemed to be missing.

But was it? In reality was it not there all the time, clear as crystal, buried in the past—in the corpse of Alexander Ricardo?

PART THREE

GUILT AND NEMESIS

CHAPTER 17

ANTIMONY FOR TWO

"CAPTAIN RICARDO died, and his body being exhumed, antimony was detected."

This was the startling revelation that came out in 1910, made in the book already referred to, by Dr. L. Forbes Winslow.* And with it light falls into the dark places, and the beginning of the story of what happened at The Priory in April, 1876, is seen to stretch back, beyond the short months of Florence's life with Charles, beyond her widowed interlude with Dr. Gully, right into the shadowy background of her first marriage.

Dr. Winslow had attended the second inquest on Charles and closely studied the whole case; and although official confirmation of his statement is lacking, the assertion of this eminent medical man can hardly be doubted. It is the more convincing because he was not making it in order to support any theory of his that either Charles or Alexander was murdered. He himself in fact thought (although he had never met him) that Charles had committed suicide during temporary insanity. And he offered no explanation of how Alexander came to take the antimony.

The doctor's statement has backing from other quarters. An issue of the *Echo* for July, 1876, carried this paragraph:

* Lyttelton Forbes Winslow, M.B., D.C.L., LL.D. (1844–1913), was a well-known alienist who founded the British Hospital for Mental Disorders and wrote extensively on insanity. He appeared as an expert witness in many notable trials here and in the U.S.A.

The *Manchester Guardian* of Friday has the following: An extraordinary report is gaining currency to the effect that the Government have thought it expedient to apply for the exhumation of the body of the late Captain Ricardo, who, it may be remembered, died at Cologne, and that the remains are at present in the Brompton cemetery, and are to be subjected to examination should it be deemed necessary.

This was suggestive. But further, during the second inquest on Charles, the Treasury Solicitor was actually instructed, in view of "certain reports connected with the deaths of Captain Ricardo and the Lady Catherine Ricardo", to make inquiries about both these deaths and submit a case to the Attorney-General and the Solicitor-General for their opinion. He did so (incurring a bill with the Ricardo family's solicitors for over £200), but what he discovered and what opinion the Law Officers formed can never be known—the papers were later destroyed. Could it have been that as part of these inquiries Alexander's body was secretly exhumed and antimony discovered, but that, as he died (however suspiciously) five years before Charles, the authorities decided not to complicate the investigation into Charles's death by dragging in that earlier death of 1871? In fact, it looks as if the Treasury Solicitor's inquiries were not completed until after the end of the inquest on Charles, for he did not receive the Law Officers' opinions until the end of November, 1876—and then it may well have seemed undesirable, and too late, to open up the whole vexed business again. As to the official interest in the death of Alexander's mother, who died in 1869, this was a new facet to the affair which could do no more than heighten the existing speculation.

Had anyone who had followed the evidence of Florence and her mother about Alexander Ricardo ever asked themselves what had really happened to this first husband of Florence's?

There he was, a dim, rather unreal figure, hovering on the very fringe of her past. Dipsomania, separation from Florence, sudden death at Cologne at twenty-eight, these people had been told, were the closing stages in the rake's progress of his short and wasted life. At best it had been a sketchy picture— and while admittedly it was all very long ago, Crown counsel and Mr. Lewis had been strangely incurious about some of the events of those years.

Yet the key to Charles's fate was to be found in the fate of Alexander Ricardo.

Two years after the second inquest, in September, 1878, the *Standard* wrote in the course of a startling editorial:

> While still almost a girl . . . [Florence Bravo] was married to her first husband, Captain Ricardo. . . . The husband and wife separated, and shortly after the separation Captain Ricardo died. It was said by his wife that he died of drink; but the peculiar symptoms were, as it was afterwards suggested, not at all incompatible with slow antimonial poisoning . . .
>
> . . . Almost immediately after the separation [from Dr. Gully] she married Mr. Bravo. . . . The second marriage was as unhappy as the first. . . . Before six months were over Mr. Bravo died, very much in the way that Mr. Ricardo had died. . . . It was impossible to avoid the terrible suggestion which the inquest raised, but which it finally left un answered. . . . The broad fact, however, remained that Mr. Bravo had been poisoned.

Two successive husbands dying within five years of each other, both having been ill with similar symptoms either immediately or some time beforehand, and one being known to have died of antimony: was this mere coincidence? What was then darkly hinted can now, after eighty years, be put forward in plainer terms.

Florence had, with antimony, hastened the death of Alexander Ricardo and murdered Charles Bravo.

When does the story of Florence's descent to murder begin? It had its roots in Alexander's drinking. Or, more basically, in her very marriage to this spoiled and dissipated young ensign of the Guards. But at nineteen, sheltered, innocent, carefully brought up, how was she to know the kind of man he was? All she could see was the tall young officer cutting such a fine figure with his sword and tunic, his gleaming pipe-clayed belt and bearskin. And there was a certain dark handsomeness about Alexander with his regular features, well-modelled nose, smooth centre-parted hair and thin line of carefully-trained moustache. It would have needed someone less in love than Florence to note the shortcomings of that face—the eyes a shade too close-set, the eyebrows a little too converging and lifting rakishly at the ends. And no doubt to her girlish eyes he had an air about him, something of the dash of his father, who, before going into business, had himself been a soldier and noted athlete, on one occasion riding a spirited horse up a staircase into a dining-room at Aylesbury.

All this gave a glamorous start to the marriage; and for Florence the glamour continued untarnished for perhaps three years. If Alexander often got drunk at this time, his adoring wife treated his weakness indulgently: after all, lots of young men in his set drank heavily. But after he had left the Army, and especially after his mother's death in 1869, the bouts got more frequent and prolonged and Alexander began to seem to her a less romantic figure. Sottish violence and boorishness were bad enough; but Alexander's first attack of delirium tremens, at Bournemouth in the spring of 1870, turned her waning love to disgust and repulsion.

And then came Malvern.

Perhaps in the early weeks of her first visit to the spa Florence still felt an obligation to stand by Alexander and try to reform him. But her resolve soon weakened under the irresistible spell of Dr. Gully. Swept off her feet by his hypnotic charm, she began to look on her drunken husband as merely an encumbrance, an obstacle in the way of her new infatuation: and as such he must be discarded. Their life together at Orwell Lodge and Stokefield, with its scenes, quarrels and recriminations as Alexander slid further into incurable dipsomania, made her every day more desperate to be rid of him; and the moment came—probably during their second visit to Malvern—when she decided on the terrible step of killing him.

Florence's nature has generally been misread. Her lack of physical robustness and a temperament which caused her to collapse when things went wrong have too often been taken as counterparts of a weak and indecisive character. Self-centred, sensuous and money-loving she has been admitted to be, but her pretty face with its crown of auburn hair, wide-spaced blue eyes and firm rounded chin betrayed (or masked) all sorts of other qualities too. It is clear that the girl who sits looking so calmly into the camera, with Alexander standing beside her, in the photographer's studio at Folkestone, is not a person to be easily dominated or taken advantage of. And did not her letter to Mrs. Cox from Kissingen in 1873 reveal her as imperious, hard, determined to have her way? She could be impetuous and passionate, but she was equally capable of acting without a shred of sentiment. It was these traits in the complex make-up of Florence that brought her to the pitch of contemplating murder.

Whether she would have been tempted to kill Alexander if she had never met James Gully is an open question. Then he would have been just a husband whom she had grown to loathe—not, in addition, an inconvenient one, standing in the way of her heart's desire. But gaining Dr. Gully was not her only incentive—though it was the chief one—for murder: there was, dangling before her and opening up a glittering prospect of wealth and luxury, the marriage settlement money, a fortune of £40,000.

A vivid picture builds up of how she planned and carried out her attempt on Alexander.

Discussing his trouble with the sympathetic Dr. Gully in the early days of her first Malvern visit, she asked how he could be cured; and learnt from the doctor that one well-known means of destroying the alcohol habit was small doses of antimony, or tartar emetic, placed in a bottle of wine or spirits; not more than two or three grains, as the drug was lethal. Whether Alexander on his arrival at Malvern received this or any other treatment from the doctor is uncertain. Florence later declared that he was a patient of Dr. Gully's, but the doctor denied it. At any rate, while noting what James Gully said, she paid no particular attention to the method—then.

Some weeks later, weeks in which her resolve to be rid of Alexander grew almost into an obsession, the doctor's words came back to her in a sudden flash of revelation.

It was one day when she was visiting the Priory House to take tea alone with him. Alexander was at Stokefield in a drunken slumber, and the way was clear for her to enjoy the thrilling intimacy of James Gully's company, that now meant more to her than anything in life. She chanced to go into the stables to look at the horses (she was a keen horse-lover) and chat with Griffith, the doctor's coachman. And there, on a shelf, she saw a packet labelled "Poison. Tartar Emetic". It was the antimony which Griffith had bought at Clark's the year before for treating the horses. At that moment Florence knew that she was going to kill Alexander—and how she was going to do it. Here, to her hand, was the "cure" that was also a deadly poison. She asked him why he had it and he told her it benefited the horses. And was it then, or a few days later, that while Griffith's back was turned she swiftly scooped a quantity of the crystals from the packet and put them in a handkerchief which she hid about her. It was a few seconds' work—but she was unlucky. Griffith saw her, not in the act, but touching or replacing the packet. Her heart racing, she answered his half-casual query with some vague remark about wanting to look at it, and Griffith dismissed the incident.

Later, in the light of what happened, he was to recall it.

Back at Stokefield, Florence locked away the crystals and decided on her next move. She would not give Alexander a single fatal dose—there was no need—but repeated small ones that would speed and intensify the effects of the spirits that were steadily killing him. In this way the symptoms of the poison would be hidden by those of the alcohol. And when he died there would be no suspicion that his end was caused by anything but drink.

So in those tense autumn weeks at Malvern Florence carried out her stealthy plan, lacing Alexander's brandy, and perhaps other drink and food, with the insidious crystals. He was too far gone in his craving to stop drinking now, even when the vomiting and prostration grew worse and more frequent. And he would certainly have died sooner than he did if the final break between them in November, 1870, had not cut short the doses of antimony. Florence, from the comfortable refuge of Dr. Gully's house, may have seen her design frustrated, but Alexander died soon enough in any case.

Little is known of Alexander's last days. About the end of March he went abroad and stayed at Cologne. With him he took a woman friend, Florentine Kemppel, probably an old flame from London; and at Cologne they lived as man and wife, lodging at No. 6/8 Franken Platz, the busy square in the centre of the city, overlooking the Rhine and near the great cathedral. And here, on 19th April, at one in the morning, Alexander died, with Florentine Kemppel beside him and attended by a Dr. Martin Meurer. His body was brought back to England and buried in the catacombs at Brompton Cemetery on 24th April.

How did Alexander die? No doubt (although no cause was given) in the throes of alcoholic poisoning or delirium tremens. But the antimony administered him at Malvern had made him more susceptible to the damaging effects of the alcohol and thereby hastened his death; and it remained in his body, according to Dr. Forbes Winslow, to tell in time its own grim tale.

With Alexander Ricardo dead, everything came wonderfully right for Florence. She was free of a drunken husband, her lover was awaiting her, and she gained £40,000.

And James Gully had what he wanted too. What part did he, who threw all caution to the winds in visiting Florence at Streatham hardly a month after Alexander's death and then gave up his life's work to be near her, play in the poisoning of Alexander? He said he was totally unaware of Griffith's buying the two ounces of antimony at Malvern in 1869 and had never while there possessed a single grain of the drug himself. But whether he was an accomplice of Florence's, knew about the poisoning only afterwards, or never knew at all, remains the greatest enigma of the case. The answer hangs largely on whether Alexander was a patient of his. If so, appearances against him are black indeed; but even if not, and even supposing that Florence acted without his help or knowledge, could he, in the four-year intimacy that followed, have remained ignorant of her secret? Perhaps in his infatuation he shut his eyes to what he knew in his heart must have happened, realising that Alexander could not have lived long in any case.

But there were others—Alexander's and Florence's families —whose blindness to Alexander's alarming later symptoms (let alone to the whole fatal course of his drinking) was indeed strange. Mrs. Campbell was to say six years later at the inquest on Charles:

"[At Malvern] I saw Dr. Foulkes. He did not tell me that Captain Ricardo was comatose and apparently suffering from an overdose of some narcotic. I always understood that he was suffering from drink. The doctor told me that Captain Ricardo had great debility of the stomach and almost uncontrollable vomiting. I did not see Dr. Phillips, of Worcester, but I heard of a Worcester doctor going to see him. Mrs. Ricardo was there when this Worcester doctor saw him.

"I saw Captain Ricardo was sick at Buscot." (This may have been after the first visit to Malvern.) "He told me that he vomited sixty times a day, and this I understood was from drink.

". . . I heard that when the illness of Captain Ricardo occurred at Great Malvern, in 1870, the coats of the stomach were said by the medical man to be gone, and if he had another attack it would be fatal."

How much of these symptoms were brought on by alcohol and how much by antimony?

So the years passed with Florence's secret buried in the grave of Alexander, unsuspected (apart, perhaps, from Dr. Gully) by any living soul. Except one. And, with George Griffith, "suspected" is possibly too strong a term. But from his stables at the Priory House he watched the situation develop that summer and autumn of 1870, and listened to the gossip. Then at some particular moment the tales of Alexander's illness brought back to his mind Florence's interest in his tartar emetic. And news of the Captain's sudden death made him ponder. But

Griffith was the sort of man who "minds his own business". It was no affair of his. Mrs. Ricardo and the doctor treated *him* well enough (she at least might have reason to!); and as, after being briefly employed by her at Malvern, he continued to serve her at Leigham Court Road and The Priory and drive them both about in her landau, he was content to forget the queer goings-on at Malvern. He was in a good steady post. Why should he worry?

When that same post was brusquely terminated with a month's notice it was another matter. With his resentment came reawakened memories. The mistress had got rid of her first husband, hadn't she? Well, this second one had better look out. "Poor fellow. I shouldn't like to be in his shoes. He won't be alive four months!" If the time-estimate was a pure fluke, events showed how right Griffith's inspired guess was in essentials. The shrewd intuition that had slumbered complacently for five years now, under the spur of grievance, voiced itself to proclaim what kind of woman he thought his mistress really was. But George Griffith passed out of the picture very soon afterwards, minding his own business to the last. He did, however, launch a parting shot against the doomed gentleman who had got him the sack: the crude anonymous letter (obviously from one of the few people who knew the truth about Florence's association with Gully) that Charles received after Christmas, 1875, was surely from him.

Florence decided to murder Charles almost on impulse. Unlike Alexander, he was no drunkard; he was not standing in the way of another lover (Gully or anyone else); he was not, despite her allegations so powerfully echoed by Mrs. Cox, jealous of her past with the doctor; nor did she kill him for money—though he left her £14,000 and by his death she came a step nearer to the £20,000 settled on him by his stepfather. Yet, like Alexander, Charles was someone with whom she could no longer bear to live. He had done her no wrong in the eyes of the world; but against him she bore a terrible secret grudge, based on a situation hardly to be talked about in reticent Victorian society.

The clue to Florence's reason for murdering Charles is to be found in that dictum of Sir James Fitzjames Stephen, quoted by Sir John Hall,* in which he says: "It is sometimes said that there is no need to look further for a motive when the parties are man and wife. . . . Married people usually treat each other with external decency, good humour and cordiality, but what lies under the veil is known only to themselves, and the relation may produce hatred, bitter in proportion to the intimacy which it involves."

"What lies under the veil . . ." Florence killed Charles because she saw no other way of cutting short the married relationship with him which had become intolerable to her and which, had it gone on, would have meant her early death or permanent invalidism—or so, in her sick, unbalanced state of mind that April, she desperately believed. Only after marrying Charles had Florence realised to the full that physiologically she was tragically unfitted for normal married life and child-bearing. And then it was too late. What had been her history with Charles? Two miscarriages in under four months. And before marrying him she had had a miscarriage in 1873, and two illnesses in 1871 and 1874, both similar, the second of which Dr. Gully had described as "a want of action in the uterine organs and suspension of the natural functions". With Alexander she had had little chance to discover this weakness, for after his descent into dipsomania it is doubtful if they lived as man and wife; and in between his drunken bouts he had, so it was said, consorted with other women. And she had banished Dr. Gully as a lover immediately after the miscarriage

* See footnote to page 256.

following the Kissingen trip. But there could be no such banishment for Charles, her lawful husband. The January miscarriage, coming so swiftly after their marriage, had been bad enough; but she was hardly over that when April brought another, leaving her weaker and more depressed, mentally and physically, than before. She asked herself in despair—and revolt—how she could go on like this. Was she to be subjected to this terrible pain and distress every few months until she was bedridden or dead? She had ousted Charles for the moment to another bedroom and taken Jane Cox in to share her bed, but he would soon be insistently demanding his rightful place again. And then what?

Such were the black thoughts that tortured Florence during those April days and nights as she lay in bed weak, shocked, emotionally disturbed. And with them was born now, as is not unknown in such cases, a personal, physical aversion to Charles—the husband whom, after all, she had married less for love than respectability and position—as the cause of all her troubles. What more natural than that in her dire need of sympathy she should confide her morbid fears and fancies, not to Royes Bell, her doctor and Charles's cousin, nor to her mother, but to Mrs. Cox as she lay beside her in the restless watches of the night?

For Jane Cox, with her own uncertainty about her future at The Priory, this renewed intimacy was like an answer to her prayers. Suddenly Florence needed her again: they were back on the old footing of pre-marriage days, but allied now in a common cause, two women against a man who in different ways threatened them both. And with comforting reassurances she pressed home her advantage for all she was worth—though she had in mind nothing more than making herself so indispensable to Florence that Florence would refuse to let Charles dismiss her if he tried. It was, for Mrs. Cox, entirely a matter of ensuring her retention at The Priory. And when one night Florence blurted out in a despairing unguarded moment that she would do anything to be free of Charles, Jane Cox merely reproved her for such wild thoughts. She knew by now the misery Florence suffered in these miscarriages and the dark moods that accompanied her pain and sleeplessness.

But for once she underestimated Florence.

Tuesday the 18th April was Florence's first full day out since her illness. Before starting for London she had felt very faint, and on her return was utterly exhausted. With such persistent weakness and malaise she had no business to be up. As she lay on the sofa in the morning-room after lunch, brooding in solitude on her broken health and the bleak future before her as the perpetually ailing wife of a husband whose attentions had become intolerable to her, the second fearful decision of her life took shape in her obsessed mind. She would get rid of Charles—just as she had set about ridding herself of Alexander. Then she would be free of men—free of the ills that they could cause, free to enjoy in unimpaired health the luxury and comfort that she had enjoyed after she had renounced James Gully as a lover and before her hateful marriage to Charles.

In that ruthless moment of resolve charged with pathological feeling against Charles, supreme egotism, self-pity, elation at her anticipated freedom, she passed the death sentence on her second husband.

"She is very fond of her horses," Mrs. Cox said of Florence at the inquest. "She goes to the stables and gives the cobs a pat, and sometimes an apple." It was a queer chance that the same love of horses that had given Florence the means of poisoning Alexander had put in her way the antimony for Charles's murder. But was it? A natural place for antimony was the stables; and Griffith, user of antimony, had worked in the stables at Malvern and The Priory alike. It was the last residue of his crystals, left undestroyed after he had departed in January (though he may well, as he said, have poured the liquid solution down the drain) that Florence had found on a visit to her cobs before Parton had arrived in February. And she had removed them to her medicine cupboard, thinking that though the next coachman might use them they ought not to lie about the stables meanwhile. If she had reflected then how she had once used the crystals there was never an idea in her mind that she would turn poisoner again. But as she lay on the sofa that Tuesday afternoon, she thanked the providence that had made her keep them. They would be put to good use now!

And this time there would be no half-measures. She would give Charles a single infallibly-acting dose that would kill at once. And as nobody knew that she had the packet, his death could never be traced to her.

She would do it that night. But how? Should she put it in his burgundy, dropping it before dinner into the decanter that would stand ready on the dining-table? No, there was the risk of being seen by Rowe (she remembered how Griffith had nearly caught her in the stables five years before); and besides, she did not want to be there when it took effect, as a powerful dose was sure to do quickly. Suddenly she saw her way. True, it depended on a bed-time habit of his, but she had never known that habit fail. At any rate, that was a chance she would have to take; and no one would be any the wiser if that night he acted differently and left the poison untouched. It would be thrown away undetected next morning and she would have to think of some other way.

How she got through dinner that night she hardly knew. Tense, silent, preoccupied, she toyed with the courses as they came. In her mind, blotting out everything else, was the single thought of what she was to do afterwards. But imbibing courage with her wine—and she drank over a bottle of sherry —somehow she kept herself steeled.

The time for action came when she got up to go to bed. A last kiss to Charles and she was out of the room, with Mrs. Cox, who had asked to come up and help her undress, close behind her. But she had to be alone for a minute—two minutes.

She stopped at the foot of the stairs.

"Jane, I'm so thirsty. Be a dear and get me a little Marsala in water and bring it up with you."

While Mrs. Cox turned back to the dining-room she hurried on upstairs. Twenty seconds in her bedroom was enough to snatch the packet of antimony from the back of her medicine cupboard, another twenty to slip into Charles's room next door, pour the poison—to the last crystal—into his full water bottle standing by the bed, and throw the packet on his fire. By this time Mrs. Cox was leaving the dining-room with the wine; and if, coming upstairs, she had seen Florence passing from the direction of Charles's bedroom to the dressing-room at the other end of the short landing she would have thought nothing of it—the lavatory was just outside Charles's room.

It was done—but the worst moment was yet to come: the moment when Charles, having gone into his bedroom and un-dressed, would, as always, lift the water bottle to his lips and drink almost to the bottom. White and shaking, despite her final night-cap just tossed down, Florence got into bed. She put her hands over her ears, waiting for the inevitable cry. Mrs. Cox looked at her anxiously. She asked what was the matter.

Florence, her face anguished, whispered Charles's name and something to the effect that she had "done it".

In a flash Mrs. Cox knew. Perhaps Florence's demeanour or the queer tension of that evening had half-prepared her for some crisis: perhaps now, in a split second, the forgotten words of the other night came back to her with a fearful significance. At any rate she knew.

In horror and consternation she asked Florence what she had done to Charles. Florence told her. And in those fateful moments Charles's life was in the balance. Mrs. Cox could have saved him—but as she stood irresolute his fate was sealed. How could she rush in and tell him not to drink that water? What explanation could she give without damning Florence as a would-be murderess? These questions raced through her mind. And there might have been time for other thoughts too: visions of herself secure now at The Priory, Florence safe from her fears of married martyrdom. At all events she did nothing. She told Florence to lie still: she herself would handle things.

The cry came soon after Mary Ann had said good night and shut the door. Both women heard it, but neither moved. Only when Mary Ann came bursting in did Mrs. Cox go to Charles, still feverishly considering what she was going to do.

She could only begin by deliberately playing for time in sending for the distant Mr. Harrison rather than Dr. Moore. And then, after misleading Mr. Harrison by talking about chloroform, she allowed the poison to get a perhaps fatal grip on Charles by delaying her poison-and-suicide tale for four hours. There was no mention of Dr. Gully now because in the emergency she had not thought up a suitable suicide motive. On that fatal Tuesday evening she had been taken badly unawares. But her sharp wits had enabled her to throw dust in the eyes of the doctors and effectively hide the truth. The price she paid afterwards was to have herself branded as a liar, even though she and Florence concocted their concerted circumstantial accounts of Charles's jealousy and violent temper to bolster up her suicide story. And the price Florence paid was to have herself condemned—largely through Mrs. Cox—as an immoral woman and a drinker. But if Mrs. Cox helped to destroy Florence's good name, at least she may have saved her neck: for was not the tarnished reputation with which Florence emerged from the inquest the only alternative to a charge of murder?

Jane Cox, even though moved partly by self-interest, did not serve Florence so badly. Becoming an accessory about five minutes before the fact, she saved the day. She got little thanks from Florence, but that tragic woman, broken by her illness, the terrific emotional strain of her act, and the remorse that followed it, was in no state to see her ex-companion as her saviour: hence the rupture between them that ensued, though in any case common sense dictated that, with suspicion pointing at them both as confederates in Charles's murder, they could never again resume their old intimacy.

So, ironically, Jane Cox, as involved as Florence in the crime and in no position to coerce her, got nothing for her pains.

Once Florence is seen as Charles's murderess her unconvincing and dubious conduct before and after his death—her wavering explanations of its cause and manner, her calling in Sir William Gull without telling him that Charles was poisoned, her mercenary and unfeeling letter to Joseph Bravo about his estate and possessions, her desire to hold the first inquest *in camera* at The Priory—becomes intelligible. And at last the Brighton incident involving Dr. Dill appears explicable. For suppose she confided to him her predicament as Charles's wife and her dread of continuing married life with him. Then, so far from wanting this brought up in court, she would have striven—as she did—to suppress it; for, if revealed, it would have provided a damning motive.

There was one moment when she nearly weakened. Lying

awake and trembling in her bed, separated only by a wall and a door from the turmoil in Charles's room and on the landing, she was feigning sleep when Mary Ann came in and called her to Charles. It was little wonder that when she stumbled into Charles's room and saw him lying on the floor, a momentary rush of horror and remorse made her cut through Mrs. Cox's delaying tactics by sending for the nearest doctor. But the mood passed and her heart hardened again. All she needed henceforth, as she acted the part of the loving wife, shocked and shattered by unforeseen tragedy, was to keep in view the stakes for which she was playing. Heaven knew, to her in her frantic, febrile state of mind they seemed high enough.

In killing Charles Bravo, Florence was acting true to character. Ruthless, self-centred, supremely unsentimental, she would go to any lengths to get what she wanted—or dispose of what she did not want. Because his death had seemed the only way out of her difficulty she had rid herself of Charles as she had brought herself to eliminate Alexander. And both times she had used the same means. It was strange that so few people seemed to see the parallel, and perceive her hand behind both deaths. The Ricardo family did: "The Ricardos thought her a bad woman," wrote the *Portsmouth Times and Naval Gazette* for 21st September, 1878, "and they found the money for the famous trial—for such it really was—before the Surrey Coroner."

Few other points remain to be mentioned. Charles's attack of sickness when leaving home one morning in March was the result of an ordinary stomach upset. It happens occasionally to everybody. And Mrs. Cox's meetings with Dr. Gully were the mere chance encounters of neighbours. Whether she was wise in engaging him so freely in conversation when communication was supposed to be over between Orwell Lodge and The Priory is another matter. But the truth is that ever since the Leigham Court Road days Jane Cox had had a soft spot for the elderly doctor.

And what of Charles himself, so traduced by Florence and Mrs. Cox in their Treasury statements and evidence? He was no saint: no doubt he had married Florence partly for her money, for he had a mercenary, ambitious and in some ways grasping nature. But he was genuinely in love with her too. And though he had a sharp temper and an occasionally boorish manner and did sometimes reproach her (when he had no business to) for her lavish expenditure over her cobs and so on, the villainous picture that she and Mrs. Cox drew of him was grossly exaggerated. As for his alleged fiery jealousy of Dr. Gully, this was never substantiated by a shred of evidence from anyone else in his intimate circle. Charles, in fact, with a past of his own, was too much a man of the world to bother about his wife's past, which he knew well was dead and buried. His *amour propre* would prevent him from admitting that an old gentleman of nearly seventy could be a serious rival to himself! The most genuine cause of resentment Florence had against her passionate, outspoken, high-spirited, devoted but sometimes moody and difficult husband was his submission to his dominating and doting mother. Yet even here, as the centre of a tug-of-war between two strong-minded women, Charles deserved a little pity.

If there is anything to mitigate Florence's murder of Charles Bravo it is that her action was partly the consequence of the emotional overstrain and nervous disorder that followed her second miscarriage in some three months and was the culmination of four years' intermittent ill-health. Impinging on a nature like hers, it made her do what she did. In a larger view, Florence Bravo was the victim of the unenlightened, patriarchal Victorian code of marriage relations in which the delicate wife, subject to the infirmities which Florence suffered, had no prospect but constant miscarriage leading eventually to the chronic invalid's bed or early death. Yet in her case "victim" is perhaps the wrong word: she was the lone rebel who, with callous cruelty, took the law into her own hands.

But she was to pay dearly for the crime that was never brought home to her.

CHAPTER 18

TRAGIC AFTERMATH

THE LAST CHAPTER in the story of Florence Bravo is the strangest and most macabre of all.

Her act brought her after all no happiness or satisfaction. Safe from the law but not from her conscience, or the mud of accusation and condemnation that was flung at her, she retired in the autumn of 1876 into an ever deeper seclusion at The Priory. She never went out, saw no one but her family. But if she hoped thus to find refuge from the remorse that now tortured her she was to be disappointed. The place was too full of the dark associations of the past. And as 1877 came and spring passed into summer The Priory became unbearable to her; and not even the returning colour of the flower gardens nor the fresh green of her prized oak in the middle of the lawn could keep her from a drastic resolve to quit it and seek total isolation in some place where she was unknown and might start a new life.

So having terminated her lease of The Priory she arranged for the sale of the furniture and effects. And at the end of August, at the Prince's Street auction rooms of Messrs. Bonham and Son, all those rich and tasteful appointments on whose choice she had lavished so much care and of which she had been so proud came under the hammer; the cherished satinwood suite and crimson hangings of the boudoir, the contents of the blue-draped drawing-room, the noble Spanish mahogany sideboard, etcetera, the pianos, *étagères*, *jardinières*, Dresden ornaments, whatnots, clocks, marble busts, candelabra, religious prints, French and Arabian bedsteads, china, cutlery, everything; even the cellarful of wines that now neither Florence, Mrs. Cox nor Charles would ever drink.

And—by one of those touches of irony that were not wanting as Florence's story closed—sale catalogues were obtainable at a shilling each from the Bedford Hotel, Balham.

So Florence Bravo put The Priory, her home for three and a half years, behind her, and Bedford Hill Road and the quiet rides of Tooting Bec Common knew her no more.

After staying temporarily at Buscot she moved in April, 1878, to Southsea. Here, in Lumps Villa, Lumps Lane, a comfortable secluded property away from the town and in sight of the sea, she found the isolation she craved. (The house still stands, but building has massively encroached on it and now it is St. Margaret's Lodge, No. 19 Eastern Parade.) To complete her cutting-adrift she took Charles's original surname and called herself Mrs. Turner; and disliking the name Lumps Villa she changed it to Coombe Lodge. But in her withdrawal she clung to the comfort which meant so much to her, employing a staff of three maids, a coachman, a gardener and his wife. (The coachman was Parton, of The Priory, and one of the maids was his wife Jane.) Only occasional visits from her family broke her solitude, and neighbours who called she peremptorily refused to see.

And did she in this retirement find the solace she was seeking?

The sequel seems to give the tragic answer.

Growing ever more introspective, morbid and hopeless, she gave way to the indulgence which her mother, Mrs. Cox and Charles had all noted and tried to curb; she took to drinking in earnest now and became, like Alexander, a dipsomaniac.

Excess soon took its toll. In May she was seized with severe vomiting and prostration. A local physician, Dr. Henry Smith, was called, and pronounced her to be "suffering from the effects of an undue amount of stimulants". On recovering, Florence managed through his persuasion to abstain for nearly two months; and when he saw her at the end of June he was pleased to find her in the best of health and spirits. But it was a state that did not last.

About this time her uncle James, who had paid her a short visit before, arrived at the Royal Beach Mansion Hotel for a longer stay. Mr. James Orr, a man of independent means who had returned from Australia some three years before, was that same uncle with whom Charles had lunched on the Tuesday of his seizure; and perhaps he came now at the instance of Florence's worried parents to keep a watchful eye on her. At any rate he visited her daily, often twice a day. But even his constant calls and kindly sympathy could not keep her from the bottle. Several times he found her intoxicated, and twice she was badly ill with violent and prolonged vomiting, recovering only through the care of her personal maid, Mrs. Everett, and his own advice. She seems to have done without Dr. Smith.

Then in September, following (it appears) a three-week drinking bout, came her third and worst attack. In an attempt to rally her, James Orr had planned to take her on a trip to Scotland, and on Friday evening, the 13th, went round to Coombe Lodge to discuss this and see how she was. He found her on the verandah, attended by Mrs. Everett and clearly the worse for drink. His heart sank.

"Florrie, keep steady," he urged, "and let us start on Sunday evening."

Mrs. Everett added her plea. "Do promise Mr. Orr not to take any more tonight."

Obstinately Florence replied: "I won't!" And she turned and went indoors and up to her room, accompanied by Mrs. Everett.

Soon Mrs. Everett came out on to the verandah again. Her face was serious. She was afraid, she said, that Mrs. Turner would not be able to start for Scotland on Sunday. And then she told Mr. Orr that she had just had a quarrel with Florence about the drinking and been summarily dismissed with a month's pay! He was staggered; but felt that there was nothing he could do then. He knew Florence in these moods: perhaps when she was sober he could reason with her.

Nevertheless Florence did not relent, and Mrs. Everett left next day, to go to her brother's at Richmond. And Florence now made the most of her new freedom.

In bed in her room on Saturday, she called another maid, Anne Spanner.

"Anne, has Everett gone?"

"Yes, ma'am, she has."

"Do you know whether she is gone out of Portsmouth?"

"I do not know where she is gone, ma'am. She did not say where she should go."

The way was clear for Florence's little ploy. "Anne," she said wheedlingly, "I want you to get me a bottle of brandy."

The girl was embarrassed. "Oh, ma'am, you know Mr. Orr said you were not to have it."

"I will have it, and you are to send for it!"

"But, ma'am, the gardener has gone for the day and the place is shut up."

"They sell it at the grocer's and you can easily get it."

But Anne, setting her face against this deception, became obstinate.

"You cannot get it. Mr. Orr said you were not to have it."

Florence flew into a rage. "Who is mistress of this house—Mr. Orr or me! I pay you your money. You do what I tell you!" She was trembling with anger.

Her small resistance broken, poor Anne Spanner left to carry out the order. And, slipping out to the Granada Arms near-by, she bought the brandy and carried it back to her mistress, who asked her to uncork it and leave it by the bed.

During the Sunday and Monday, with only the inexperienced Anne and Jane Parton to watch over her, Florence sank steadily into an alcoholic stupor. On Monday the bottle was gone from her bedside and Anne, tidying her mistress's wardrobe, found it hidden away in a corner—empty.

That morning James Orr had looked in to see how Florence was, and being told she was dozing said he would return later. But when he called that evening he was so shocked at her condition that he stopped with her until eleven-thirty and arranged with the two maids to stay up all night with her.

At six next morning he was back at Coombe Lodge, to find Florence worse and the maids worried out of their wits. During the night she had brought up blood. And now her laboured breathing, extreme pallor and continued vomiting told their alarming story. Leaving only to snatch a hurried breakfast at his hotel, James Orr returned at eight. Weakly Florence begged him for brandy.

"I don't think you want any, Florrie. I think you have had enough already."

"I shall die if you don't give me a little." Florence's craving was now all-dominant.

Mr. Orr could not resist the pitiful entreaty. He took a small flask of brandy from his pocket and gave her a spoonful in water, which seemed to comfort her. But this was only a palliative: she must see a doctor. On Monday night—as on several other occasions when she had been ill before—he had pressed her to have Dr. Smith but she had emphatically refused. Now he implored her once more.

She shook her head. "No, I won't see him."

James Orr shrugged in despair. In the face of this what could he do? And throughout that anxious morning as he and the two maids stood helplessly by, he asked her again and again. But always the reply was no.

At two there was a change for the worse—a sudden calamitous attack of vomiting and then a collapse. Again her uncle entreated her to send for Dr. Smith but the answer was the same. He even suggested telegraphing for her mother, but in vain. Then, a little later, another fearful paroxysm, and a gasping cry: "I can't breathe, I can't breathe, save me!" and James Orr saw that the end was near. While Jane Parton held her head he tried to give her a teaspoonful of brandy, but she was beyond swallowing: she could neither move nor speak. And soon afterwards, at about four o'clock, she was dead.

But the pitiful story was not quite over. The final intrusion on the privacy that Florence had so desperately sought was yet to come: post-mortem; inquest; viewing of remains ("Her face presented a livid appearance. There was a very marked curl of the lip, but beyond that there was nothing to indicate the agony which the deceased must have undergone"); evidence with its repellent details; notoriety that now flared up again to shatter her anonymity and dog her even to her grave.

The inquest was held next day, Wednesday the 18th September, at the Granada Arms Hotel: the Coroner was Mr. Garrington, J.P. And after James Orr, Anne Spanner, Jane Parton and Dr. Smith had been heard, the Coroner summed up and the jury recorded a verdict that "the immediate cause of death was hæmorrhage from the lining coat of the stomach, accelerated by disease of the heart, liver, and kidneys, produced by an undue partaking of alcoholic stimulants."

In plain English—and according to the official finding—Florence Bravo had died of drink.

But had she? About her end were certain very peculiar features that could not be ignored. In the first place both Anne

Spanner and Jane Parton said, curiously, that before the final attack they had never seen their mistress the worse for drink; and neither had known of any spirits coming into the house. If Florence had died of drink, how had she got it—with Mrs. Everett supposedly so closely guarding her? Perhaps only Mrs. Everett could have answered this; but she, so recently dismissed, was not called to give evidence. It seemed odd that so vital a witness was passed over. As it was, it was from James Orr and Dr. Smith, neither of them living in the house, that the reports of Florence's drinking had come. Then there was the failure to call the doctor. Did not Florence's desperate condition justify Dr. Smith being summoned whether she wished or not? Further, suspicious-minded people noted that the one person who had been with both Charles and Florence during or immediately before their fatal illnesses was James Orr. And finally there were the symptoms that had preceded her death; so like those of both Alexander and Charles.

What had been happening in those last four months in the unapproachable seclusion of Coombe Lodge? Had the whole truth come out or was there some sinister secret behind those walls? Once again speculation played around the name of Florence Bravo; and with the surmise about her sudden sordid end were linked the unsolved enigma of two years back and the uncertainties of her more distant past. But now there was a difference: there was freedom to speak out as there had not been before. And one newspaper, the *Standard*, voiced the suspicions and the queries in a dramatically candid leader:

> The sudden death of Mrs. Bravo, under circumstances which are, to say the least, peculiar, suggests the possibility that we may have not yet heard the last of the so-called Balham Mystery.
>
> ... No sooner was Captain Ricardo dead than his widow

forsook her family and her friends . . . and for some years travelled from one town on the Continent to another . . . in Dr. Gully's company.

How or why this disgraceful connection came to be broken off is matter of conjecture. . . . Anyhow, we find her separated from Dr. Gully, and living, as the handsome fortune left her by her first husband enabled her to do, in a well-appointed establishment. Almost immediately after the separation she married Mr. Bravo. . . .

How she has lived since [Mr. Bravo's death] there is no evidence to show. All that is clear is that she changed her name, and passed as "Mrs. Turner"—a title to which, as the widow of Mr. Turner-Bravo, she had a certain right. It is said that she not only drank to excess, but that she practically became a dipsomaniac. Anyhow, we find her residing at Southsea, under the charge of a certain Mrs. Everett . . . who no doubt was specially skilled in the management and treatment of such cases.

. . . On a Friday evening she is suddenly taken ill—the symptoms being exactly similar to those which had preceded the deaths of her two husbands, and the cause suggested being intemperance. On Saturday, we are told, she quarrels with Mrs. Everett, and dismisses her on the spot with a month's wages in lieu of notice. On the Sunday and during the early part of the Monday she slightly rallies. On the Monday evening she becomes suddenly worse. On Tuesday afternoon she dies—the symptoms being again the same as before.

It might have been thought that a series of coincidences thus singular would have been held proper matter for a most searching inquiry. Instead, however, of any such investigation, we have an inquest of the most perfunctory kind. An uncle of the deceased woman is the first witness, and we do him no injustice when we say that he seems to know literally nothing about the matter. . . . A couple of maidservants in the household give evidence, which—so far as it went— really tended to disprove the theory of dipsomania.

The last witness was a medical man . . . whose knowledge of the deceased woman is, to say the least, extremely limited. . . . And he adds that she was young and "well nourished". . . . The body of a woman who has killed herself with drink is not, as a rule, "well nourished".

It is, from every point of view, a very strange, and, indeed, startling fact, that the symptoms of Mrs. Bravo's last illness should be almost identical with those that marked the deaths of both her first husband and of her second. Whatever may have been the faults, or even vices, of Captain Ricardo, Mr. Bravo, at any rate, did not kill himself with brandy. He was killed by tartar emetic—a slow poison, the action of which is not easily to be distinguished from chronic gastritis, produced either by habitual intemperance, or any other cause.

It is impossible not to ask ourselves why the one witness who might have let some real light on the matter should not have been called. Mrs. Everett was the one person in a position to state, of her own knowledge, whether Mrs. Bravo drank or not. . . . And yet, singularly enough, neither is this woman called to speak to facts which in any case must have been within her knowledge, nor is the inquiry adjourned to enable her to be present.

. . . There is really no proof whatever, or next to none, that the unlucky woman died of habitual intoxication. Such a verdict, however, just fits into all the circumstances of the case. It is eminently safe. It offends nobody. . . . Nor, indeed, is it altogether improbable that Mrs. Bravo should have died from the cause alleged. She was a miserable woman, who had led a miserable life, and of whom it might have reasonably been expected that she would, sooner or later—as the saying is—"take to drink".

Admitting this, however, we find ourselves confronted by the more than usually strange circumstances with which the case is surrounded. How is it that Mrs. Bravo should have suddenly died under circumstances which, like those attending the death both of her first husband and her second, are compatible with delirium tremens, but perfectly consistent with slow poisoning?

How has she been living since her second husband's death? Has she been leading a secluded life, or has she taken up again with her old companions and associates? Who is Mrs. Everett; where is she; how long has she known Mrs. Bravo; how did she come to suddenly leave her employment; and has she ever known her late mistress to suffer from similar attacks?

. . . In default of a properly conducted investigation all that can be said is that a miserable and wretched life has suddenly come to a strange end, and that the perfunctory inquiry which has been held is altogether unsatisfactory and incomplete.

Thus did the *Standard* voice its vague and ominous conjectures. It hit the mark but at the same time overshot it, and in getting near the heart of the mystery added a further complication (by hinting that antimony had found *three* victims) that only fogged the issue. Yet it was right to criticise the proceedings at the Granada Arms Hotel; but "unsatisfactory and incomplete" as Mr. Garrington's inquest—like Mr. Carter's first one—may have been in its failure to sift every possibility, there never was another inquiry into the death of Florence Bravo. What Mrs. Everett could have said remains for ever a mystery, as does her real part in the drama of those final months at Coombe Lodge. Did people think that she might have been a tool of Mrs. Cox—or even of Dr. Gully—hired to perform some act of vengeance? Or, more far-fetched still, that she was in league with Florence's own uncle, who wished to murder her for some unguessed reason? Though nothing like this can be seriously contemplated, it was grossly negligent not to call this lady as a witness.

However, Dr. Smith effectively routed the suspicion that Florence was herself a victim of antimony by declaring that there were no symptoms of any irritant poison having been administered to her. And so, though she carried the truth to her grave, it seems that she did indeed drink herself to death, finding forgetfulness of her secret, ironically enough, in that same solace which she had so bitterly deplored in Alexander— and which he himself, perhaps, had taught her.

A touch of irony linked her, in her death, to Charles too. "Poor miserable woman," wrote a columnist in the *Portsmouth Times and Naval Gazette* of the 21st September, "so her remains too, like those of her ill-starred husband, have been sat upon by a jury." And unpitying fate saw to it that on her death-bed she did not escape the self-same sufferings that had afflicted both Alexander and Charles. She had eluded the long arm of the law but not the equally long arm of coincidence.

Florence had remade her will in February, 1877, leaving substantial legacies to her nephews and nieces; £1,000 to her goddaughter (James Gully's granddaughter) Florence Gully; her pictures, silver and glass to Augusta; and the residue, about £60,000 to her brother William in trust for his descendants. There were three other legacies—£100 each to Mrs. Cox's three sons; but to Jane Cox, erstwhile companion, friend and intimate, Florence left not a penny.

Jane Cannon Cox fades from the story now. She seems to have gone to Jamaica after all; and is said to have survived to an old age, being spoken of affectionately by an elderly friend whom she visited with fruit and flowers. (It is odd how Joseph Bravo's native island figures in the background of the story: for it was in Kingston that James Gully was born.) And for Dr. Gully, the price of his association with Florence was, as he had so clearly foreseen at the second inquest, professional and social ruin. How heavily he was made to pay for his transgression is shown by his expulsion from all the medical societies of which he had been a member. And Florence's death brought him fresh abuse. A scurrilous news-sheet then wrote: "Meantime, by means of cold water and cool temperament, a fellow-delinquent still enjoys a frosty and kindly old age. Dr. Gully, at whose door in reality lies this wretched death, trots up and down in health and vigour, the sun shining benevolently on his white head and ruddy face. At the famous Bravo enquiry he came into the room 'smiling'. Does he still smile? Serene and beautiful old man! How we envy his retrospections, and, since he is an ardent spiritualist, the shining apparitions which he is able to conjure up!" Even after his death in 1882 the stigma stuck to his family. Years later, when his distinguished son took the Chair as Speaker of the House of Commons, unruly Irish members greeted him with shouts of "Bravo! Gully!"

Florence's grief-stricken parents had her body brought home and buried in Buscot churchyard. It was almost exactly fourteen years since she had stood as a radiant bride in Buscot Church. A golden future had seemed her lot then. Instead, here she was in her coffin, her short life blighted and her memory shrouded by mystery, scandal and darkest suspicion.

And as a monument to this tragic unhappy woman The Priory still stands at the top of Bedford Hill and on the edge of the common, its chimneys now masked from that "dreaded innovation", the railway, by the red-brick villas that have so closely encroached on it since 1876. But though its cream stucco is a little faded and its small surviving piece of garden overgrown, it retains a semblance of the elegance and character it had when Florence and Mrs. Cox and Charles sat down in its dining-room to their last dinner together over eighty years ago. Its conversion into flats has not much changed the internal lay-out; and the impression received from actual sight of the interior is of compactness—even smallness: the same feeling that one has when revisiting as a grown-up a house one has known in childhood. Mounting the stairs one visualises power-fully the drama that was enacted on the bedroom floor that Tuesday night; and standing half-way up as Mary Ann, trans-fixed by Charles's cry, must have stood, one is struck by the nearness to one another of Charles's and Florence's bedroom doors. They are just four feet apart. It is indeed a tell-tale near-ness, which seems to explode once for all the possibility that anyone in the bedroom next to his could have failed to hear his anguished shout. And the silence and immobility that reigned on that landing immediately afterwards proclaim that behind the green baize door of the best bedroom two pairs of ears were wilfully closed to his cries. Thus from the past The Priory still silently offers its damning and incriminating murder-clue.

POSTSCRIPT

When in 1974 the BBC commissioned me to write three television plays, *The Poisoning of Charles Bravo*, I consulted my friend, the celebrated crime writer Christianna Brand, who generously supplied me with a mass of original Victorian research material which formed the basis of my work.

Amongst this was a reference to an intriguing postcard in the files at Scotland Yard, which I believe provides strong confirmation of John William's solution to this strange affair. I reproduce it here with the original spelling:

The Balham Mystery

What are you about? Why in the world do
you not have Mrs. Bravo's first husband,
the Captain, exhumed and his intestitines
annalised? Fire away!! You will work it.
Never mind the £500 reward.

That modest final disclaimer, the writer's anonymity and above all the style suggested at once that this was from the hand of George Griffiths, even before I noted the postmark – Canterbury, 24th May, 1876. By this date, some five months after his abrupt dismissal from The Priory, Griffiths was in service with Lady Prescott at Herne Bay. No doubt he made regular journeys to Canterbury where, amongst other duties for her ladyship, he possibly resumed his old habit of buying drugs for veterinary purposes. I am convinced we have in this relic the proof that Griffiths was the source of the tartar emetic which killed both Captain Ricardo and Charles Bravo – though whether these were truly acts of wilful murder by Florence may never be finally established.

KEN TAYLOR
1988

INDEX

FOR THE BEST IN PAPERBACKS, LOOK FOR THE

In every corner of the world, on every subject under the sun, Penguin represents quality and variety – the very best in publishing today.

For complete information about books available from Penguin – including Pelicans, Puffins, Peregrines and Penguin Classics – and how to order them, write to us at the appropriate address below. Please note that for copyright reasons the selection of books varies from country to country.

In the United Kingdom: Please write to *Dept E.P., Penguin Books Ltd, Harmondsworth, Middlesex, UB7 0DA*

In the United States: Please write to *Dept BA, Penguin, 299 Murray Hill Parkway, East Rutherford, New Jersey 07073*

In Canada: Please write to *Penguin Books Canada Ltd, 2801 John Street, Markham, Ontario L3R 1B4*

In Australia: Please write to the *Marketing Department, Penguin Books Australia Ltd, P.O. Box 257, Ringwood, Victoria 3134*

In New Zealand: Please write to the *Marketing Department, Penguin Books (NZ) Ltd, Private Bag, Takapuna, Auckland 9*

In India: Please write to *Penguin Overseas Ltd, 706 Eros Apartments, 56 Nehru Place, New Delhi, 110019*

In Holland: Please write to *Penguin Books Nederland B.V., Postbus 195, NL–1380AD Weesp, Netherlands*

In Germany: Please write to *Penguin Books Ltd, Friedrichstrasse 10–12, D–6000 Frankfurt Main 1, Federal Republic of Germany*

In Spain: Please write to *Longman Penguin España, Calle San Nicolas 15, E–28013 Madrid, Spain*

In France: Please write to *Penguin Books Ltd, 39 Rue de Montmorency, F-75003, Paris, France*

In Japan: Please write to *Longman Penguin Japan Co Ltd, Yamaguchi Building, 2–12–9 Kanda Jimbocho, Chiyoda-Ku, Tokyo 101, Japan*

CRIME AND MYSTERY IN PENGUINS

Deep Water   Patricia Highsmith

Her chilling portrait of a psychopath, from the first faint outline to the full horrors of schizophrenia. 'If you read crime stories at all, or perhaps especially if you don't, you should read *Deep Water*' – Julian Symons in the *Sunday Times*

Farewell, My Lovely   Raymond Chandler

Moose Malloy was a big man but not more than six feet five inches tall and not wider than a beer truck. He looked about as inconspicuous as a tarantula on a slice of angel food. Marlowe's greatest case. Chandler's greatest book.

God Save the Child   Robert B. Parker

When young Kevın Bartlett disappears, everyone assumes he's run away . . . until the comic strip ransom note arrives . . . 'In classic wisecracking and handfighting tradition, Spenser sorts out the case and wins the love of a fine-boned Jewish Lady . . . who even shares his taste for iced red wine' – Francis Goff in the *Sunday Telegraph*

The Daughter of Time   Josephine Tey

Josephine Tey again delves into history to reconstruct a crime. This time it is a crime committed in the tumultuous fifteenth century. 'Most people will find *The Daughter of Time* as interesting and enjoyable a book as they will meet in a month of Sundays' – Marghanita Laski in the *Observer*

The Michael Innes Omnibus

Three tensely exhilarating novels. 'A master – he constructs a plot that twists and turns like an electric eel: it gives you shock upon shock and you cannot let go' – *The Times Literary Supplement*

Killer's Choice   Ed McBain

Who killed Annie Boone? Employer, lover, ex-husband, girlfriend? This is a tense, terrifying and tautly written novel from the author of *The Mugger*, *The Pusher*, *Lady Killer* and a dozen other first class thrillers.

CRIME AND MYSTERY IN PENGUINS

Call for the Dead   John Le Carré

The classic work of espionage which introduced the world to George Smiley. 'Brilliant . . . highly intelligent, realistic. Constant suspense. Excellent writing' – *Observer*

Swag   Elmore Leonard

From the bestselling author of *Stick* and *La Brava* comes this wallbanger of a book in which 100,000 dollars' worth of nicely spendable swag sets off a slick, fast-moving chain of events. 'Brilliant' – *The New York Times*

Beast in View   Margaret Millar

'On one level, *Beast in View* is a dazzling conjuring trick. On another it offers a glimpse of bright-eyed madness as disquieting as a shriek in the night. In the whole of Crime Fiction's distinguished sisterhood there is no one quite like Margaret Millar' – *Guardian*

The Julian Symons Omnibus

The Man Who Killed Himself, *The Man Whose Dreams Came True*, *The Man Who Lost His Wife:* three novels of cynical humour and cliff-hanging suspense from a master of his craft. 'Exciting and compulsively readable' – *Observer*

Love in Amsterdam   Nicolas Freeling

Inspector Van der Valk's first case involves him in an elaborate cat-and-mouse game with a very wily suspect. 'Has the sinister, spellbinding perfection of a cobra uncoiling. It is a masterpiece of the genre' – Stanley Ellis

Maigret's Pipe   Georges Simenon

Eighteen intriguing cases of mystery and murder to which the pipe-smoking Maigret applies his wit and intuition, his genius for detection and a certain *je ne sais quoi* . . .

PENGUIN CLASSIC CRIME

The Big Knockover and Other Stories Dashiell Hammett

With these sharp, spare, laconic stories, Hammett invented a new folk hero – the private eye. 'Dashiell Hammett gave murder back to the kind of people that commit it for reasons, not just to provide a corpse; and with the means at hand, not with handwrought duelling pistols, curare, and tropical fish' – Raymond Chandler

Death of a Ghost Margery Allingham

A picture painted by a dead artist leads to murder . . . and Albert Campion has to face his dearest enemy. With the skill we have come to expect from one of the great crime writers of all time, Margery Allingham weaves an enthralling web of murder, intrigue and suspense.

Fen Country Edmund Crispin

Dandelions and hearing aids, a bloodstained cat, a Leonardo drawing, a corpse with an alibi, a truly poisonous letter . . . these are just some of the unusual clues that Oxford don/detective Gervase Fen is confronted with in this sparkling collection of short mystery stories by one of the great masters of detective fiction. 'The mystery fan's ideal bedside book' – *Kirkus Reviews*

The Wisdom of Father Brown G. K. Chesterton

Twelve delightful stories featuring the world's most beloved amateur sleuth. Here Father Brown's adventures take him from London to Cornwall, from Italy to France. He becomes involved with bandits, treason, murder, curses, and an American crime-detection machine.

Five Roundabouts to Heaven John Bingham

At the heart of this novel is a conflict of human relationships ending in death. Centred around crime, the book is remarkable for its humanity, irony and insight into the motives and weaknesses of men and women, as well as for a tensely exciting plot with a surprise ending. One of the characters, considering reasons for killing, wonders whether the steps of his argument are *Five Roundabouts to Heaven*. Or do they lead to Hell? . . .'

FOR THE BEST IN PAPERBACKS, LOOK FOR THE

A CHOICE OF PENGUINS

A Better Class of Person   John Osborne

The playwright's autobiography, 1929–56. 'Splendidly enjoyable' – John Mortimer. 'One of the best, richest and most bitterly truthful autobiographies that I have ever read' – Melvyn Bragg

Out of Africa   Karen Blixen (Isak Dinesen)

After the failure of her coffee-farm in Kenya, where she lived from 1913 to 1931, Karen Blixen went home to Denmark and wrote this unforgettable account of her experiences. 'No reader can put the book down without some share in the author's poignant farewell to her farm' – *Observer*

In My Wildest Dreams   Leslie Thomas

The autobiography of Leslie Thomas, author of *The Magic Army* and *The Dearest and the Best*. From Barnardo boy to original virgin soldier, from apprentice journalist to famous novelist, it is an amazing story. 'Hugely enjoyable' – *Daily Express*

The Winning Streak   Walter Goldsmith and David Clutterbuck

Marks and Spencer, Saatchi and Saatchi, United Biscuits, G.E.C. . . The U.K.'s top companies reveal their formulas for success, in an important and stimulating book that no British manager can afford to ignore.

Mind Tools   Rudy Rucker

Information is the master concept of the computer age, which throws a completely new light on the age-old concepts of space and number, logic and infinity. In *Mind Tools* Rudy Rucker has produced the most charming and challenging intellectual carnival since *Gödel, Escher, Bach*.

Bird of Life, Bird of Death   Jonathan Evan Maslow

In the summer of 1983 Jonathan Maslow set out to find the quetzal. In doing so, he placed himself between the natural and unnatural histories of Central America, between the vulnerable magnificence of nature and the terrible destructiveness of man. 'A wonderful book' – *The New York Times Book Review*

A CHOICE OF PENGUINS

Adieux: A Farewell to Sartre   Simone de Beauvoir

A devastatingly frank account of the last years of Sartre's life, and his death, by the woman who for more than half a century shared that life. 'A true labour of love, there is about it a touching sadness, a mingling of the personal with the impersonal and timeless which Sartre himself would surely have liked and understood' – *Listener*

Business Wargames   James Barrie

How did BMW overtake Mercedes? Why did Laker crash? How did MacDonalds grab the hamburger market? Drawing on the tragic mistakes and brilliant victories of military history, this remarkable book draws countless fascinating parallels with case histories from industry world-wide.

Metamagical Themas   Douglas R. Hofstadter

This astonishing sequel to the bestselling, Pulitzer Prize-winning *Gödel, Escher, Bach* swarms with 'extraordinary ideas, brilliant fables, deep philosophical questions and Carrollian word play' – Martin Gardner

Into the Heart of Borneo   Redmond O'Hanlon

'Perceptive, hilarious and at the same time a serious natural-history journey into one of the last remaining unspoilt paradises' – *New Statesman* 'Consistently exciting, often funny and erudite without ever being over-whelming' – *Punch*

The Assassination of Federico García Lorca   Ian Gibson

Lorca's 'crime' was his antipathy to pomposity, conformity and intoler-ance. His punishment was murder. Ian Gibson reveals the truth about Lorca's death and the atmosphere in Spain that allowed it to happen.

The Secrets of a Woman's Heart   Hilary Spurling

The later life of Ivy Compton-Burnett 1920–69. 'A biographical triumph . . . elegant, stylish, witty tender, immensely acute – dazzles and exhila-rates . . . a great achievement' – Kay Dick in the *Literary Review*. 'One of the most important literary biographies of the century' – *New Statesman*

FOR THE BEST IN PAPERBACKS, LOOK FOR THE

A CHOICE OF PENGUINS

Fantastic Invasion   Patrick Marnham

Explored and exploited, Africa has carried a different meaning for each wave of foreign invaders – from ivory traders to aid workers. Now, in the crisis that has followed Independence, which way should Africa turn? 'A courageous and brilliant effort' – Paul Theroux

Jean Rhys: Letters 1931–66
Edited by Francis Wyndham and Diana Melly

'Eloquent and invaluable . . . her life emerges, and with it a portrait of an unexpectedly indomitable figure' – Marina Warner in the *Sunday Times*

Among the Russians   Colin Thubron

One man's solitary journey by car across Russia provides an enthralling and revealing account of the habits and idiosyncrasies of a fascinating people. 'He sees things with the freshness of an innocent and the erudition of a scholar' – *Daily Telegraph*

The Amateur Naturalist   Gerald Durrell with Lee Durrell

'Delight . . . on every page . . . packed with authoritative writing, learning without pomposity . . . it represents a real bargain' – *The Times Educational Supplement*. 'What treats are in store for the average British household' – *Books and Bookmen*

The Democratic Economy   Geoff Hodgson

Today, the political arena is divided as seldom before. In this exciting and original study, Geoff Hodgson carefully examines the claims of the rival doctrines and exposes some crucial flaws.

They Went to Portugal   Rose Macaulay

An exotic and entertaining account of travellers to Portugal from the pirate-crusaders, through poets, aesthetes and ambassadors, to the new wave of romantic travellers. A wonderful mixture of literature, history and adventure, by one of our most stylish and seductive writers.

Beyond the Blue Horizon   Alexander Frater

The romance and excitement of the legendary Imperial Airways East-bound Empire service – the world's longest and most adventurous scheduled air route – relived fifty years later in one of the most original travel books of the decade. 'The find of the year' – *Today*

Voyage through the Antarctic   Richard Adams and Ronald Lockley

Here is the true, authentic Antarctic of today, brought vividly to life by Richard Adams, author of *Watership Down*, and Ronald Lockley, the world-famous naturalist. 'A good adventure story, with a lot of information and a deal of enthusiasm for Antarctica and its animals' – *Nature*

Getting to Know the General   Graham Greene

'In August 1981 my bag was packed for my fifth visit to Panama when the news came to me over the telephone of the death of General Omar Torrijos Herrera, my friend and host . . .' 'Vigorous, deeply felt, at times funny, and for Greene surprisingly frank' – *Sunday Times*

The Search for the Virus   Steve Connor and Sharon Kingman

In this gripping book, two leading *New Scientist* journalists tell the remarkable story of how researchers discovered the AIDS virus and examine the links between AIDS and lifestyles. They also look at the progress being made in isolating the virus and finding a cure.

Arabian Sands   Wilfred Thesiger

'In the tradition of Burton, Doughty, Lawrence, Philby and Thomas, it is, very likely, the book about Arabia to end all books about Arabia' – *Daily Telegraph*

When the Wind Blows   Raymond Briggs

'A visual parable against nuclear war: all the more chilling for being in the form of a strip cartoon' – *Sunday Times* 'The most eloquent anti-Bomb statement you are likely to read' – *Daily Mail*

The Diary of Virginia Woolf
Five volumes edited by Quentin Bell and Anne Olivier Bell

'As an account of intellectual and cultural life of our century, Virginia Woolf's diaries are invaluable; as the record of one bruised and unquiet mind, they are unique' – Peter Ackroyd in the *Sunday Times*

Voices of the Old Sea   Norman Lewis

'I will wager that *Voices of the Old Sea* will be a classic in the literature about Spain' – *Mail on Sunday* 'Limpidly and lovingly Norman Lewis has caught the helpless, unwitting, often foolish, but always hopeful village in its dying summers, and saved the tragedy with sublime comedy' – *Observer*

The First World War   A J P Taylor

In this superb illustrated history, A J P Taylor 'manages to say almost everything that is important for an understanding and, indeed, intellectual digestion of that vast event . . . A special text . . . a remarkable collection of photographs' – *Observer*

Ninety-Two Days   Evelyn Waugh

With characteristic honesty Evelyn Waugh here debunks the romantic notions attached to rough travelling; his journey in Guiana and Brazil is difficult, dangerous and extremely uncomfortable, and his account of it is witty and unquestionably compelling.

When the Mind Hears   Harlan Lane
A History of the Deaf

'Reads like a suspense novel . . . what emerges is evidence of a great wrong done to a minority group, the deaf' – *The New York Times Book Review* 'Impassioned, polemical, at times even virulent . . . (he shows) immense scholarship, powers of historical reconstruction, and deep empathy for the world of the deaf' – Oliver Sacks in *The New York Review of Books*

FOR THE BEST IN PAPERBACKS, LOOK FOR THE 🐧

A CHOICE OF PENGUINS

The Big Red Train Ride   Eric Newby

From Moscow to the Pacific on the Trans-Siberian Railway is an eight-day journey of nearly six thousand miles through seven time zones. In 1977 Eric Newby set out with his wife, an official guide and a photographer on this journey. 'The best kind of travel book' – Paul Theroux

Star Wars   Edited by E. P. Thompson

With contributions for Rip Bulkeley, John Pike, Ben Thompson and E. P. Thompson, and with a Foreword by Dorothy Hodgkin, OM, this is a major book which assesses all the arguments for Star Wars and proceeds to make a powerful – indeed unanswerable – case against it.

Somerville and Ross   Gifford Lewis

Edith Somerville has a talented artist and illustrator, her cousin Violet Martin had a profound political insight. Together they created the master-piece *The Real Charlotte* and the witty tales of *The Irish R.M.* This is Gifford Lewis's colourful account of their lives.

PENGUIN CLASSICS OF WORLD ART

Each volume presents the complete paintings of the artist and includes: an introduction by a distinguished art historian, critical comments on the painter from his own time to the present day, 64 pages of full-colour plates, a chronological survey of his life and work, a basic bibliography, a fully illustrated and annotated *catalogue raisonné*.

Titles already published or in preparation

Botticelli, Caravaggio, Cézanne, Leonardo da Vinci, Manet, Picasso, Piero della Francesca, Raphael, van Eycks, Vermeer.

PENGUIN TRUE CRIME

A series of brilliant investigations into some of the most mysterious and baffling crimes ever committed.

Titles published and forthcoming:

Crippen: The Mild Murderer   Tom Cullen
The famous story of the doctor who poisoned his wife and buried her in the cellar.

Who Killed Hanratty?   Paul Foot
An investigation into the notorious A6 murder.

Norman Birkett   H. Montgomery Hyde
The biography of one of Britain's most humane and respected judges.

The Complete Jack the Ripper   Donald Rumbelow
An investigation into the identity of the most elusive murderer of all time.

The Riddle of Birdhurst Rise   R. Whittington-Egan
The Croydon Poisoning Mystery of 1928–9.

Suddenly at the Priory   John Williams
Who poisoned the Victorian barrister Charles Bravo?

Stinie: Murder on the Common   Andrew Rose
The truth behind the Clapham Common murder.

The Poisoned Life of Mrs Maybrick   Bernard Ryan
Mr Maybrick died of arsenic poisoning – how?

The Gatton Mystery   J. and D. Gibney
The great unsolved Australian triple murder.

Earth to Earth   John Cornwell
Who killed the Luxtons in their remote mid-Devon farmhouse?

The Ordeal of Philip Yale Drew   R. Whittington-Egan
A real life murder melodrama in three acts.